WHY PARTIES MATTER

CHICAGO STUDIES IN AMERICAN POLITICS

A series edited by Benjamin I. Page, Susan Herbst, Lawrence R. Jacobs, and Adam J. Berinsky

Also in the series:

Neither Liberal nor Conservative: Ideological Innocence in the American Public by Donald R. Kinder and Nathan P. Kalmoe

Strategic Party Government: Why Winning Trumps Ideology by Gregory Koger and Matthew J. Lebo

The Politics of Resentment: Rural Consciousness in Wisconsin and the Rise of Scott Walker by Katherine J. Cramer

Post-Racial or Most-Racial? Race and Politics in the Obama Era by Michael Tesler

Legislating in the Dark: Information and Power in the House of Representatives by James M. Curry

Why Washington Won't Work: Polarization, Political Trust, and the Governing Crisis by Marc J. Hetherington and Thomas J. Rudolph

Who Governs? Presidents, Public Opinion, and Manipulation by James N. Druckman and Lawrence R. Jacobs

Trapped in America's Safety Net: One Family's Struggle by Andrea Louise Campbell

Arresting Citizenship: The Democratic Consequences of American Crime Control by Amy E. Lerman and Vesla M. Weaver

How the States Shaped the Nation: American Electoral Institutions and Voter Turnout, 1920–2000 by Melanie Jean Springer

The American Warfare State: The Domestic Politics of Military Spending by Rebecca U. Thorpe

Changing Minds or Changing Channels? Partisan News in an Age of Choice by Kevin Arceneaux and Martin Johnson

Additional series titles follow index

WHY PARTIES MATTER

Political Competition and Democracy in the American South

JOHN H. ALDRICH

JOHN D. GRIFFIN

THE UNIVERSITY OF CHICAGO PRESS

Chicago & London

The University of Chicago Press, Chicago 60637
The University of Chicago Press, Ltd., London
© 2018 by The University of Chicago
Published 2018
Printed in the United States of America

27 26 25 24 23 22 21 20 19 18   1 2 3 4 5

ISBN-13: 978-0-226-49523-1 (cloth)
ISBN-13: 978-0-226-49537-8 (paper)
ISBN-13: 978-0-226-49540-8 (e-book)
DOI: 10.7208/chicago/9780226495408.001.0001

Library of Congress Cataloging-in-Publication Data
Names: Aldrich, John H., 1947– author. | Griffin, John David, 1968–
   author.
Title: Why parties matter : political competition and democracy in the
   American South / John H. Aldrich and John D. Griffin.
Other titles: Chicago studies in American politics.
Description: Chicago : The University of Chicago, 2018. | Series:
   Chicago studies in American politics | Includes bibliographical
   references and index.
Identifiers: LCCN 2017022086 | ISBN 9780226495231 (cloth : alk.
   paper) | ISBN 9780226495378 (pbk. : alk. paper) |
   ISBN 9780226495408 (e-book)
Subjects: LCSH: Political parties—Southern States—History. |
   Democracy—Southern States—History. | Elections—Southern
   States—History. | Southern States—Politics and government—
   History.
Classification: LCC JK2295.S6 A43 2018 | DDC 324.2730975—dc23
LC record available at https://lccn.loc.gov/2017022086

⊗ This paper meets the requirements of ANSI/NISO Z39.48–1992
(Permanence of Paper).

For
Cindy and David
and
Amy, Natalie, Jack, and Elizabeth

CONTENTS

TABLES

FIGURES

PART ONE

WHY PARTIES MATTER

1 "EXCEPT IN THE SOUTH"

The South has long differed from the North in the United States, a set of differences that were already deeply rooted over the century and a half between the arrival of the British to the American colonies and the founding of the American Republic.[1] The South had the same federal Constitution, of course, and the differences in state constitutions and governmental organizations between North and South were slight (Thorpe 1909). Indeed, even upon secession, the eleven states that formed the Confederacy adopted a constitution remarkably similar to the one from which they were seceding (Coulter 1950, 23; Jenkins 1999). Yet the paths of southern and northern political development after the founding differed dramatically, as secession attests.

THE PARTY SYSTEM, ELECTIONS, AND RACE

The most obvious regional difference in politics over much of the nation's history was that the North generally enjoyed a well-defined two-party system. In contrast, the South has had more weakly developed parties, as was true during the Democrat-Whig party era (1836–52), or, often, no "system" of parties at all, as was true during most of the Jim Crow era. The southern "party system" most often consisted of a single political party, and even that one party was typically not very well organized. For example, during the Confederacy, there were no political parties at all (one of the few major differences between the constitutions of the Union and the Confederacy). After Reconstruction and what southerners then called "Redemption," that is, when the southern white Democrats retook power, the South had a single-party system. From about 1900 to 1965, it was a lily-white southern Democratic Party, with much of the action concentrated in whites-only primaries. Even after the Civil Rights Act of 1964 and the Voting Rights Act of 1965 were enacted and desegregation and Jim Crow ended, the Republican Party was not able to begin to make real inroads into the South, outside of presidential elections, for another fifteen years. Not until about 1980, that is, did a genuine two-party system develop in the South, and that development took even longer to mature. It wasn't until 2012 that the Republican Party was finally able to win unified majority control in North Carolina for the first time since Reconstruction, an event that sounded one final death note to the "solid South."

This macro view of the absence of a competitive two-party system in the South has some exceptions, exceptions that we exploit in these pages. One period is the 1830s to 1850s in which the (Jacksonian) Democratic Party and the Whig Party competed in both the North and the South. This nascent two-party system collapsed, primarily due to the failure of the Whig Party in 1852–54. That failure was owing in large part to the fact that the regional division of the Whigs proved simply too large to survive as the slave issue grew in importance during and after the passage of the Kansas-Nebraska Act (1854). Once the Republicans emerged as the new alternative major party to the Democrats in the nation, the old two-party system in which both parties consisted of interregional alliances was gone. The Republicans were exclusively a northern party, and the South refused to be a part of a national two-party system that included a party that could win national majorities entirely without them.

Once more, at the end of Reconstruction, there was potential in the South for a two-party system, most prominently for an alliance between the remnants of the Reconstruction-era Republican Party (victorious as long as former Confederates were excluded from voting) and the emerging Populist Party. Such a coalition would tie together the remaining Republicans, especially the freed slaves, and poor whites who might well benefit from such an alliance and form an electoral majority. But more well-off white Democrats fought back (in some cases literally), re-disenfranchised former slaves, effectively sweeping a good number of poor whites out of the electorate along with them. In doing so, they enshrined a one-party system as a key piece in forging the Jim Crow South.

That these two different moments of at least potential two-party-ism in the South failed, and failed so spectacularly, as planter and middle-class white southerners first seceded and then essentially subverted democracy (or at least the intention of the Civil War Amendments) indicates just how large were the stakes involved—and how fragile the near successes of full-bodied, competitive mass party politics proved to be.

The great scholar of southern political parties, V. O. Key Jr., in his masterpiece, *Southern Politics in State and Nation* (1949), believed that the solid Democratic South was not even so much as a one-party system in the late Jim Crow era. He believed that, at least in the states (but not in the nation), the South instead "has no parties" (1949, 299) at all. And, he believed, the absence of a competitive multiparty system was closely associated with the complete failure of democracy in the South.

In our view, white southern Democrats were seeking to solve a difficult political problem. How could they win elections consistently, over a long period of time in a majoritarian electoral system, when they constituted no more than a minority? The strategy they chose was simple—subvert democracy. In particular, they chose to subvert the ability of any actual or potential competing political party to form and endure in opposition to the Democratic Party. In this, at least in the Jim Crow era, they chose a structure that looks a lot like an authoritarian political system using a single party as a vehicle for enforcing their authority on the public, albeit one embedded within a national democratic system (e.g., Garreton 1995; Lawson 2000; Mickey 2015).

The southern Democrat Party differed from its northern branch in many ways throughout the first two hundred years of the nation. In the post–World War II era, and especially the civil rights era, southern Democrats acted both in the state and in the nation very differently from their northern counterparts. Nationally, they voted differently, they fought to block much of the agenda of their own party, and they presented a picture of democratic politics in which political parties communicated extraordinarily diffuse signals about what they stood for to the public (except on Jim Crowism). By the 1960s, for example, the Democratic Party was the champion of civil rights for African Americans, and leaders of the southern Democratic Party stood in schoolhouse doors, blocking the desegregation that the Supreme Court declared to be the law of the land, indeed elevated to the level enshrined in the Constitution. George Wallace had emerged as first among such leaders via his inaugural address weeks earlier, saying, "In the name of the greatest people that have ever trod this earth, I draw the line in the dust and toss the gauntlet before the feet of tyranny . . . and I say . . . segregation today . . . segregation tomorrow . . . segregation forever."[2] So different had the one-party Democratic South become from the northern party in the 1940s, 1950s, 1960s, and 1970s that most papers on American electoral behavior included the recurring phrase, "except in the South" (e.g., Huntington 1974; Rusk 1974; Nagel and McNulty 1996; Fiorina 1997; Newman and Ostrom 2002; Carson and Roberts 2005).

While the northern and southern Democrats differed dramatically from each other in Washington, DC, it was in the states where parties and politics really differed, and it is this set of differences that will be the main story of this book. National politics, even if roughly a third of the Congress was selected via means we might call nondemocratic, was still understood as primarily democracy at work. As Key showed, that wasn't true in his no-party South. Here, we want to investigate party politics in much of the rest of the nation's history, particularly those periods when there was a budding second party seeking to establish itself as a major political party in the region and, with that, a competitive party system. We look here particularly at the Jacksonian Democrat and Whig Party era, the era between Reconstruction and the coming of Jim Crow, the period that Key studied up until the Civil Rights and Voting Rights Acts, and the recent era of the successful emergence of the Republican Party in the South, over a century after it had become a major party in the North, and at last creating a genuine two-party system in the South.

It was not, of course, just that the southern politician felt that competitive democracy was something to be avoided while his northern counterpart felt it was something to struggle for. There was a reason that the South chose rarely to accept a competitive party system. The South differed from the North, that is, more than merely in having a less competitive party system. Perhaps the most important line Key wrote in *Southern Politics* was "whatever phase of the southern political process one seeks to understand, sooner or later the trail of inquiry leads to the Negro" (1949, 5). And it is in understanding racial politics in the South that we can come to understand the actions of the southern politician. It is the politics of slavery, racial exclusion, and Jim Crow that explain the motivations that lead to the avoidance of competitive party politics. Thus, in our story, political parties and race will be inextricably intertwined.

UNIVERSAL SUFFRAGE, DEMOCRATIC PRACTICES, AND RACE

Another similarity of this intertwining is the public justification given by southern Democratic leaders for the absence of democracy in the South—and in particular for not extending full citizen rights to African Americans. They were not "ready" for democracy, or so at least went the claim. This is a standard argument of those who seek to maintain power in an authoritarian system, and our claim about the South, especially in the Jim Crow era, is that the South was much closer to an authoritarian, one-party system, even if embedded in a democracy with a fully competitive party system nationally, than it was to an effective democracy.

On February 10, 2011, Benjamin R. Barber wrote a blog post entitled "'The People Are Not Ready for Democracy!' Announces the Tyrant."[3] He was writing about demonstrations that helped lead to the overthrow of Hosni Mubarak in Egypt's version of the Arab Spring, and the reaction from then Vice President Omar Mahmoud Suleiman. He went on to point out that, in the absence of appropriate supporting features of civil society, the claim is well grounded in history and political philosophy, to which we would add political science. He went on to say:

> But here's the rub: what is wise counsel coming from independent observers rooting for democracy becomes reactionary stalling when prescribed by interested players rooting against democracy. We can only scorn autocrats who are suddenly repositories of prudence concerning the sociology of democracy. They are obviously using such arguments as a pretext for staying in power and thwarting popular aspirations. "The people are not ready for democracy!" announces the tyrant.

As we write this, Egypt remains murky as to just what its Arab Spring actually will lead to, but it does not look like it is leading toward democracy. It also remains murky just how much of its difficult move toward democracy (if that is what it will be) is due to resistance of elites, lack of the infrastructure of civil society, or both.

The claim of a people not ready for democracy is not limited to Egypt. In a blog post about China on February 27, 2012, entitled "China Isn't Ready for Democracy—Vote Buying, Low Quality People, and Other Excuses," the author goes on to say:

> The idea that democracy doesn't fit China's national condition seems to be a weekly feature in the Global Times. . . . The Party argues that this is another reason that Democracy shouldn't be expanded. The poor are simply too easy to buy, and the rich would just buy the elections leading to a Chinese Oligarchy. . . . As popular blogger Han Han argued at the start of the year, China isn't ready for democracy, because the people aren't capable of making their own good decisions.[4]

Here is a quote from Eman Al-Nafjan about his country, Saudi Arabia:

> In an absolute monarchy such as ours, political awareness, never mind democracy, is hard to come by. Democracy as a form of government

is a completely foreign concept. This lack of awareness and experience among the people has been used by academics, political analysts, and even the people themselves to postpone the inevitable. "Saudi people are not ready for democracy," is heard practically everywhere.[5]

As a final example, Larry Diamond makes a general claim about arguments concerning the unsuitability of the people for democracy, writing about these claims made in the context of the Arab Spring:

> The warnings and reservations were variations on a theme: Arabs are not ready for democracy. They have no experience with it and don't know how to make it work. Islam is inclined toward violence, intolerance, and authoritarian values. People will vote radical and Islamist parties into power, and the regimes that ultimately emerge will be theocracies or autocracies, not democracies.[6]

He goes on to discuss them in the context of less developed and/or newly freed countries in virtually every region of the world. He concludes,

> But the data show that popular attitudes and values are not the principal problem, and there is little evidence to support the claim that postponing democracy in favor of strongman rule will make things better. The people of Burma have made that point repeatedly at the polls and on the streets, and finally their rulers seem to be listening to them. The best way to democracy is through democracy.

These arguments are not unique to less developed countries and newly decolonized nations. They were common in the American South. At the founding, the argument went, slaves could not be freed and become citizens because they purportedly lacked the ability to exercise the prerequisites of democracy as citizens (Finkelman 2014). This argument was again put forth in the post-Reconstruction South (Woodward 2001), as helping to justify limiting participation, such as requiring literacy tests, and thus ensuring that most freed slaves and many poor, rural whites would be unable to vote, making the white middle- and upper-class minority in the South into an effective majority.

Were these arguments only made to rationalize the disenfranchisement of blacks? No. As we just suggested, they were also made to support the political exclusion of poor, less educated whites during the Populist era. But convincing the North that blacks' access to the ballot box properly could be limited was probably an easier task than making a similar case for income-based exclusion. In this way, racial differences were a vehicle for a subset of southern elites to maintain a stranglehold on political office well beyond its natural demise.

In both instances, that is, these appeals to rationalize southern ways to northerners were politically strategic. Northerners might agree in sufficient numbers with permitting racial and income differences in political inclusion. If southern elites had more candidly acknowledged that the maintenance or reintroduction of political inequality in participation was the only mechanism that would allow for minority rule, that would be a principle with which few northerners could agree.

This book, then, can be read as a defense of the central place of open political competition for instantiating the effectiveness of democratic governance. It has become somewhat fashionable of late to call into question the importance of electoral competition. Some contend that political competition is simply unnecessary for the maintenance of a healthy democracy (Buchler 2005). Others go even further, claiming that electoral competition has ill democratic effects (Brunell and Buchler 2009). For instance, some suggest that electoral units, be they municipalities or counties or congressional districts, should be drawn or redrawn to maximize the political homogeneity of the population. This will ease the burden, so the argument goes, of officials elected to represent the unit's interests, and it will maximize the satisfaction of citizens with the representation they receive. This book argues the contrary and indeed is a full-throated argument that electoral competition is necessary for democratic governance to work effectively. Electoral competition, born of a healthy system of political parties, induces the government to be responsive to the public.

In this we join a number of other recent defenders of parties' role in a healthy democracy (e.g., Rosenblum 2010; Muirhead 2014). However, we hope that we go further than others in demonstrating in rich factual detail the benefits to democracy of political parties. We take full account of the emergence of national, two-party competition and show that this development is, on balance, a very good thing.

A ROADMAP

Chapter 2 concludes part 1 of the book and lays out our theoretical argument. In brief, we contend that an effective democratic politics is the politics of regularized party competition for control of the offices of government. More precisely, our position is that when in-equilibrium, party systems convert public preferences into competitive elections, and such a competitive party system is a necessary condition for effective democratic politics.

Part 2 of the book, consisting of four chapters, evaluates the state of the party system in the South, generally in comparison with the North, in four historical periods. In doing so, we follow Key's tripartite conception of the three spheres of party activity—the party in government, the party as an organization, and the party in the electoral arena. That is, how distinct from each other were the officeholders affiliated with the parties in each region? How developed were the capacities of the parties to work in service of their candidates? How strong were the attachments of citizens to the parties? In chapter 3 we address these questions in the second party system, or the period between 1832 and 1852. There, we will see that legacies of the pre-Jacksonian era stunted the development of a southern party system somewhat, but that the region was catching up to the North in the years prior to the collapse of the Whig Party.

In chapter 4 we focus primarily on the period from Reconstruction until the turn of the century, or 1876 to 1900. There, we will see that a nascent two-party system was abruptly and dramatically thwarted by the "Redemption" of the South by the lily-white southern Democratic Party. In chapter 5 we briefly revisit and extend the period upon which Key focused in *Southern Politics in State and Nation*, that is, from 1900 to 1965. There, we will observe that southern parties, to the very limited extent there could be said to have been a Republican Party in the South at all, were much less distinctive than were the two northern parties in this era. We also document the divergence in electoral turnout between the two regions.

Chapter 6 concludes part 2 with a comprehensive examination of regional party development in the modern era. There, we have access to a much wider array of primary data to investigate the development of a southern party system in government. We report the results of surveys we and our colleagues have recently conducted measuring the parties' organizational capacities and operations, and we have at our disposal public opinion surveys to track the parties in elections. We will see that by virtually every measure, the southern party system has today caught up to the party system in the North, a process that appears to have accelerated around 1980.

In part 3 we turn to an examination of the consequences of party-system development for electoral competition and for effective democratic politics. In chapter 7, our focus is threefold—assessing the electoral competitiveness of the North and South during each of our historical eras and using various metrics, describing the process by which parties become competitive with a focus on the role of the ambitious politician climbing the political opportunity structure, and comparing the qualifications of elected officials in the two regions over time. We will see that the South has become more competitive, especially since 1980, and that the region at last has reached parity with the North on this score. What is more, we will see that when and where political parties became more developed in the South (in government, as organizations, and in elections), more competitive elections followed. That is, we observe considerable support for our claim in chapter 2 that party systems in equilibrium yield competitive elections. We also see in chapter 7 that a competitive party system in the South, and voter support of Republican candidates, emerged primarily, but not exclusively, from the "bottom up"—that is, from lower (state) to higher (federal) levels of office holding. This is not to say that there were not early successes for the GOP at the presidential or congressional level, but this support was not so sustained and systematic to conclude that the southern GOP was built from the "top down" (Aistrup 1996). Third, chapter 7 effectively shows that in terms of qualification for office (age, experience, family legacy), it was not until the modern period that officeholders in the South rivaled their northern counterparts.

Chapter 8 examines a key consequence of competitive elections, namely, more responsive elected officials. We chiefly do this by assessing whether the roll call behavior of southern elected officials reflected the same level of responsiveness to variation in citizen opinion as was observed in the North. We will see that during the Whig and post-Reconstruction eras, and from 1948 to 1980, the responsiveness of elected officials in the South was either nonexistent or did not come close to approaching the level of responsiveness seen in the North. Only in the last three decades has the responsiveness of southern officeholders caught up to that of their northern peers. We observe a parallel trend when we examine other forms of legislator responsiveness beyond roll call voting—appropriations, constituency service, and so on. In sum, where it was for most of its history true that southerners did not enjoy the same level of representation as did northerners, today the two regions are indistinguishable on this score.

Finally in chapter 9 we have several objectives. The first is to evaluate how, over time, democratic attitudes and behaviors in the South have evolved as compared to the North as the region has acquired a more developed party system and more competitive elections. We will see that southern whites' and southern blacks' democratic attitudes such as support for free speech, equality, and political efficacy, as well as their democratic behaviors such as participation in elections, have over the last half century converged with the attitudes and behaviors of their northern compatriots. We also assess the effectiveness of government in the two regions over time. We will see that regional gaps in government performance in such areas as combating illiteracy, school attendance, family size, and life expectancy have narrowed or disappeared altogether. The final objective of chapter 9 is to conclude our story. In doing so, we will address the question of whether the South has become a one-party region with the GOP now dominant, whether the nation's convergence with the South is more a "southernization" of the nation than a "nationalization" of the South, and, thus, whether the South remains a distinctive political region.

2

POLITICAL PARTIES, ELECTORAL COMPETITION, AND EFFECTIVE DEMOCRATIC GOVERNANCE

Democracy is the worst form of government, except for all the others, to paraphrase Winston Churchill.[1] His point, of course, was that governing is very difficult, but that a government based on citizen sovereignty has the best chance of working effectively and thus being the best form of government. Our question follows from his by asking under just what conditions does it really have a better chance of succeeding and when does it not? Our answer is that it arises to its Churchillian "least worst," level precisely when there is an established, competitive, multiparty system.[2] Or to put it more positively: Effective democratic governance arises consistently in the presence of regularized party competition for control of the offices of government. That is our central claim in this book.

The purpose of this chapter is to develop an understanding of why this may be true. That is to say, we seek to provide a logic that tells us why democracies are more effective when there is such a party system, and why governments are less effective when there is not. The rest of the book will investigate whether the data from the South and more generally in the United States support this claim. And thus, this chapter develops a theory of party systems and democratic governance that is then tested as a means of understanding the politics of the American South.[3] Our claim, to put it more precisely, is that when in equilibrium, party systems are the only tool we have to reliably convert public preferences into competitive elections, and regularly competitive elections are required for effective democratic governance. There must be regularized party competition in elections, or else governance will not be effective and democracy will fail sufficiently as to no longer be worth that name. And, in the South, there have been a few times when there has been such a party system and many times when there has not been. When there has been no "equilibrium" party system, democracy has failed there.

While we are by no means original in making a claim similar to this, not everyone agrees that political parties are central to the proper functioning of democracies.[4] For instance, Schumpeter (1962) and Sen (1999) instead emphasize the significance of individual freedom in democracies. Others relatedly stress the central role of mass participation in democratic politics: "Democracy provides opportunities for 1) effective participation, 2) equality in voting, 3) gaining enlightened understanding, 4) exercising final control [by the people] over the agenda, and 5) inclusion of adults" (Dahl 1998, 38).

Other scholars go beyond simply failing to specify a prominent role for political parties in a democracy to specifically disavow their necessity: "It would be too much to argue that institutionally strong parties are a necessary condition for consolidating democracy or maintaining its vitality" (Diamond and Gunther 2001, 1).[5] Some claim that party factions may stand in for full-blown parties (Grynaviski 2004; Caughey 2014), a point we discuss below. Others have contended that interest groups can perform many of the functions parties do in a democracy (Clemens 1997). For proponents of this view, it was no accident that the reforms of the 1880s and 1890s that were intended to limit the role of political parties in elections coincided with an uptick in the creation and activity of interest organizations (Clemens 1997; Wiebe 1967). However, most would agree that while interest groups compete with parties in some ways, they do not offer a real alternative because they fail to field a broad array of candidates for office (Schattschneider 1942). In our view, there may be times when interest groups serve as a substitute for parties, as Hansen (1991) argues, but these are specialized and likely transient instances and differ relatively little in their structures and practices from a political party as we understand the term. More commonly, interest groups combine with parties to help create the conditions for parties to succeed, as when the religious right aligned with the Republican Party and when the unions and civil rights groups aligned with the Democratic Party. Similarly, party factions may serve as temporary substitutes, but they are likely to fail or to develop from faction to full party status rather quickly, with respect to the time frame we are using.

Other scholars have recognized the *coincidence* of democratic politics and political parties, without necessarily elaborating why they go hand in hand. For example, studies have asserted that political parties are "inevitable" (Sartori 1968), "desirable" (Dahl 2003, 30), "critical" and "essential" (Levitsky and Cameron 2003, 1, 5) for democracy, or "endemic" (Stokes 1999, 246) to it. Democracy is "unthinkable" (Schattschneider 1942, 1), or perhaps just "unworkable" (Aldrich 2011, 3), without political parties. The studies that perhaps come closest to our claim are those that suggest "parties create[d] democracy" (Schattschneider 1942, 1; see also Aldrich 1995; Levitsky and Cameron 2003).[6] However, even these studies have not followed up their bold proclamations with a rigorous explanation of how, exactly, party systems engender effective democratic governance.

We contend that effective democratic governance is created and sustained in the electoral competition that occurs *specifically between political parties* and in the information and incentives that this competition promotes. Stated more direly, absent this organized, repeated competition between or among several political parties, there is no democracy. Politicians may claim to want to be independent of all political parties, abhor partisan "bickering," and seek to "rise above" the partisan fray (e.g., Herbst 2010; Coleman and Manna 2007). Indeed, Washington's warning of the "baneful effects" of political parties was typical of the prevailing views of the Founders. But politicians very quickly discovered that they needed political parties to achieve the desired benefits of a democracy. So, let us take this notion seriously and explore *how* a system of political parties generates political competition and *why* electoral competition rooted in a party system is indeed necessary to make democratic governance effective.

OUR ARGUMENT OVERVIEWED

Figure 2.1 summarizes our argument that electoral competition is required for effective democratic governance and that a party system in equilibrium is, while perhaps not necessary, the only alternative we have seen to reliably produce competitive elections over time. Below, we develop this series of expectations, somewhat unconventionally from the last to the first of the relationships. Our argument will be:

1. Democracies govern effectively when they a) perform well on so-called valence issues where there is greater consensus among citizens, and b) represent citizens' preferences on more controversial issues, those on which there is a possibility for parties to choose positions;[7]
2. Regularly competitive elections in which voters can hold elected officials accountable are necessary to induce elected officials to follow through on 1a) and 1b);

3. When a party system is in equilibrium, it will yield competitive elections in which voters are able to hold officials accountable.[8] A party system is not a necessary condition for competitive elections, except in the sense that we know of no alternative.

4. A party system is in equilibrium when there are at least two "major" political parties that are sustained as fully developed over time. "Major" indicates that at least two parties offer candidates across a very wide swath of available offices, and contest strongly for most of them. They are able to do so, in part, because they attend to points 1 through 3 above when in office. Finally, the system is in equilibrium where at least two of these major parties have these qualities for a sustained period of time.[9] To these points we can add the characteristic that they induce, that a party in equilibrium designs its strategies in light of the anticipated behavior of the candidates and others in the other major party or parties.

ELECTORAL COMPETITION AND EFFECTIVE DEMOCRATIC GOVERNANCE

In this section we define effective democratic governance, define electoral competition, discuss prior research on electoral competition and effective democratic governance, and provide our account for why the two are linked.

Defining Effective Democratic Governance

In our view, democracies govern effectively when a) elected officials capably produce the conditions that citizens broadly expect the public sector to provide, or what are sometimes referred to as "valence issues," and b) elected officials represent the citizens', even if only their particular constituents', preferences on more controversial issues. As Key famously stated, "Unless mass views have some place in the shaping of policy, all the talk about democracy is nonsense" (Key 1961, 7).

On some issues, citizens are in general agreement about the desired policy outcome. There is little disagreement that longer life expectancies are preferred to shorter ones and that educated children are better prepared for life, for example. There is also a good deal of agreement that there is a governmental role to be had in facilitating these outcomes. In a comparative context, Janda et al. (2012) has termed this "country governance," or "the extent to which a state delivers the desired benefits of government at acceptable costs." In these domains, as we argue more comprehensively below, political parties compete to offer and implement a program that will achieve the consensus-desired

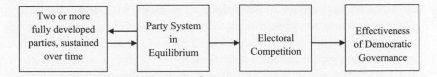

Figure 2.1 Summary of argument

result. These programs could be identical, or nearly so, and the parties merely compete over their ability to implement them effectively, or, in common parlance, to govern and to govern well. Or the means to achieve the commonly desired end can be quite different in their design, and presumably also the results.

There may be little difference over ends on many things. Neither party will campaign for reducing employment or decreasing economic growth. But they—and many citizens—differ regularly and sometimes passionately about whether the government is a means to economic growth or whether it is a hindrance, harming the economy in ways that should be left to the market alone.

Voters evaluate party performance by observing outcomes, attributing those outcomes to whichever party is thought to be responsible for them, and rewarding or punishing the parties accordingly at the ballot box. Or, as Janda et al. (2012) found in a comparative context, governance is better where citizens are able to press their desires on government. To this we would add that a central way that citizens press their desires on government is through their judgment that the party controlling the levels of government has or has not succeeded in the act of governing. So, we contend that a democracy is operating effectively on valence issues when in the areas that government might reasonably be expected to produce public goods, it is reliably able to do so.

But perhaps this is insufficiently demanding. According to Key:

> When two distinct groups with some identity and continuity exist, they must raise issues and appeal to the masses if for no other reason than the desire for office. Whether the existence of issues causes the formation of continuing groups of politicians or whether the existence of competing groups causes issues to be raised is a moot point. Probably the two factors interact. Nevertheless, in those states with loose and short-lived factions campaigns often are the emptiest sorts of debates over personalities, over the means for the achievement of what everybody agrees on. . . . A disorganized politics makes impossible a competition between recognizable groups for power. (1984, 304)

On other issues, perhaps most of them, citizens do not agree about the desired outcome. On these issues, "dimensions" of disagreement exist in the mass public and among elected officials that divide them on so-called ideological grounds (e.g. Converse 1964; Poole and Rosenthal 1997). Usually, these divisions are on economic or moral policies where some prefer the status quo while others wish to see it changed. There may be considerable disagreement as well as to which direction the status quo should be changed.

These are so-called ideological issues, because it is not obvious, in many cases, whether the issue position is "liberal" or "conservative" until the party leaders choose sides (Karol 2009). Thus, for example, in the 1950s, it was not at all obvious whether the pro–civil rights position was best found on the liberal (and Democratic) side or the conservative (and Republican) side of the status quo. Only after the northern liberal, Democratic majority had embraced civil rights, such as through the passage of the Civil Rights Act of 1964, and the conservative, Goldwater wing of the Republican Party had opposed it, did it become clear which ideological camp would become home for the pro–civil rights supporters. Similarly, before *Roe v. Wade*, the liberal Democrats tended to be more pro-life, while the conservative Republicans were more pro-choice, but there was plenty of support for both positions on each side of the ideological and partisan divide. It was only after *Roe v. Wade* that the contemporary affiliation of pro-life with conservative ideology and Republican partisan politics and pro-choice with liberal ideology and Democratic partisan politics emerged.

On these combative issues, effective democracies find a way for the citizens who prefer the status quo in a given policy domain to be represented in the main by elected officials who work to retain it while the citizens who desire policy change (even if they be in the minority) to be represented by elected officials who work (at least at the electoral stage) for that to occur. This comparison of elected official behavior to constituency attitude has been termed "dyadic representation" (e.g., Miller and Stokes 1963; Ansolabehere, Snyder, and Stewart 2001). One way to assess the degree of dyadic representation in a political system is to measure its *responsiveness*, or whether more conservative electoral districts are represented by more conservative elected officials and more liberal districts by more liberal officials (Achen 1978). Or we might look to see if those in office change their behavior when citizens' preferences shift; for example, do elected officials vote more liberally after constituents had voted more liberally in the preceding election?

Defining Electoral Competition

We claim that an election writ large is competitive when incumbents across the full range of offices stand a reasonable chance of failing to maintain their seats. The presence of competition is usually easiest to assess after an election is over, by observing the proportion of the vote received by the challenger for the office, by the spending patterns of the candidates, and perhaps also by the objective credentials of the challenger (Holbrook and Van Dunk 1993). We might also evaluate the degree of competition by focusing instead on the proportion of seats won by challengers in a given election (Ranney 1965, 1976). Doing so helps to head off concerns that some challengers might perform better in an election for reasons that have little to do with their attractiveness as a candidate. For instance, the backers of challengers (as a group) might strategically focus their resources on a subset of challengers in hopes of maximizing the share of seats secured rather than the average vote proportion won.

The essential, and seemingly simple, point is that politicians in the presence of electoral competition need to attend to the business of winning votes and thus attend to the concerns of those who cast them and so can ultimately put them in office or keep them there. So by "competitive" we mean that politicians, incumbents or those from the same party who are nominated in their place, have a realistic concern about being defeated in the coming election. And, therefore, they choose to act on that concern so as to win the election. That is achieved only by appealing directly or indirectly to the "great body of the people" to vote for her or him. Once they actually do take the requisite action, they may win reelection almost all the time, but failure to attend to the will of the people puts that apparently safe seat at real risk.

Competition and Democracy

The literature on electoral competition and democratic governance contains, on the one hand, studies of political competition that are not explicitly tied to democratic politics, and, on the other hand, studies of democracy that are not explicitly tied to competition *among parties*. Contemporary studies of the former variety tend to reside in the realm of American politics, where there is great variation in electoral competition but less variation in the "level" of democratic effectiveness. Some have investigated whether political competition stimulates citizens to voice their preferences to governing officials through the electoral process (e.g., Cox and Munger 1989), which may promote accountability. Research has also asked whether electoral competition enhances the responsiveness of policy to public opinion (Griffin 2006). In this study, Griffin showed that the responsiveness of elected officials' roll call behavior to the opinions of their constituents was much sharper within districts that were electorally competitive than in less competitive districts.[10] Jones (2013) also finds that states with greater political competition have greater levels of voter knowledge of, and responsiveness to, congressional representation. He also finds that unrepresented voters will only tend to desert the incumbent in competitive races, giving legislators in uncompetitive districts greater leeway to shirk from public opinion in making policy decisions.

Meanwhile, studies of the latter variety, focusing on government performance in democracies, tend to be cross-national. For example:

> Modern political democracy is a system of governance in which rulers are held accountable for their actions in the public realm by citizens, acting indirectly through the competition and cooperation of their elected representatives. (Schmitter and Karl 1991, 76)

> Democratic systems [are] . . . characterized by competitive elections in which most citizens are eligible to participate." (Powell 1982, 3)

> Democracy is a competitive political system in which competing leaders and organizations define the alternatives of public policy in such a way that the public can participate in the decision-making process. (Schattschneider 1960, 141)

Others put a finer point on it—linking political competition to specific aspects of government performance. Several studies have found a strong and positive association between the extent of political competition and outcomes such as government efficiency and corruption, the provision of public goods, tax compliance, and per capita income (e.g., Grzymala-Busse 2007; Besley et al. 2010; Rodrik 1999). So, many scholars conclude that electoral competition is a key ingredient of democratic governance, but do not take the next step of asking how institutions have been (or might be) designed to promote regularized competition.

A final line of studies fingers political parties as central to effective democratic governance, as in Przeworski (1991), but in these the mechanism remains underdeveloped:

> Democracy is a system in which parties lose elections. There are parties: divisions of interest, values and opinions. There is competition, organized by rules. And there are periodic winners and losers. (10)

> The competitive electoral context, with several political parties organizing the alternatives that face the voters, is the identifying property of the contemporary democratic process. (Powell 1982, 3)

> In competing with each other for votes, parties are in fact vying to better represent the general public. (Scheiner 2006, 7)

These studies tend to ignore the question of why, exactly, competition among political parties facilitates democratic governance.

Our Argument

Our theoretical argument linking effective democratic governance to electoral competition runs as follows: On some policy issues there is consensus in the public regarding the desired outcome such as reducing infant mortality, living in a healthy environment, and having a low crime rate. We assume that voters will prefer the candidate who offers the most convincing program to achieve these outcomes, all else equal, and that in the aggregate voters are able to distinguish better from worse programs. So when elections are competitive or voters prefer the candidates in equal numbers, we can infer that the candidates are offering comparably attractive programs. Not only that, we can conclude that the offered programs in a competitive election are also highly attractive to voters, because strategic candidates will take advantage of opponents who offer unattractive programs leading to a less competitive result. So, on valence issues competitive elections are coincident with candidates and incumbents seeking to deliver attractive programs.[11] Regardless of which candidate is elected in a competitive election an attractive program will be implemented.[12] And finally we assume that more attractive (and, per above, better) programs yield more effective outcomes.

On nonvalence issues where voters are much more likely to disagree, electoral competition also promotes effective democratic governance. Above, we define an effective democratic government as one that is responsive to differences in the policy preferences of voters. The electoral system might be said to be perfectly responsive when each district's median voter is represented by a like-minded elected official. We assume that the median voter in an electoral unit will prefer the candidate whose ideological platform is closest to her own. In the extreme case, the median voter will be indifferent between the candidates (and by extension the remaining voters will be evenly divided and elections will be perfectly competitive) when the candidates are equidistant from the median voter's ideal point. As above, candidates will exploit opponents' distance from the median so both candidates will be as close to the median as other constraints permit. So, a competitive outcome suggests that the candidates were as close as possible to the median voter. In this way, competitive elections promote responsiveness and effective democratic governance on contentious issues as well.

Another way to see this is that when incumbents enjoy a built-in, nonpolicy advantage over their challengers, they can choose not to be as like-minded while maintaining a sufficiently high probability of re-election (Wittman 1983). Per Wittman (1983, 146) "policy-motivated legislators can trade off some added probability of winning for a more desirable policy position." Empirical analyses of this claim have found that elected officials who represent competitive districts are less loyal to their parties—presumably defecting to support roll call alternatives that their constituents preferred (e.g., Froman 1963; MacRae 1952). Subsequent studies indicated that state assembly members were more responsive to constituents when they represented competitive districts, but only on some issues (Kuklinski 1977), and that only among competitive districts, the House candidate closest to the constituency mean was more likely to win the election (Sullivan and Uslaner 1978). More recent studies claiming to support the marginality hypothesis showed that congressional candidates' policy positions tend to converge in ideologically balanced districts, especially in races involving high-quality candidates or candidates who face tough primary challenges (Ansolabehere, Snyder, and Stewart 2001; Burden 2004), and that incumbents whose expected vote share is near 50% tend to vote more moderately relative to other members (Erikson and Wright 2000). Finally, Griffin (2006) found that the responsiveness of House members representing more competitive districts was substantially greater than those representing less competitive districts.[13]

Effective Democratic Governance without Competition?

In a one-party system that lone party may be "fully developed" while elections are not competitive. However, this is not a stable equilibrium due to the absence of an opinion consensus about partisan politics among citizens. Indeed, this is precisely the connection that Key drew between the national one-partyism of the Jim Crow South and the local fragmentation and factionalization of that one party in individual southern states (1949). Another example of this strong tendency is the rapid "disintegration" of the Jeffersonian party along regional lines after the collapse of the Federalists, making the "Era of Good Feelings" short-lived (Jenkins and Weidenmier 1999, 232; see also Gamm and Shepsle 1989).[14]

Although "one-party democracy is not supposed to happen" (Scheiner 2006, 210), others contend that democratic governments can persist even in the absence of political competition or a consensus among citizens. Japan, for example, "is a democracy" and yet "a single party . . . dominated Japan throughout most of the postwar period" (Scheiner 2006, 12). In our view, Japan was only putatively a democracy so long as the Liberal Democratic Party (LDP) was effectively uncontested for power, regardless of the extent of factional competition with it. As Scheiner argues, it was only through a system of clientelistic politics—material side payments—that the widely unpopular LDP was able to remain the single, dominant political party. He concludes that "the lack of competition . . . appears to have promoted policy immobility, even in the face of serious economic and political problems" (Scheiner 2006, 218). It is telling indeed that more often, single-party governments are observed in authoritarian systems (Magaloni and Kricheli 2010).

Others take more direct aim at political competition as the purported engine of democracy (Buchler 2005, 2007; Brunell 2006, 2008; Brunell and Buchler 2009; Adams et al. 2013). According to this view, voter satisfaction and the representation of public opinion are maximized when voters are organized into homogenous groupings represented by a like-minded elected official. As one author put it, "it is easier to represent homogenous districts than it is to represent heterogeneous districts" (Buchler 2005, 449). Conversely, "drawing districts with relatively equal numbers of Democrats and Republicans maximizes the number of losing voters," because a single legislator cannot appeal to both groups of partisans simultaneously (Brunell 2006, 83). What is more, voters do not appear to place great intrinsic value on elections being competitive, so long as they are not on the losing side of election outcomes (Brunell and Clarke 2012).

Almost as an afterthought, drawing district lines to maximize the political homogeneity of voters would lead to noncompetitive general elections: "If, say, all citizens are Democratic partisans, then both candidates will appeal on policy grounds to these partisans, since there are no others. Therefore . . . margin-maximizing candidates will converge to identical positions in this 'perfectly' uncompetitive scenario" (Adams et al. 2013, 335). Rather than seeing this product of a homogenous districting scheme as a drawback, for these scholars the lack of competition is to be embraced: "ideologically homogeneous districts structured in such a way as to minimize competition in congressional elections can do a better job than competitive districts in achieving representative outcomes. These non-competitive districts produce legislators that are closer to their district medians and more representative of everyone in their districts" (Buchler 2005, 457). Conversely, "in competitive districts, each candidate is motivated to appeal in large part to his/her own partisan constituency, which motivates increased divergence of the candidates' positions" (Adams et al. 2013, 335), or what is labeled the "*competitive polarization result*" (337, italics in original).

As evidence in support of this argument, one study compared the roll call behavior of Democratic and Republican congressional winners who represent ideologically similar districts (Adams et al. 2013). Detecting little descriptive evidence of convergence in moderate as compared to one-sided districts, they conclude that "partisan polarization has tended to be as great or greater in districts that are the most competitive" (Adams et al. 2013, 347). They also point to a study by Ansolabehere, Snyder, and Stewart (2001) that found, in passing, little difference between the ideological gap between congressional winners and losers in competitive and uncompetitive districts. Based on this type of evidence, these scholars conclude that "the assumption that competitive general elections make representatives more responsive is . . . wrong" (Brunell 2006, 83),[15] and more sweepingly, competitive elections are bad for America (Brunell 2008).[16]

We could point out several problems with these arguments against the value of political competition.[17] For instance, we might ask why it is that ideologically similar districts (as measured using presidential voting behavior) are not electing representatives sharing the same political party. This is particularly curious among the districts that are not ideologically moderate. Moreover, knowing the gap between legislators tells us little about where they stand relative to their district median voter. However, we need not undermine entirely this perspective to maintain that competition among parties is necessary for a healthy democratic politics.

We contend that, rather than eliminating political competition, homogenous districting schemes merely displace and mask it. To homogenize district elections is to displace competition downward by diverting ambitious politicians to party primary fights. That is, when incumbents can so readily reflect constituent opinion and enjoy the benefit of the district's preferred party label, it is hard to imagine unseating the incumbent in the general election. This leaves ambitious politicians little recourse but to target the incumbent's party primary. We will detail our contention that this is an inferior form of political competition due to the lack of continuity inherent in party factionalism. Here, we simply add that political competition can be relocated from the general to primary election environment through the manner of districting.

An effort to remove competition from general election races also cannot prevent the disagreements among the public from appearing in the legislature. That is, even if districts are drawn so as to maximize voter agreement within districts, the legislators representing these districts will, so long as voters disagree across districts, need to compete within the legislature. In this way, the competition between voters over the direction of policy is transferred, and actually best observed, in the partisan balance of the state legislature or the state's congressional delegation.

PARTY SYSTEMS AND ELECTORAL COMPETITION

In this section we provide a comprehensive account of how a party system in equilibrium yields regularly competitive elections. We begin by defining the political party and a party system. We then explain what we mean by a party system in equilibrium, including the role that citizens and politicians play in the movement of a party system toward equilibrium. Finally we show how a party system in equilibrium will yield competitive elections.

What Parties Are

In our task to link the party system to electoral competition we begin by defining what we mean by a political party, by a party system, and by a competitive party system.

Many groups and organizations can be considered or even call themselves political parties, creating such a diversity of groups that might be expected to be included under a comprehensive definition as to render an inclusive definition nearly meaningless. We are interested in the major political party, a term clear enough in the United States, although it may be rather less clear in comparative contexts, particularly in systems using proportional representation that generate a large number of often very small parties. A party is or aspires to be a *major political party* when it competes (i.e., offers candidates) for many, even most, electoral offices up for election at any given time, when it competes for such offices repeatedly over time, and when a reasonable observer would conclude that many of these candidates competed strongly (had a reasonably high probability of success) for a substantial number of the offices they contested.[18]

A political system is said to have an associated system of political parties (i.e., *a party system*) when each of the major political parties is at a self-enforcing equilibrium, the nature of which we discuss below. It has proved useful to denote a party system primarily by the number of major political parties at this equilibrium, and that typically means "two" or "more than two."[19] Our definition requires the sustained competition between at least two "fully developed," that is, "major," political parties. That is, we focus on the party here and see the party system as the aggregation of major parties. This contrasts with those such as Cox (1997) who derive the number of parties in a system that is in equilibrium, that is, he derives whether a system has two or more than two parties as the major part of the definition of a party system in equilibrium. In this view, a system is in equilibrium when all the parties have chosen to compete or not, perhaps when they have chosen spatial positions, and when all individuals agree on the first two points and on the probabilities with which each candidate is expected to win. This idea of party system equilibrium is the game-theoretic one in which all parties are effectively members of a system of political parties if they condition their behavior on that of the other parties, and those parties condition their behavior on that of the party, in turn. That is, a party system is one in which there are two or more parties engaged in ongoing strategic interaction (see Aldrich 2011).

Aldrich and Lee (2016) provide an example that reflects a multi-party system satisfying the above conditions. In their model, there are two "major" parties who condition their behavior in an n-dimensional space to prevent the possibility of entry of a third party. The positions they choose are those that ensure that there is no platform a third party can adopt and win the election, but also ensures that the two major parties are located so that they are ensured a tie with each other in expectation. The interesting features of this model, therefore, are that the two parties strategically choose to diverge from the median voter equilibrium position, appropriate if there were exactly and only two parties and that the divergence is designed to block entry of a third party. The model yields a rationale for the persistence of two parties in a plurality or, more generally, "first-past-the-post" (FPTP) system, and, most importantly for here, provides a system-level equilibrium (or conditions when such exists) in which two parties are observed, but the parties act as if there are four players, voters, the two "major parties," and a hypothetical third party.

Finally, while we could spend considerable time outlining what scholars have meant by a "competitive party system" (Ranney 1965, 1976; Holbrook and Van Dunk 1993) let us simply state it as meaning that there are at least two political parties competing over the full range of elective political offices for lengthy durations. By "competitive" we mean that no one party is given distinct advantage in elections by the laws of the nation (and/or state) and that every party that wins any given election has a realistic risk of losing that office to another party or parties in the near future. Under this definition, a party might win, say, the U.S. presidency repeatedly, but it would enter each election with a serious concern about losing.[20]

To return to our story, there are two major sets of actors in a party system, citizens and ambitious politicians, a set that is in turn divided into office seekers and political and partisan activists.[21] In the next section we discuss how both citizens and politicians benefit from the construction of and adherence to clear party labels in a self-enforcing equilibrium.

Citizens

Many scholars have asked whether and how citizens learn a sufficient amount about the candidates in campaigns to make an informed choice between them (e.g., Delli Carpini and Keeter 1996). Among the sources of information available to citizens are challengers (Kingdon 1989; Arnold 1993), the media (Lodge, Steenbergen, and Brau 1995; Hutchings 1998; Arnold 2004), and cues adopted by the candidates themselves (Erikson 1971; Lupia and McCubbins 1998). This information may be conveyed directly to any particular citizen (who may have, e.g., watched a televised commercial) or indirectly, through the two-step flow of communication, from source through an opinion leader to one or more other citizens (Lazarsfeld, Berelson, and Gaudet 1948). Of the cues available about candidates, it may be that none convey any more information to voters than the candidates' party affiliations, although they may convey much more.

Citizens receive value from a label, including a party label, when it helps them decide how to vote. It helps them decide how to vote when the label has content. We consider two illustrative cases that are particularly prominent in the context of programmatic parties.[22] The party label might stand for ideas, values, or policies, and the voter might therefore choose to support politicians who stand for the same ideas, values, or policies the voter does (e.g., Abramowitz 1988). In this case, the voter is choosing prospectively, in the hopes that those who stand for what the voter desires will be elected and will carry those ideas, values, or policies into practice.

The second case is that in which the party label has content that consists primarily of what prominent politicians of that party have done while in office. That is, parties in government work to advance a policy agenda that is unique from the competing party's agenda, which helps to improve the clarity of each party's label (Cox and Mc-Cubbins 1993). Party organizations contribute to this construction of party labels by working to recruit candidates for office who either hold personal preferences for the direction of policy that are consonant with the mainstream of the party (Gibson et al. 1983), or who are willing to contribute to the development of a meaningful brand or party label by supporting the party line regardless of their own preferences (more on this below). Thus, there may be considerable latitude for candidates and elected members of the party to vote freely on many issues, but not (if the brand name is to convey meaningful information) on those issues that unite the party and distinguish them from their opposition, in equilibrium.

In this second case, the voter is choosing retrospectively, especially in the sense in which retrospective voting is used by Downs (1957) and Fiorina (1981). She might be choosing based on outcomes realized while that party held office—Key's "rational god of vengeance or reward" (Key 1964, 568). She might, instead, use that evidence as the basis for inference about what current candidates of that party could be expected to do if in office, in comparison to what candidates of the other party might do.

In either case, a party label's meaning and its clarity are products of the cohesiveness of the candidates and associated activists the voter has come across who affiliate with the party.[23] If a voter is aware that the policies espoused by the Democrat running for office in her district are out of step with the policies espoused by another Democratic candidate in a neighboring district or state or region, the voter's certainty about the meaning of the party label declines (Grynaviski 2010). Importantly, the meaning of the label declines for all the Democratic candidates the voter encounters, whether it be in this election or the next.

In both cases, the party label is useful to the voter because it carries with it political content. But having content that guides the voter into understanding what the candidates stand for in the election, while necessary, is insufficient for the label to be useful. The party label is useful to the voter only if it conveys political meaning *and* if it is a useful guide to what the candidate would actually do if elected to office (or at least try in good faith to do so), and thus it conveys content about the major outcomes the political system produces. This is a measure of the way in which the party label has both content and accountability built into it, to be effective for the voter and (as we develop below) therefore effective for the candidate running affiliated with a party.

Consider an example of the failure of the party label, due to the second factor, drawn from the nineteenth century (Woodward 1971

[1951], 237). In the 1890 election, a number of southern states saw competition that included an Alliance, allying farmers and laborers of the Populists with some Democrats, those who favored the "wool hats" over those who supported the "silk hats." Tennessee, for one, elected their state Alliance president, John P. Buchanan, governor, as well as electing numerous Alliance men to the legislature. The radical change called for by the Alliance did not appear, however, because, according to Woodward, Buchanan turned out to be as conservative as the former administration he was elected to replace. Governor John Young Brown, who won election in Kentucky in 1891, said he "went the whole way" with Alliance in that election, but he not only failed to deliver on that promise, he actually reversed a mandate for railroad regulation, supported by the Populists, that a constitutional convention had recently handed down. The Democratic state chairman of Virginia promised the Virginia Alliance a railroad commission in exchange for their support in 1890, but the Democratic assembly defeated it.

The lesson is that the value of the party label may lie in ideas, values, or policies, but it loses all of that value to the voter when politicians are elected on those promises but fail to deliver on them—and especially so when politicians actively choose to oppose them. Thus accountability also requires the ability of the voter to reflect back, even if making prospective choices, on the performance of the candidate or those who affiliate with the candidate's party. That is, accountability requires the value of the party label to extend over time, even for the same office. Similarly, Woodward does not say, in his example of the Virginia state party chairman, whether the chairman was unfaithful to his promise or whether he was unable to deliver in the legislature. For the voter, it does not matter which is true.[24] The value of the party label must extend not only over time but also across space, across the range of offices necessary to translate those ideas, values, or policies into governmental outcomes.

Politicians

Our perspective argues that the central components of the political party are the activists and the candidates and officeholders who adopt the name of the party, and it is the name of the party—and what meaning that label carries—that makes the party valuable to the voter. That electoral value is always one of the reasons, and it is perhaps the only reason, that a political aspirant, that is, the activist and office seeker/holder, finds affiliation with the party valuable. It is necessary for the party label to be meaningful to the public, and it is necessary for it to have a meaning that is sufficiently positively evaluated by sufficiently large numbers of voters for a political aspirant to imagine winning election under that label.

It might be the case that these are also sufficient reasons for an ambitious politician to affiliate with a party. They are sufficient, for example, if the politician's ambition extends only to the winning of office, which is also to say that the politician herself does not particularly care about the meaning of the label. Such politicians are referred to as pure office seekers in the theoretical literature (see, e.g., Downs 1957).[25] Put in other terms, pure office-seeking politicians, those who find the electoral benefits of adopting a party label both necessary and sufficient for affiliating with the party, are those whose personal ambitions for office entirely override their political concerns as a voter (Strom 1990).

Other ambitious politicians may reap value from affiliation with the party for the same reasons that a voter does—they value what the party stands for (Calvert 1985). Such politicians have multiple motives (Strom 1990). They care about winning office, and they care about how those offices are used, what policies they seek to implement, how much power they can acquire in the chamber, and so on. But they are still ambitious politicians who value office, if for no other reason than that they, or those whom they are backing, need to win elections to be able to control office. Whether, that is, the office seeker and those elites who back them are pure office seekers or have mixed motives, the electoral benefits of a strong and popular party label are of great value.[26] Aldrich and Bianco (1992), for example, examine the case of affiliation decisions when both the particular political parties and the party system are "out of equilibrium" (both in our sense of the term and in the sense of Cox as described above).

Schlesinger (1966) has long argued that democracy works better when politicians are ambitious in the office-seeking sense and not ambitious in the policy sense: "Ambition lies at the heart of politics. Politicians thrive on the preferments that office brings" (1). In the former but not necessarily in the latter case, the politician's ambition is harnessed to the wishes of the general public. It has become fashionable to refer to the politician who chooses policies to win votes rather than wins votes to choose policies as one who "panders" to the wishes of the public (see, e.g., Canes-Wrone et al. 2001). If that "pandering" continues into the use of office to do what the public finds valuable, then pandering is precisely what the electoral connection is supposed to achieve—a tie between what the candidate advocates, the voters support, and the governing official enacts (at least in what Riker [1982] calls the "populist" view of democracy). The panderer, most of all, is that politician who is harnessed to the public, by which one can only mean that the panderer-in-office chooses that which he believes he can most effectively run on in the next election. If they pander for election and choose differently when in office, they will lose their support, as assuredly as did the Alliance victors in 1890–91.[27] We could put this point in the cloak of contemporary game theory. From the voter's perspective, she observes a candidate who has adopted a party affiliation and runs, therefore, as a partisan. Either that label has meaning to the voter or it does not. If it has no meaning, then the voter decides on the basis of whatever can be gleaned about the individual candidate, which would be the identity of any groups they fortuitously bring to politics, any policies they demagogically appeal on, or their own record as lone-wolf operator, or the friends and neighbors effect of appeals within their own little bailiwicks (to paraphrase Key 1949). That they are, let us say, a Democrat is by definition irrelevant, since the label has no meaning—what some Republicans today refer to as "Rino," or "Republican in name only" (and similarly for "Dino").

If, instead, the label has meaning, then that meaning (for good or ill) is part of what enters into the voter's calculations about whom to support. The voter cannot tell from the fact of affiliation whether the candidate values the goals, principles, and policies of the candidate's party, or is merely using the label to seek office for its own sake. If the label has no meaning to the candidate, as seems to be the case with Woodward's accounting of Alliance men, then the voter soon learns that fact, and the label loses value to the voter, as well. Indeed, it was precisely the reversal of promises that (perhaps intentionally on the part of the winning candidates) caused the demise of the Alliance and the end of the populist (and Populist) hopes in the South as well as in the nation. Certainly, we would expect that this might be the case for a politician who desires to hold office for one term and then retire from politics (perhaps seeking to be governor as the capstone of a career). Once elected, there is no longer any electoral sanction that matters, and the politician is freed to do whatever he or she might like. To stand for one thing in the campaign and do another when in office is not a recipe for reelection.

Therefore, it follows that if the label is to have meaning, it must translate into at least some level of guidance for conduct while in office. The voter, even then, cannot distinguish between a candidate who adopts a party affiliation for expediency and one who adopts that label out of belief. It will not distinguish between candidates, for both stand for office affiliated with that party. It will not (greatly) distinguish between officeholders, for the panderer will still pander to the public by being reasonably faithful to the content of the label that elected him, otherwise the label will lose meaning and not be able to help reelect him, while the true believer will be at least modestly faithful to the content of the label that elected her—and her partisan affiliates—otherwise she would acting against her beliefs *and* putting any reelection hopes at risk as well.[28] This case of a meaningful label that attracts candidates who value the policy encoded in the party reputation because of its meaning to voters and that attracts candidates who desire to win those voters is a type of equilibrium outcome known as "pooling"—one cannot distinguish one type of candidate from the other, one cannot distinguish the pure office seeker from the candidate who also values policies, ideas, or principles.

There is one exception to the above case that helps to prove the rule. It may be that the purely office-seeking candidate originally wins election in part with the aid of the party label, but once in office is able to develop within the electorate sufficient knowledge of who he is and what he stands for that he can "rise above party" and campaign on the strength of his own personal qualities in his quest for reelection. Given what we know about voter knowledge of candidates, however, this strategy is available only to those who hold among the very highest offices (remember how few can identify their own member of the U.S. House; see, e.g., Mann and Wolfinger 1980), hold it for a long time, and are mostly restricted to those who hold executive offices, except in unusual circumstances. This strategy is most evidently *not* available to those just entering politics, those holding less visible offices, and those not otherwise able to distinguish themselves in politics or in some high-salience position in an earlier career (or, as Canon [1990] calls, them, the "astronauts, actors, and athletes" who turn to elective office). Thus, affiliation with a party, adopting a party label that is meaningful to the voter, is most valuable to the new entrant to politics, the (usually) young, striving, ambitious newcomer, and those holding the least well known and closely followed offices.

Of course, this exception, which comes to a fair number of U.S. senators, and a few members of Congress (MCs) in the U.S. House, also is distinctive to majority electoral systems with single-member districts, and separate elections. That is, only in such institutional circumstances is it possible for a legislator to develop a personal vote (Cain, Ferejohn, and Fiorina 1984; 1987). Even in the United States, which has the combination of conditions that make candidate-centric politics feasible, it was not until late in the nineteenth century that the first glimmerings of candidate-centered elections emerged in the U.S. Congress (see McGerr 1986; Carson and Roberts 2013), and even then it paled in comparison to that of the 1960s and 1970s, when a substantial number of MCs developed what we might call a personal vote (to use the Cain, Ferejohn, and Fiorina's [1984; 1987] term) rather than a partisan one, presumably primarily due to technological changes that enabled them to develop the "nucleus" of an effective electoral campaign organization (to use Schlesinger's [1966] term) of their own and to strengthen it through the various advantages unique to incumbency.

Party Systems and Electoral Competition

As should be evident from our account of the fully developed major political party, a two-party system in which both parties are fully developed will be a competitive party system (Downs 1957). That is, a party is in equilibrium when its label conveys meaning to voters (i.e., the party stands for something), and is sufficiently attractive to enough voters so as to attract ambitious politicians to affiliate with the party label. From the office-seeking, ambitious politician's perspective, "enough" voters is half the electorate. So, the individual party is in equilibrium when it can offer its candidates something approximating an even chance of election. In a two-party system, then, each of the parties is in equilibrium when elections are competitive.

In a party system with relatively few parties, the task of affording party candidates an even chance of winning an election requires the forging of broad coalitions (Cohen, Karol, Noel, and Zaller 2008; Carmines and Stimson 1989). It is the thorny task of party leaders to identify a set of policies and recruit a set of candidates that would build an ongoing, competitive coalition in this complex terrain of public preferences. As Key (1949) so elegantly put it,

> The decline in the Negro population, the growth of cities, and the dilution of an agricultural economy . . . occur only slowly . . . it is not to be supposed that these fundamental trends automatically bring political change. They only create conditions favorable to change that must be wrought by men and women disposed to take advantage of the opportunity to accelerate the inevitable. (674–75)

To summarize our linkage of party systems and electoral competition, political parties seek to control public offices (Downs 1957). To do so, parties need sufficient voters and candidates. Party labels, or reputations, inform voters of what a party will do in office (Grynaviski 2010). Candidates are drawn to parties able to obtain voter support (Schlesinger 1966). A single party is fully developed when it can attract sufficient voters and candidates to be broadly competitive.

A party system is in equilibrium when each of its component parties is in equilibrium (i.e., competitive). We anticipate a two-party system, given the single-member district requirement in the United States. Thus, a party system in equilibrium generates electoral competition between two parties. This two-party system, when in equilibrium, generates conditions in which office-holding politicians seek to realize the wishes of the voters who brought them to office in the first place and are likely to be the basis of the voting coalition that will seek to return them to office in the second place. It is this set of incentives that leads a democracy with a competitive party system to be in equilibrium and achieve effective governance, yielding Churchillian "least worst" status among all forms of government that have yet been tried.

Competition without Parties?

An objection to our argument might be that in the absence of a party system, intraparty competition among party factions might serve the same purpose. The suggestion is that these factions might play the same role as parties in tying government policies to citizens' interests. For instance, one assessment of mid-nineteenth-century factionalism in the United States concluded that "factional competition provided another opportunity for the public, and especially active partisans, to influence policy" (Benedict 1985, 386).

Perhaps the fullest explication of this argument is by Caughey (2014). Caughey contends that in the South,[29] during the V. O. Key era of 1930–60, there was vigorous competition in Democratic Party primaries; for instance, between 1932 and 1952 about half of all Democratic congressional primaries were contested. One factor that boosted the level of competition was voters' ability to coordinate on a few viable candidates (Grynaviski 2004). Then, using a subset of roll calls, data from Gallup, and an item-response model, Caughey modeled the relationship between white liberalism and roll call liberalism in the U.S. House and Senate. He found that northern U.S. House members were more responsive to public opinion than were southerners between 1936 and 1952. On the other hand, "in the Senate . . . there is no evidence that responsiveness differed across regions." Based on this and other evidence, Caughey concludes that "partisan competition is not necessary for effective representation."

Our rejoinder includes the idea that there are a lot of ways to organize for specific elections, but to do so across the broad swath of offices, so people can hold someone responsible for, say, a state government's legislation, and especially to do so over time, requires the kind of broad and encompassing organization that we call a mass-based political party. This was Key's point that we elaborate below—there were organizations for folks to win office, but not party organizations. A faction can organize for a few offices—the Tea Party, if it was a separate organization from the Republican Party in 2010, ran for only a smattering of seats; it has yet to run for most offices over the medium term, let alone long term, and thus cannot be held accountable. As another example, a Liberal Democrat member of Parliament in Britain might be able to be held accountable for her actions in the Commons but not for policy, and indeed the party cannot, so it needs also to win a lot of offices, not just run for a lot. Even if one disagrees with this point, the competition was over a very restricted range of policies than would be supported in the full electorate, if everyone were eligible. In particular it was competition over how best to preserve Jim Crow and keep the primary and all of southern politics lily-white. And that was necessary to be able to compete in all-white primaries.

To return to and elaborate Key's argument, the politics of faction were to Key thoroughly negative and precisely the negative of the politics of party (1984, 302–6). Factions were "ill-designed to meet the necessities of self-government" (1949, 310–11). Factions, he claimed, lack continuity in name and in the makeup of their leadership and the political candidates they presented to the public. As a result, factions lack continuity in voter support. The electorate becomes confused because it does not have as clear a set of options, sustained over time, as with parties. Parties, he believed, were able to be held responsible and therefore exercised at least a modicum of responsibility. Factions cannot be held responsible and therefore will not exercise responsibility. With factions, there is no consistent out-group. Thus the benefits of a loyal opposition, searching for issues to bring up in their attempt to oust the governing party, are lost. Issues are generally not brought up by factions, as Key had just demonstrated for the southern states. They lack "collective spirit," a sense of duty and obligation, and any sense of "joint responsibility" between governor and legislature as well. In sum, factional politics undermines each part of his party triad (i.e., party in the electorate, in government, and as an organization), both in the short term and, more worrisomely, in the long term.

Key is also justly famous for developing a different view of elections, that of retrospective voting based on the successes or failures of the incumbent administration (1966). It might seem that the voter in a one-party, even if factionalized one-party (or, to Key, a "no-party"), system could still be a "rational God of vengeance or reward." Not so, he argued. At the same time, he extended his argument about how the

lack of organized parties also undermines the development of responsible leadership and affects the choices of those ambitiously seeking to
enter politics (1984).

> American politics is often cynically described as a politics without issues
> and as a battle between the "ins" and the "outs." In a system of tran-
> sient factions—in its most extreme form—it is impossible to have even
> a fight between the "ins" and the "outs." The candidates are new and,
> in fact, deny any identification with any preceding administration. . . .
> Party responsibility is a concept that is greatly overworked, but in a fluid
> factional system not a semblance of factional responsibility exists. A gov-
> ernor serves his tenure—fixed either by constitution or custom—and the
> race begins anew. The candidates are, as completely as they can manage
> it, disassociated from the outgoing administration. The "outs" cannot
> attack the "ins" because the "ins" do not exist as a group with any col-
> lective spirit or any continuity of existence. Moreover, the independence
> or autonomy of candidates means that legislative candidates are disasso-
> ciated from the gubernatorial races, and if the electorate wants to reward
> the "ins" by another term or to throw the rascals out—if electorates
> behave that way—it has no way of identifying the "ins."
>   The lack of continuing groups of "ins" and "outs" profoundly influ-
> ences the nature of political leadership. . . . Enemies of today may be
> allies of tomorrow; for the professional and semiprofessional politician
> no such barrier as party affiliation and identification exists to separate
> the "ins" from the "outs." . . . Not only does a disorganized politics
> make impossible a competition between recognizable groups for power.
> It probably has a far-reaching influence on the kinds of individual lead-
> ers thrown into power and also on the manner in which they utilize
> their authority once they are in office. Loose factional organizations are
> poor contrivances for recruiting and sifting out leaders of public affairs.
> Social structures that develop leadership and bring together like-minded
> citizens lay the basis for the effectuation of majority will. Loose factions
> lack the collective spirit of party organization, which at its best imposes
> a sense of duty and imparts a spirit of responsibility to the inner core of
> leaders of the organization. While the extent to which two-party systems
> accomplish these ends are easily exaggerated, politicians working under
> such systems must, even if for no other reason than a yearning for office,
> have regard not only for the present campaign but also for the next. In
> an atomized and individualistic politics it becomes a matter of each
> leader for himself and often for himself only for the current campaign.
> (303–4)

Factional politics was lacking in every positive virtue he felt partisan politics did, or at least could, offer. Most serious among these,
however, was its effect on the ability of the public to exercise their sovereignty effectively. For Key democracy worked from bottom up (his

own words) while southern politics operated from the top down, and it was the creation and maintenance of factional rather than party politics that intentionally destroyed the ability of the public to govern. The solution to the problem of factions was clear—organized and sustained competition. And, if there be organized and sustained competition, then there were political parties, for that is precisely what Key meant by political parties.

The problem Key identified with factional politics was that they did not, that is, stand for any of three things that we might believe partisan contests for control of electoral offices to be about. They did not stand for ideas or policies that would help the voter distinguish one from another in the voting booth.[30] Neither did they stand unified with others for control of a large swath of offices, and therefore could not be seen as bound together across the legislature, the executive, and whatever other offices were chosen directly, by election, or chosen indirectly, by political appointment by elected officials. Nor did they typically, in Key's account, stand for control of the same office over time, making the transition from one occupant of that office to the next, and thus stand accountable for conduct while in office.

As another example that elections may be competitive even in the absence of electoral parties, we turn to contemporary state elections. Approximately three in four states use nonpartisan elections to choose some of their public officials (Desantis and Renner 1991), and these races certainly can be competitive. However, the available evidence suggests that nonpartisan elections are generally less competitive. In a study of intermediate appellate court elections by Schaffner, Streb, and Wright (2001), the authors found that in nonpartisan contexts judges were less likely to face an opponent, and when they did, incumbents received an additional 6% of the vote on average, compared to judges in partisan contexts. One reason for this is that turnout decreases significantly in nonpartisan contests (Schaffner, Streb, and Wright 2001; Hall 2007), and greater voter turnout is strongly associated with greater competition (e.g., Milbrath 1965).

A final critique concerning the importance of parties in producing electoral competition is that political competition instead emanates from the heterogeneity of the population. Berkowitz and Clay (2011) contend that a region's geographic conditions yield a degree of occupational heterogeneity that is fundamental to creating political competition. They show that in locations where elite occupations were more evenly divided, for instance, between agricultural and manufacturing pursuits, the parties were more evenly balanced in the state legislature. Their argument unfolds as follows:

> For most of the nineteenth and twentieth centuries, seats in state legis-
> latures were allocated on the basis of geographic units such as counties
> and not population. Counties typically had a comparative advantage in
> either agriculture or trade. Thus the wealth of local elites was typically
> grounded in one of these two areas. Local elites tended to control who
> served in the state legislature. The two types of elites tended to have dif-
> ferent interests and thus to support different political parties. . . . States
> with more occupationally diverse elites had higher levels of political
> competition in the state legislature than states where the elites were
> more homogenous. (8)

This perspective is consistent with a notion we have articulated,
namely, that when the public lacks consensus on the issues of the day,
a single-party system is not likely to be sustained for long, and/or democracy is not likely to be terribly effective.

True though the Berkowitz and Clay account may be, it still leaves
a critical role for political parties to play. As we argue above, political
parties confront a set of preferences that is more complex and cross-
cutting than the view of Berkowitz and Clay allows. The political divisions within the South (and indeed the nation) went beyond concern
about occupation to matters of race and religion. It was the thorny
task of party leaders to identify a set of policies and recruit a set of
candidates that would build an ongoing, competitive coalition in this
complex terrain of public preferences.

Sufficiency

We do not go so far as to claim that a party system in equilibrium is
a sufficient condition for competitive elections. What we mean by this
is that a party system in equilibrium can be disrupted, or thrown out
of equilibrium, such that it can no longer be counted on to regularly
yield competitive elections.

The equilibrium is not, in this sense, self-reinforcing or at least sufficiently self-reinforcing to withstand all disruptions. For a disruption to
throw the system out of equilibrium it must be significant, for parties
are adaptable to minor alterations in the political system. An alteration
in the rules of the political game, for instance, can be sufficiently dis-
ruptive, as we will see in the chapters that follow.

CONCLUSION

We have contended that electoral competition, historically born of a
durable, mature party system, is a necessary ingredient of effective
democratic governance. To summarize our view, meaningful party la-

bels allow voters to play a substantial role in selecting the direction of policy and holding politicians accountable over space and time. Ambitious politicians affiliate with parties that create meaningful and popular labels. A party will be competitive when its label attracts a sufficient number of voters and ambitious candidates. A competitive party system consists of two or more parties each of which is in equilibrium.

In each of the subsequent four chapters, we test several empirical implications of our argument using four historical eras—the Democratic-Whig period of 1832–52, the period during and after Reconstruction (1868–1900), the Jim Crow years (1900–1965), and the period after World War II to the present day (1948–2012). After an introduction to the historical context, each chapter proceeds with a similar empirical framework, as follows.

First, in each of these chapters we document the extent to which the parties were in equilibrium in the South. To do so, we gather the available evidence on the activity of the parties in government, the party organizations (except the Jim Crow chapter where Key [1949] has already done this comprehensively), and the parties in elections (Key 1964). First, we consider the manner in which political parties improve the meaning of the party label once in government (Snyder and Ting 2003). Governing parties are concerned about both the uniqueness and the cohesiveness of their membership. Parties in government work to advance a policy agenda that is unique from the competing party's agenda, which helps to improve the clarity of each party's label (Cox and McCubbins 1993; Grynaviski 2010). In addition, parties in government often seek to gain the support of a greater than minimum number of their members to advance the party's policy agenda. One important reason to do this is to clarify the party's label—the fewer dissenters from the party majority the more meaningful will be the party's label for voters.

Party organizations contribute, among other things, to the construction and usefulness of party labels. First, party organizations work to recruit candidates for office who either hold personal preferences for the direction of policy that are consonant with the mainstream of the party, or who are willing to toe the party line regardless of their own preferences (more on this below). A party organization that is successful in recruiting a homogenous group of candidates that is distinctive from the candidates of the competing party succeeds in improving the meaning of the party label.

A second way in which party organizations serve to improve the usefulness of the party label is by mobilizing citizens on election day. That is, citizens may have a clear sense of the policies that a party stands for (if the party in government is successful), and may even support those policies, but may not participate in the election. As we have argued, citizen participation, and more specifically full and equal participation is critical for a party system to reach equilibrium. If parties recruit quality candidates but cannot mobilize their supporters to show up on election day, they will face increasing difficulty recruiting future candidates to challenge for office. In sum, party activities while in office and party organizations work together to advance the role of the party in elections—to encourage voter identification with the party and an ability to recognize a meaningful difference between the parties, and finally to do what is necessary to get supporters to the polling booth.

As our benchmark for comparison in each of these domains we take the state of political parties in the North. We ask, were northern parties more cohesive and differentiated in government compared to those in the South? Were they more organized? Were they more effective at mobilizing voters? We are able to bring more data to bear on these questions in some chapters than in others, and it is perhaps not surprising that the earlier periods are the most challenging. While measures of party distinctiveness and cohesiveness are available for all three periods to aid our assessment of the party in government, measures of party organization and voter attitudes/behavior are more scant in the first two eras. Where necessary, we rely on the conclusions of historians to round out our story.

PART TWO

THE EXCEPTIONAL SOUTH

At the founding, one of the major cleavages among the new states was regional. Early on, there were three regions: New England, the Middle Atlantic States, and the South. But even then it was understood that the cultural, economic, social, and political differences between the South and the rest of the colonies were greater than those between New England and the Middle Atlantic States.[1] And thus, not very long after the founding, the three regional cleavages became primarily a division between North and South. This deeper cleavage was due in large part to slavery, but not only to that. The southern colonies had been settled by different waves of émigrés (at the extreme, Georgia by convicts), explaining some of the religious and cultural differences.[2] The nature of the economic bases of the North and South were sharply different. And, of course, there were about 150 years of separate development of the colonies to allow the lines of cleavage to appear or to strengthen. But slavery was very much a part of almost every other potential source of regional division, as well as being a major line of cleavage itself.

Enslaved Africans arrived in what would become the Carolina colony (which consisted mostly of what was to become both North and South Carolina) in 1526, when the land was Spanish territory. The first African slaves in an English colony, brought by Dutch slave traders, arrived in Jamestown, Virginia, in 1619 to serve the already emerging tobacco economy. The Dutch also supplied slaves of African origin to what was still their nation's land of New Amsterdam, that is, present day New York City, and the Puritans were the first to codify slavery in 1641. So, slavery was a part of the social context of life in all three regions more than a century before the Revolution.

Slavery's importance varied, however, and proved to be a singular boon to the southern, plantation economy in ways it would not be so valuable in other parts of the economy and, hence, in other parts of the colonies. Slaves, and African slaves in particular, were critical early on in the South's development, as the low country around Charleston, the most important city in the South (and arguably in the colonies), was both productive and malarial—whites, and many Africans for that matter, could not survive there. The rice plantations there required slaves (all too often short-lived) to be remunerative. Later, of course, it was the large number of dirty, difficult, and repetitive tasks such as picking cotton that made slaves particularly valuable economically, unlike the smaller farms and artisan industries of the North. It thus took a good part of the colonial period, but eventually it become clear that slavery had become essentially a southern thing on more or less purely economic grounds (Franklin and Moss 2000).

Early on, the slave trade from Africa competed with indentured servitude and with enslaving Native Americans as sources of unpaid labor, making some analogue to slavery multiracial.[3] It was, of course, the growth of the slave trade from Africa, principally to the Caribbean colonies, that made slaves of African origin so widely available. The declining "competitiveness" of indentured servitude for whites and of enslavement for Native Americans over the seventeenth century meant that slavery did, after the first fifty years of the colonial period, become a thing visited mostly upon Africans and their offspring, African Americans.

The final piece that made slavery so different in the South, the transition of slavery from a more limited degree of enslavement to the true chattel nature of nineteenth-century southern slavery, also culminated at about the end of the eighteenth century although it continued to structure developments in legal frameworks further, well into the nineteenth century. South Carolina, for example, passed the first full slavery code in 1696, a more fully developed and chattel-based code than the Puritan code of 1641. Virginia criminalized interracial marriage in 1691. They ended African American rights to vote or to hold office shortly thereafter and constructed their state's legal basis of slavery in 1705. But it was really not until around the time of the Jackson presidency that the full, chattel-based, legal structure for slavery was developed in the South.[4]

Thus, it took a great deal of time for slavery to become a truly southern, nearly purely African American, and fully chattel-based system. These dynamics to the deepening, increasingly southern-focused slavery system served to make the division between North and South grow ever deeper from the seventeenth century, over the eighteenth century, through the founding, and into the first half of the nineteenth century. With a slave-based tobacco economy developing first as early as the beginning of the seventeenth century in Jamestown, the centrality of slavery to the social, economic, and hence political life of the South was over a century and a half old by the time of the founding, by which time its unique effects in the South distinguished that region from the other two.

This history was consequential to this account of politics in at least two respects. First, the North-South regional differences were sharper and deeper than other of the many potential divisions in early America. For example, the divisions between the coast and interior that served as the social and economic basis of the partisan divisions of the Democrat-Whig era were clearly consequential, but not as critical. Second, it is understandable, if regrettable, that the Founders feared that doing something as precipitous as actually abolishing slavery in the new Constitution would so threaten the former southern colonies as to end the Union before it began. It is for this reason that the Founders could (or at least did) go no farther than permitting the ending of the slave trade after two decades and compromising on the Enumeration Clause, also known as the three-fifths rule. And, perhaps, this fear explains why the founding included compromises on slavery that would not be resolved until the Civil War seventy years hence or even until the civil rights era another century later.

At the founding, the South was undergoing a dramatic economic reshaping, largely because the Revolution came during a fundamental transformation that left the South much weaker, relative to its former economic status in the colonies. At the start of the Revolution, real income per capita was higher in the South than in the other two regions (126% of the national average in 1774, whereas New England was at 67% and the Middle Atlantic States were at 89% of the national average; Lindert and Williamson 2012). By 1800, the three regions neared parity, although the South was still the richest of the three by this measure. Its growth was therefore the smallest between 1774 and 1800, and indeed, per capita income actually declined. By 1840, the South was the poorest region, reaching only 77% of the national average income. It is understandable that economic issues were paramount in the confederal and early federal Congresses, and that the assumption of state debt loomed large (see Aldrich, Jillson, and Wilson 2003). Aldrich (2011) details how handling of the debt and the location of a permanent capital for the nation were the two most critical issues for creation of the new Constitution and for formation of the first political parties, and that these were issues inherited by the new Congress from their confederal predecessor. Indeed, he suggests that it was largely due to the inability of the confederal Congress to solve the economic issues flowing from the Revolution that led to the creation of the new Constitution and final resolution of the issues under it. At the same time, it generated the first political parties. In both cases, it tended to be the South, with some northern allies, against the rest of the country. Our first presidents, in spite of John Adams, formed the Virginia dynasty, after all. In any event, the take-home message is that the South was noticeably richer than the rest of the nation for much of the colonial period, but that this reversed dramatically, and before long, the South had become the poorest of the three regions. So not only was the nature of the southern economy unique, the region was differentiated by economic growth and decline as well.

The South's relative population was also shrinking. In terms of the number of citizens, the South was, at the founding, nearly as large as the North. Excluding the territories of Kentucky, Maine, and Vermont, as of the 1790 census, the total population of northern states was just over 1.84 million, while the population of the southern states (including Maryland) numbered 1.79 million.[5] The region's relative position declined, however, so that by 1840 the total population of the South was approximately 5.5 million (about 3.8 million free citizens), compared to nearly 11.5 million in the North.

Religion also tended to separate the North and the South, although this often was a result of, rather than a cause of, slavery and other regional divisions. Only the Friends (Quakers, located primarily in the Middle Atlantic States) were antislavery in eighteenth-century America. Late in the eighteenth century, Methodists and Baptists took early steps against the institution of slavery, and those were steps almost always taken by churches in the South. But it was not until the nineteenth century that most mainline religious organizations confronted the question of slavery head on. The result, generally, was that religious organizations split. Early in this period, it was often southern churches or their leaders who took antislavery positions. After all, this was where the issue was serious. The abolitionist movement, concentrated in the North and especially New England, however, tended to reverse positions with the South, such that by the 1830s and 1840s, southern churches rarely took antislavery positions, while northern ones increasingly did. The division of many of the mainline Protestant denominations, particularly the Baptists, Methodists, and Presbyterians, was largely due to slavery. As slavery became increasingly seen as unethical and even immoral around the world (or at least in Europe), religious groups in the South faced the unenviable task of balancing the belief that slavery was wrong and should be abolished with the need to maintain support of the congregations they served.[6] To summarize, thus far we have seen that in the nation's first half century, the South as a region became increasingly distinctive from the remainder of the country based on the nature and growth of its economy, its population, and its religious practices.

Political institutions also set the South apart by structuring its relationship with the remainder of the country. The Articles of Confederation included nothing about slavery, in part because representation was by state, and states were sovereign. Three provisions in the new Constitution in particular helped shape the role of the South in national politics in the antebellum period. The first was the fugitive slave provision that became relevant in national politics at the end of the Jacksonian-Whig period, a period to which we shall soon turn.

The second was the clause concerning the importation of slaves. The Constitution prohibited ending importation of slaves before 1808, and Congress passed a law to end such importation at the earliest opportunity, on January 1 of that year. This had two consequences. As many northern states had abolished slavery by 1808, the standard practice was for northern slaveholders to sell their slaves to (or at least intended for) a southerner, and thus the proportion of African Americans in the North fell, while it grew in the South. Second, ending importation of new slaves obviously increased the selling price of those slaves still able to be bought and sold, that is, those already in the United States. As the price of slaves increased, it became increasingly important for the slaveholder to figure out where he could continue to obtain a sufficient number to remain economically viable. One answer was reproduction, and in part for this reason, the practice of slavery ending either after a fixed period or at least at the slave's death began to give way to the practice of making slavery perpetual and of making offspring born into slavery slaves themselves.[7]

Finally, the Enumeration Clause, which defines apportionment of House seats by population, therefore requiring a census, resulted in slaves being counted as "other persons" (other than citizens, that is) and being counted as three-fifths of a whole person for purposes of allocating House seats. According to Humes et al. (2002), the three-fifths rule added fourteen seats to the slaveholding state apportionment as the First Congress under the new Constitution opened, getting it to near parity with free-state apportionment (46% of the total House rather than the 38% the South would have held without it, that is, if counting only citizens and thus not counting slaves at all).

These provisions, and especially the three-fifths rule, are justly famous for recognizing slavery without providing its end. Even the provision that ended up supporting the abolition of the slave trade in 1808 actually only said that trade could not be ended before then; it did not say it would ever end. It thus took (and takes) on symbolic power of great significance, well beyond the specifics of the wording. Thus, the Constitution might not have said that the slave trade would ever be abolished, but it was understood that its purpose was to give the South twenty years to adjust to the end of the trade. And it was in fact ended at the first possible moment.

Another provision in the Constitution that greatly affected the South, and indeed gave them great leverage over national affairs from 1820 to 1850 especially, was not specifically about North-South relations or about slavery. Indeed, the South, like the North, was split on the issue in Philadelphia. That is the so-called Connecticut Compromise, under which bicameralism was used to provide representation by population in one chamber and representation by state in the other chamber. This, of course, was designed to assuage fears of small states that they be overwhelmed in a population-based Congress. For this reason, large states, such as Virginia most notably, and some smaller states such as Georgia that hoped to grow to be large, opposed it, while Delaware joined with Rhode Island in supporting it.

What this meant when the First Congress opened was that the South had the largest number of states of the three regions, but a large minority rather than an actual majority when considered as divided into the North and the South. This close parity was maintained in the early years of the Republic. By 1820, the South had come to see the value of state representation, especially through the efforts of Henry Clay in reaching the Missouri Compromise (aka Compromise of 1820).

The direct effect of the Missouri Compromise was to limit slavery in the Louisiana Territory north of the parallel 36°30' except for Missouri. The practical effect in terms relevant here was that it assured that there would be as many states in the South as in the North. As a result the South would have as many senators as the North. This was known as the "Balance Rule." This gave the South a veto over legislation (or nearly so as discussed below), and it used its status in the Senate to stop any challenge to slavery, as it did by defeating the Wilmot Proviso, passed in the House in both 1846 and 1847, and also its close analogue that was a part of the Treaty of Hildago in 1848. As it could reasonably have feared, the North, holding a majority in the House, would, someday, find an issue on which it was united as a region and in opposition to the South. When it did, as it did over territories expected to be won in the Mexican-American War, the North would need merely to vote its preferences and it would defeat the South. And once defeated—in this case barring slavery from any lands gained from Mexico with whom we were then at war—the South risked total defeat on slavery. The Wilmot Proviso, for instance, did not affect slavery where it existed, "only" prohibiting it from any lands we would win from Mexico (in the current war or into the future). But a reasonable interpretation was that, in the long term, this spelled doom for slavery in the South. As the United States expanded, the conditions that made slavery economically viable in the South were not found in many places in the American territories. It was hard to see, therefore, where there was land that, once formulated as a candidate for statehood, would want to enter the union as a slave state.[8] If there were to be any, they would be in the Mexican territories. Even more, the land the United States did acquire in the following years was so vast as to be able to come in only as several states. If many of these could not come in as slave states, it was unclear how the Balance Rule could be maintained. Indeed, the efforts that finally led to the Compromise of 1850, which, while a compromise like that of 1820, failed in finding a way to keep an equal or greater number of slave as free states. And, as soon as these states were admitted, the Balance Rule was gone forever. One loss for the South, and, in fact, it really would be over.

So balanced was the Balance Rule that it was actually insufficient to give the South the lock on a veto point it felt it needed to be secure about the future of slavery. As Aldrich showed (2011), it had to be coupled with party tickets that balanced nominations for president and vice president with one from (and, even more importantly, standing for) the South and one from the North to give the South either a vote to the vice president to break a tie in the Senate in favor of the South, or an actual presidential veto in the White House. And thus, the Democratic Party created an actual veto for the South in its party proceedings by enacting (from 1832 until 1936) a two-thirds rule for the selection of the presidential and vice presidential nominees. This meant that the southerners in attendance could stop any nomination they cared to stop, and thereby assure that they would either have a vice presidential candidate who would break any tie vote in the Senate in their favor and thus stop a northern House majority, or they would have a president in the White House who would support them, thereby vetoing any such legislation that snuck through the Senate. And, of course, the Balance Rule in the Senate was more than sufficient to guarantee that the North could not override a presidential veto the South did not want overridden.

The final piece of context is the South and the first two parties. As is well known, political parties were not yet on the scene at the founding but appeared very soon thereafter. According to Aldrich (2011), they were founded first over the remaining difficulties in resolving the two major policy issues that undermined support for the confederal Congress under the Articles—getting the United States on a sound economic footing and locating the capitol. The Founders (who almost universally condemned parties) were their creators. The Democratic-Republican (D-R) Party (soon to be today's Democratic Party) was essentially southern, its founders being Jefferson and Madison. They forged an alliance with New York (and especially Aaron Burr) to create an intersectional coalition and hence the makings of a truly national party. Hamilton with others founded the Federalist Party (including Washington, an asserted nonpartisan, who is thought of as a Federalist in practice). The typical description is that the Democrats favored a weaker, and the Federalists favored a stronger, national government. While accurate, recall that the context is that both sides agreed that the national government needed to be stronger than it was under the Articles, so it is a relative question in which the Democrats favored some strengthening, while the Federalists favored even more strengthening of the central government.

Both parties were born of intersectional alliances, rather like the Democratic-Whig era to which we will soon turn. And like it, the Federalists (as would the Whigs) tended to draw from the cities, and thus from the coastal region, while the Democrats tended to draw from rural and mountain regions making up the frontier. The Federalists, in favoring a stronger national government, reflected the views of its founder, Hamilton, in favoring conditions that would create a stronger national economy and business community. Thus, they tended to draw support from Virginia, North Carolina, and around the important city of Charleston in South Carolina.[9] The Federalists favored paying for a stronger national government through tariffs, which an emerging cotton trade led their erstwhile supporters in the South to oppose. The Federalists essentially died out as a national force early in the 1800s and last ran a candidate for president and vice president in 1816, albeit noncompetitively. Of course, the D-R Party headed by the Virginia dynasty until 1824, and then by Tennessean Andrew Jackson until 1836, maintained strong roots in the South from its founding through the late twentieth century.

The first parties quickly adopted structures associated with all aspects of political parties as we have come to know them. The D-R defeat by Hamiltonians on the economy, for example, led to an at least rudimentary electoral and campaign arm of the party in the early 1790s, one that the Federalists mimicked, and certainly the 1800 presidential election was one of the bitterest partisan affairs in our history (Aldrich 2005; Larson 2007; Sharp 2010). The parties were sufficiently organized electorally by that time to require adding the Twelfth Amendment to the Constitution to adjust the government to the realities of partisanship. That is to say, the two parties organized their activities by 1800 in such a way as to seek to coordinate campaigns to win elections, what we today call the party as organization. This included, for the 1800 election, organizing over candidate selection (coordinating over presidential and vice presidential picks, when there was no such constitutional distinction for the electors) and ensuring that state legislatures they controlled passed laws that aided the party's ability to maximize its electoral votes (moving from a districting plan to a statewide winner-take-all plan, or moving from selection via public election to selection by the state legislature).

Hamilton, as secretary of the treasury, was part of the executive branch. Even so, it was clear that he won his first partisan victory for his party on the floor of Congress in enacting parts of his economic plan, thus symbolizing the use of parties to coordinate activities of elected officials across the branches of government. It is common to take the partisan meaning of the 1800 election of Jefferson by illustrating that party's ability to coordinate across their majorities in the House, the Senate, and in the presidency. Thus, by 1800, each party had shown a degree of organizing ability as the party in government.

One early sign of the D-R Party's appearance was the hiring of a newspaper editor, Philip Freneau, in the early 1790s, thus reflecting an electoral, campaign arm of the party. What were then called "committees of correspondence" provided the bulk of that sort of work—along with partisan presses, of course, like Freneau's. These were used to motivate Jefferson supporters to vote for their party's contenders for Congress. The revealed success of the early Hamiltonian floor organizing in Congress meant that the Jeffersonian floor minority could no longer expect to defeat Hamilton's initiatives. One way to change that was to organize elections so that the Jeffersonians would have a majority in the next Congress. This is in part what lead to the meeting between the Virginians (Jefferson and Madison) and the New Yorkers (Burr and George Clinton), and it worked in that they did indeed win a majority in 1794. Through these means they (and in response the Hamiltonians) sought to develop a party in elections.

The point of this litany is that early versions of nearly every piece of the modern mass political party (the party in government, the party as organization, and the party in elections; see Key 1942; Aldrich 2011) that would appear in the 1830s and would continue into the twentieth if not the twenty-first century was invented in some form or another in the late eighteenth and very early nineteenth centuries. They were, however, rudimentary. That is to say, the forms were evident, presumably because their creators observed the tasks that could be— and needed to be—done to have a viable, competitive political party in a competitive party system. By general consensus in the scholarly community, these were considered too preliminary to appear anything like the "roaring flood of new democracy" that the "modern mass political party" the Jacksonian era would be associated with (Beard and Beard 1933; McCormick 1960, 288–301).[10] And, as our chapter on Jacksonian Democracy and the Whigs opens, the Federalist Party has long been noncompetitive nationally, the D-R Party is in chaos over who is to be its presidential nominee, or even how that person might be chosen. That is, there is no party system, and in many respects no parties at all, or only the vestige of a competitive party looking for a second one against which to compete. In other words, we are witnessing at this time something very similar to what Key described for the South in the 1940s—the consequences of having only one party for the organization. We are witnessing, that is, the declining organizational vigor of a party with no one to contest.

A roadmap. The following four chapters are concerned with two questions. First, in each historical period we consider the question of the situational and historical context in the South, particularly in comparison to the North, and how that shaped partisan politics. Second, we ask whether in the South, as compared to the North, the party system appeared to be moving toward "equilibrium" or at least was settling down in its development, as if it were reaching equilibrium. Settling in what ways? Most important, we believe, are the ways in which each of the parties communicated to voters a clear sense of what it stood for, most often through the actions of its elected officials. In addition, we ask how well the parties were organized in terms of recruiting members and in focusing the ambitions of its candidates and officeholders. Finally, we look to see if the party was mobilizing voters effectively in support of these candidates. These three overlapping spheres of party activity have come to be known as the party in government, the party as organization, and the party in elections, respectively (Key 1964; Aldrich 2011). We turn to assess the implications of a developed party system for electoral competitiveness and effective democracy in part 3 of the book.

In these four chapters, we also present evidence on the development of the three dimensions of the individual parties to supplement the analyses of the South's respective historical contexts. For the party in government, we examine the extent to which the two parties were relatively more or less differentiated, or polarized, by party and by region. A measure of polarization speaks to the extent to which the two parties present a coherent message to the public as a pair of contending and differentiable forces, and the stability of that pair of signals over time.[11]

The party as organization is harder to assess, due to the lack of regularly measurable aspects over time in the nineteenth century. There are many measures of the extent of party organization in the contemporary era, and these will be used to provide a rich and detailed account of the development of the parties, particularly the Republican Party in the South, in the post–World War II era (see chapter 6). While such measures are lacking in the earlier periods, we are fortunate to have numerous detailed studies of party organization in various places at various times conducted by historians, and we rely upon assessments of these studies for this and the next chapter.

The central question about the success of the party in elections is whether the parties are able to mount successful campaigns. One measure of the success of both parties in organizing and creating effective campaigns is voter turnout (e.g., Aldrich 1995). If both parties are strongly and effectively campaigning, turnout is expected to increase. We also believe that the degree of competition as revealed by the choices of the electorate, across regions and over time, is a measure of the electoral arms of the parties, but also reflects (as Key [1984] argued) on the strength of the party organizations. In a one-party dominant area, even the dominant party's organizational strength declines with less and less threat from the other party. In this way, electoral competition is a cause, as well as a consequence, of party organization.

3

DEMOCRATIC-WHIG PARTIES
IN THE JACKSONIAN ERA

The era of the "second party system" in the United States (1828–52, for our purposes) included the invention of what historians like to call the "modern, mass political party." Such parties are considered the first political parties to be structured around the purpose of winning support from the electorate. This is so because, while it is debatable whether there had yet been organized political parties or a coherent party system before this period opened, as noted above, it is consensual that there were both by the 1840s. As McCormick (1986) showed, most states entered this period with at most one organized political party or with none at all. By 1840, most states could claim to have two parties. Even more, in virtually all states, it was the same two parties as in every other state, and thus the nation could be said to have a fully developed, two-party system, the first fully developed system of two mass-based parties in the world. They appealed to the mass public (which is roughly translated as the full set of white male citizens) because suffrage had largely become fully extended to them. There was, however, substantial variation in the timing and extent to which such a level of party development occurred. Given that both parties were intersectional alliances, the continuation of the Democrat-Whig party system was contingent on keeping issues related to slavery off the agenda. The inevitable rise in salience of such issues eventually shattered those alliances and led to the demise of the Whig Party. That event did not end the incentives for ambitious politicians to act so as to create and maintain a two-party system. Shortly after the collapse of the Whigs, the Republicans emerged to take their place. The transformed content of that new system, however, disadvantaged the

South, sufficiently so that southern politicians could only choose to disrupt that party system by extralegal means, in this instance, through secession.

HISTORICAL SETTING

Jacksonian Democracy began in 1828, with the election of Andrew Jackson to the presidency. That seems obvious, but there are critical events that led to his election and the development of the party he led. But even by the end of his first term, there were other, equally critical components of a fully developed, mass-based political party that were still missing. For the former, Jackson's campaign in 1828 in many ways rested on his defeat in 1824. In that year, the congressional caucus, which had been the exclusive means of selecting the Jeffersonian Democratic-Republican Party's candidates for president and vice president, collapsed. Multiple candidates were nominated. William Crawford of Georgia was the caucus's selection, the last via this method. He suffered a stroke that effectively ended his candidacy. Whether he would have succeeded to the presidency remains, therefore, unknown. We do know, however, that state legislative caucuses also nominated candidates for president, including Jackson, John Quincy Adams, and Henry Clay.[1] All who agreed remained viable contenders, with "viability" requiring only that electors, whether selected by voters or state legislatures, would vote for them.[2] With no one winning a majority in the Electoral College, Adams's, Clay's, and Jackson's names were forwarded to the House, using the new procedures from the Twelfth Amendment for the first time.[3] Clay withdrew in favor of Adams, who subsequently selected him as secretary of state, the then most common steppingstone to the presidency. Jackson's supporters claimed this to be a "Corrupt Bargain" and used it as a rallying cry for creating an opposition to the Adams administration.[4] The 1826 elections had a strong pro-administration, anti-Adams division among candidates. The anti-Adams faction fared well in the elections and served as the core of the Jacksonian "campaign" for presidency in 1828.

Jackson, like all eighteenth- and nineteenth-century presidential contenders, did not overtly campaign for nomination and election. This fell to his supporters, including Martin Van Buren who would become his second vice president (John C. Calhoun serving as his first) and succeed him to the presidency. Van Buren drew from his experience in organizing opposition, what became known as the Albany Regency, to the Tammany Hall political organization in New York State. He sought to bring the South (especially Virginia) in coalition with his part of New York and with other strong Jackson areas. In this he would be recreating the New York–Virginia alliance of the Democratic-Republican Party of Jefferson and Burr. In this period, however, he needed only to rely on existing state and local political organizations, united around the clear personal popularity of Old Hickory, the hero of the War of 1812, and also to rely on antipathy to the Adams administration, waving the claim of a corrupt bargain for its existence, much as Civil War veterans later in the century would waive their bloody shirt to symbolize the Civil War. Like them, Jackson could claim heroic status and, as it happened, win office without staking out positions on the actual political issues of the day. Adams was never especially popular personally in the public. He and Clay in 1828 (and again in 1832) had a competing political organization of sorts, the National Republicans, but it was much more similar to the old Federalists in organization—a grouping of political elites—than the Jefferson-Jackson coalition Van Buren was forging, with roots extending much more deeply into the American public. Thus, while Van Buren and others could organize around Jackson through 1832, they did so without a counterorganization that reflected the growing role of the American electorate and the emerging urban middle class.

Jackson could remain purely a heroic figure without policy stance while campaigning for office, but once in office, he could no longer avoid public positioning on issues. Perhaps the most controversial issue of the nineteenth century, except for slavery and its related manifestations, was the tariff. Overall, the South was mostly exporting, and the North was, in net, importing, so that tariffs had regional dimensions. Adams had raised the tariff in 1828, which hurt the South, perhaps especially South Carolina, from which Jackson's first vice president, John C. Calhoun, hailed. Calhoun pushed hard for tariff reductions and eventually resigned from office not long before the 1832 elections. Jackson did secure a tariff reform bill shortly thereafter, which Calhoun saw as too little, too late. South Carolina called a convention that declared that the state believed the 1828 and 1832 tariff bills were unconstitutional and unenforceable in South Carolina. In 1833, the national government passed a tariff acceptable to South Carolina but also a "force bill," authorizing the use of federal troops to enforce federal law. South Carolina backed down and repealed its declaration, ending the confrontation. While South Carolina won on the tariff, they lost on the issue of state versus national government power; that is, they lost on the question of the supremacy of the Union. The tariff (and the relative balance of state versus national power) was an ingredient soon used to help organize an opposition party to the Jacksonian Democrats. And, of course, this confrontation had a number of elements that reappeared as regional divisions in the run-up to the Civil War.

A second division that helped motivate the organization of the Whig Party was the crisis of the Second National Bank, founded during the Madisonian administration. Nicholas Biddle, president of the bank, pushed for early rechartering in 1832, a bill that was favored by Clay but that Jackson vetoed. In 1833, after defeating Clay, Jackson withdrew federal funds from the bank, and a "bank war" followed that Jackson eventually won, but not until 1836 and not until the Whig Party had formed.

After the 1832 election, Jacksonian opposition began to coalesce around the above-noted issues, some of which, like the tariff, tapped regional divisions, others like the bank less so. The opposition also coalesced around personalities, notably Clay, Calhoun, and Daniel Webster. It also was aided by personal politics, as Jackson's changes in cabinet personnel after the Eaton affair caused some erstwhile supporters among southern elite politicians to move toward or even fully into opposition (Folsom 1973).[5]

By 1834, the Whig Party was forming as the major opposition to Jackson, replacing the National Republicans. They won seventy-six seats as the major opposition to Jackson and his party, an increase of fifteen seats over what the National Republicans held after the 1832 elections. In 1836, the Whig Party was fully established and ran its first presidential candidates. Webster and Calhoun might seem to have had relatively little in common, and this symbolized the Whig Party, which was as much organized as an opposition as it was organized in terms of a positive assertion of political goals. It is symbolic, for example, that it would run candidates first for Congress, because it favored congressional over presidential (especially over President Jackson's) power. It is perhaps even more symbolic of the reach the Whig coalition was stretching to achieve that it ran three candidates for president in 1836: Webster, William Henry Harrison, and Hugh White (TN).[6] Van Buren, never personally that popular with the public, lost a great deal of support because of the very deep Panic of 1837, and the Whig Party carried a congressional majority in 1838, which they held for four years, reflecting both the Democratic-Whig cleavage over economics and the tariff, and (again) the Whig preference for congressional over presidential power. In 1840, the Whigs selected Harrison as their candidate for president, and he became one of two Whigs to be elected to the presidency, both of whom were war heroes, relatively inexperienced in politics, and unfortunate enough to die in office. But it was, to most historians, the 1840 election that saw the completion of two mass-based parties.[7] In either case, in that two-year period, the creation of a full two-party system was completed, and led immediately to the "full flowering" of democratic politics in the United States. Flowers, however, are short-lived, and so was the Whig Party. Its birth from the remnants of the National Republicans, aging Federalists, and others to its complete collapse covered a mere twenty years. But in its completion of the first, full, mass-politics-based, competitive two-party system in history, its historical importance transcended its relatively brief life span.

ORIGINS OF DEVELOPED PARTIES

The accounts offered to explain the emergence of a two-party system in the 1830s are numerous. Some claim that conflict over the presidency was critical to the creation of sustained two-party competition in each state (McCormick 1986). As McCormick (1986, 13) put it, "the most influential factor determining when alignments appeared within a particular region was the regional identifications of the presidential candidates." For instance, a party system arrived in New England just in time, because, otherwise, the region's support for Clay was not as uniform as its support for Adams had been and thus with the aid of organized Jacksonians, in New England, the Clay-Jackson race became reasonably competitive. Similarly, parties took root in the South when the region's support for Van Buren was less widespread than had been its support for Jackson.

One difficulty for this account is that considerable support for Whig congressional candidates emerged in 1834, before Van Buren was nominated. "In many states, the incipient opposition parties did far better in 1834 when Jackson's tyranny and alleged responsibility for the recession were the issues, than in 1835 and 1836 when the focus was on the impending presidential election" (Holt 1999, 50). Of course, by 1834 the Nullification Crisis had occurred, and many southerners had turned away from Jackson. In the end, we agree that southern support for the Whig presidential candidate Hugh White in 1836 was important for the party's development at other levels of office. However, we build on McCormick's observation that party organizational development tended to coincide with a region's disagreement over the presidential candidates to explain why this might be.

In our view, the reason that Whig success at the presidential level was important for party development was that it signaled to ambitious office seekers that there was electoral support for the Whig label. These candidates had to capitalize on local issues to sustain the party's early success. As Holt (1999, 49) put it, "Almost invariably the key to Whigs' success at the state level lay in their ability to go beyond questions stemming from national politics. Success instead depended on Whigs taking appealing stances that differed from those of Democrats on concrete matters stemming from the agendas of state politics and governance."

A very different factor that has been offered to account for regional variation in party system development is state differences in transportation and communication (McCormick 1986). Aldrich (2011) emphasized the new opportunity that improved communications and transportation offered for the creation of mass-based parties in the 1830s. To the extent that these advancements varied by region, they might explain at least a portion of the different rate by which state parties developed. "The half century before the Civil War was a period when most Northern and Western states eagerly embraced new forms of transportation. But the South, well supplied with navigable streams and coastal waterways, was rather consistently opposed to any national system of internal improvements" (Stover 1969, 109–10). There was less railroad mileage in the South, relative to the North, and the rails of the South were more fragmented (Ward 1973; Majewski 1996). In the end, we allow for the possibility that the stunted development of southern parties stemmed from multiple causes, and now turn to recount those regional differences in more detail.

PARTY DEVELOPMENT IN THE WHIG ERA

Having set the historical stage, we next investigate the regional development of party systems during this era. In doing so, we will be especially attuned to whether there is evidence supporting, or disconfirming, two expectations borne from our discussion above. First, at the outset of this period we expect to observe that the party system in the South was less developed, or was further from equilibrium, than the party system in the North. Recall that a party system is in equilibrium under our account when each of the parties is able to credibly compete for the wide variety of public offices within a region. As we discuss in chapter 7, because the first party system in the South was less competitive, and this perhaps owing to the lesser economic heterogeneity in the region and the need for cohesion on civil rights matters, we expect a legacy of this lack of competition that extends into the second party system. With somewhat less reason to be optimistic about their chances for success in the South, the Whigs had less reason to organize state parties in the region and to expend effort mobilizing voters.

Second, we expect that by the end of this twenty-four-year period we will observe some regional convergence in party system development. That is, if the North began the period with a party system much closer to equilibrium, we would not expect great strides in northern party development as the party system moved ever closer to, and even perhaps reached, equilibrium. In contrast, we would expect to observe greater and more rapid change in southern party development because there was a further distance to travel in that region for the parties to reach equilibrium. This is not to claim that the party system in either or both regions reached equilibrium by 1852, but only that the relative progress toward equilibrium converged. And as this account suggests, the convergence should have occurred chiefly due to party development in the South rather than only due to any erosion of the party system in the North.

We begin these assessments by studying the distinctiveness of the parties in government, measured primarily using the roll call behavior of elected officials. We then compare the extent to which the parties were well organized in each region using, as we indicate above, secondary historical accounts. Finally, we use the limited data available to us to compare the electoral role of the parties in the two regions.

Party in Government

The concern with developing a party label through the activities of officeholders should have been especially pressing in this period, due to the practice of rotation in office (Kernell 1977; Struble 1979). Whether motivated by an idealistic sense that, as Cooper put it, "contact with the affairs of state is one of the most corrupting of the influences to which men are exposed" (Cooper 2010, 56) or a more pragmatic sharing of the spoils system's benefits in district nominating conventions for the U.S. House, or even a simple desire among ambitious politicians to be where the most important action is—which in nineteenth-century America was in the state rather than national government—a system of rotation developed and was enforced. In an election environment with substantial rotation, voters more frequently considered candidates who were not incumbents and thus had no voting history of their own for voters to use in forming a signal as to what a victorious candidate might do once in office. And, of course, voting for office was in public and not by secret ballot. The ballot was usually of the "party strip" form (and often provided by the parties themselves), making write-in and split-ticket voting difficult (Carson and Roberts 2013). With this in mind, we commence our discussion of the pattern of roll call voting across parties and regions during this era.

To evaluate the distinctiveness, or interparty heterogeneity, of parties we first calculate the absolute difference between the roll call liberalism of the mean Democrat and the mean Whig in a given Congress and region using House members' first-dimension DW-NOMINATE coordinates (Poole and Rosenthal 1997; Aldrich, Berger, and Rohde 2003). According to Poole and Rosenthal (1997, 35), the first dimension of roll call voting reflects conflict over the role of the government in the economy. In the 1840s, the first dimension largely reflected disagreements between the parties over tariffs to promote industrialization and internal improvements such as roads and canals (35). The Whigs championed both programs, while the Democrats supported maintaining an agricultural economy (Wilson 2000). Poole and Rosenthal orient the DW-NOMINATE coordinates in this period such that legislators most supportive of a strong government role in the economy took on positive scores while those opposed took on negative scores, where positive scores indicate conservatism. In other words, somewhat counterintuitively for those who associate a small role for government rather than a pro-business orientation with conservatism, the Whig Party was the more conservative of the two parties according to this measure. In any event, what we are interested in are the regional differences between the parties, regardless of the valence of the positions taken.

Figure 3.1 displays the trends of these measures from 1836 through the 1852 elections. That is, the data in the figure reflect the roll call behavior of officials in the term following the election year denoted on the x axis (e.g., 1851–52 for MCs elected in 1850, and so on). We use this convention in the remainder of our analyses below. These data indicate that the difference between the average Democrat and Whig was quite a bit greater in the North than in the South from 1836 to 1850. In the last Congress we examine, however, the regional difference in the gap between the parties disappeared, in part due to a decline in the difference between the northern wings of the parties, but growing differences in the South over the entire period were the primary cause of regional convergence.

To further probe the source of these trends, in figure 3.2 we report the House DW-NOMINATE means by party and region. According to these data, the main reason that the gap between the parties was so much smaller in the South for much of this period was that southern Whigs voted much more liberally than northern Whigs, who were the most conservative of the four groups. Indeed, from the mid-1830s to the early 1840s, the southern Whigs were ideologically closer in their roll call voting to southern Democrats than to northern Whigs.[8] The

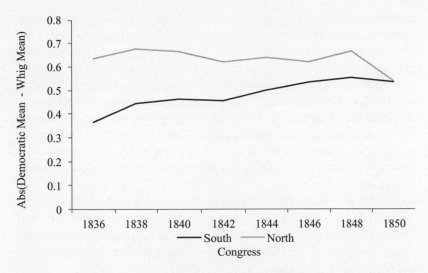

Figure 3.1 Difference in House party DW-NOMINATE scores by region, 1836–52

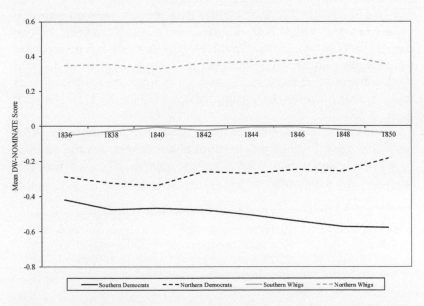

Figure 3.2 Mean House DW-NOMINATE score by party and region, 1836–52

average southern Whig was very close to the center of this roll-call-voting-induced policy space. The convergence of the gap between the regional parties seen in figure 3.1 is principally due to more liberal voting among southern Democrats over the entire time span, coupled with more conservative voting by northern Democrats from 1848 to 1852 and somewhat more liberal voting among northern Whigs during the same four-year period. Thus, the convergence between North and South at the end of this party system is due as much to differences among Democrats as among Whigs. But the most important observation is that the first, commonly understood as the major "liberal-conservative" dimension of DW-NOMINATE, has at least as large a regional as a party effect. And recall that the point of the duopoly between the two parties in the nation in this period was to ensure that the *second* dimension did not divide the nation, so that party division would occur along the lines of tariff policy and the like, issues that were less threatening to the survival of the union.

We also examined interparty heterogeneity in the U.S. Senate (see figure 3.3). To do so, we pooled senators for the entire period because there were relatively few senators in a given Congress by party and region. Upon doing so, we found that the ideological gap between northern Democrats and Whigs was larger than the gap between southern Democrats and Whigs. Not only that, but the gap between the two parties was only "symmetric" in the North—in the South both parties were ideologically liberal on this economic dimension, it was just that the Democrats were more so. In this respect, the makeup of the parties in the Senate mirrored the pattern we observed for the U.S. House in figure 3.2.

In sum, there was considerable polarization in the Democratic-Whig era Congresses. It was a polarization, however, that was the product of *both* party and region, overlaying one another. The evidence thus supports Holt's judgment (1999):

> The Whig and Democratic parties advocated specific policies in order to gain office. They attempted to enact those policies once elected. And they expended enormous effort to educate voters about what officeholders had done. Voters knew what the parties stood for in terms of both specific legislation and general goals. They could judge the expected results of those programs because of recent experience with both. And they responded in rational ways to the contrasting programs and party images presented to them. (83)

However, with respect to each characteristic, these were more pronounced in the North than in the South, and in any event, region

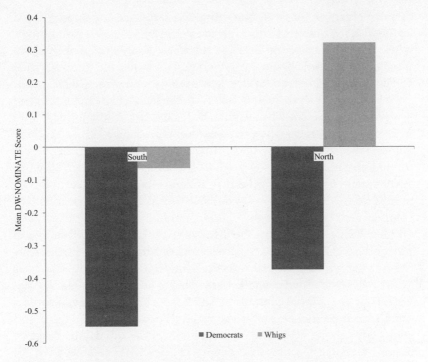

Figure 3.3 Mean Senate DW-NOMINATE score by party and region, 1836–52

rivaled party even on the first or liberal-conservative dimension of roll call voting. Whereas the Democratic Party initially was less regionally divided than the Whigs, as events associated with the Mexican War, and thus the growth of the nation and the consequent inability to maintain a southern veto, became more apparent, the Democratic Party began to act increasingly differently between northern and southern members of House and Senate, much like the Whigs long had.

Party Organization

Next, we compare the development of party organizations in the South and in the remainder of the country during this period. In doing so, we rely on McCormick (1986) supplemented by Folsom (1973) and Holt (1999). In New England, "party organization was highly developed and characterized by the centralization of control in a state committee and a mixed legislative caucus" (McCormick 1986, 87). The unusual use of the state as the election unit in New England and the requirement that winning candidates be elected by a majority encouraged the development of party organizations in this region. The structure of party organization in all New England states except Rhode Island included a legislative caucus empowered to make statewide nominations, elect a central committee, and enforce party discipline (93). In the Middle Atlantic States of New York, New Jersey, Pennsylvania, Delaware, and Maryland, party organizations were somewhat less centralized than they were in New England, the legislative caucus was less powerful, and, predictably, the state was a less important political unit.

In the South, meanwhile, parties organized more slowly. According to McCormick (1986, 178), "Even after the new alignments had formed and politics was conducted on the basis of contests between fairly matched parties, southern practices remained distinctive. The parties were slow to adopt the extensive organization of their northern counterparts." In place of party organizations, candidates often relied on their own organizations. For McCormick, this was attributable in part to the legacy of the first party system, during which organized parties were much less prevalent in the South. Holt (1999, 50) concurs: "In the West and South, where state Whig candidates depended most heavily on presidential coattails in 1835 and 1836, Whig organizations often remained inchoate or nonexistent." Folsom also concurs and adds (1973, 218), "From 1800 to the 1830s, the South was beset by intense factional politics on the state and local scenes and a listless one-party system in national politics. By 1840, a relatively balanced national two-party system existed throughout the South and the nation—a system unique in ante-bellum America." He goes on even further to say about the Eaton affair in the Jacksonian administration, "This description of Southern party formation suggests that Jackson's cabinet reorganization helped trigger a political rebellion which ultimately destroyed his one-party hold on the Old South" (triggering defections to the new Whig Party; 223–24). Note that Folsom uses these data as a way of revising McCormick's emphasis on presidential elections as a force in party organizing, as he says in conclusion (229) that not only was southern Whiggery arising out of antipathy to Van Buren, "Neither was it the revival of the contest for the presidency, which was a result rather than a cause of party divisions. Instead, party formation was influenced by Jackson's failure to placate personally or ideologically an influential coterie of Southern leaders."

Party in Elections

To evaluate the effectiveness of parties in elections during this period, we examine turnout data. In the present day, citizens who vote are much more likely than those who do not to say that they observe a difference between the parties and to identify with one of the parties (e.g., Campbell et al. 1960; Rosenstone and Hansen 1993; Verba, Schlozman, and Brady 1995; Fowler 2006). There may be reasons that this relationship was weaker (or stronger) historically, but we have no basis for thinking the relationship was reversed or even did not exist. Rather, it appears likely to exist and, indeed, the ability of both parties to turn their faithful out on election day is the hallmark not only of strong parties in elections generally, but especially so in this era (see, e.g., McCormick 1986; Holt 1999). Thus, we rely on turnout data to reflect the value of party labels to the electorate. Greater turnout in a region may also reflect a greater organizational capacity of the electoral arm of the political parties, that is to say, reflect strength of party organizations, per se. Indeed, Rosenstone and Hansen (1993) argue that the failure of party mobilization efforts was one of the principal causes of the decline in turnout in the 1970s and 1980s. We take evidence of sustained increases in turnout as evidence of the success of a competitive party system, whether that is due to the mobilizing efforts of the party organization, the vigor of contests between the two parties in elections, or the sharpness of party platforms and thus the policy consequences voters see at stake in the elections.

Figure 3.4 reports the regional difference in mean turnout in presidential elections from 1832 to 1852. According to these data, there was a very large regional difference in turnout at the beginning of this period of nearly 30 percentage points. This difference fell in 1836 to about 5 percentage points, in part because turnout declined in the North, but more so because turnout rose dramatically in the South, from approximately thirty-six thousand to nearly sixty thousand voters. The Whig candidacies of Hugh White and Willie Mangum may explain the rise in southern interest, particularly in White's home state of Tennessee, and in Georgia, Alabama, and North Carolina where White and Van Buren competed closely. Thereafter, there was somewhat greater turnout in the North than the South, except in 1848. Pooling across all years, turnout in the South was about 7 points lower than it was in the North during the second party system. In absolute terms, in the South, "despite the lack of competitive, organized parties, and the general absence of 'issues' in elections, voter participation was at a relatively high rate. Indeed, except for Virginia, where the suffrage was drastically limited [by voter eligibility laws], participation compared favorably with that in states where the parties were highly developed" (McCormick 1986, 248). Folsom (1973) shows the breadth of these effects, noting that turnout in the South was as high or higher in state and local contests than in presidential contests, and these local peaks generally preceded those in the presidential elections.

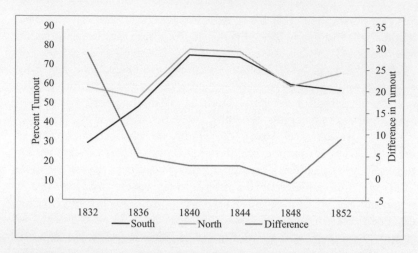

Figure 3.4 Regional difference in presidential year turnout, 1832–52

CONCLUSION

This chapter lays out the development of the first pair of mass-based political parties. It is of course a rich and complex set of steps toward that development. When it did happen, it happened rather quickly, at least nationally, with the Whig Party reaching national level formation in something like two to three congressional elections. This was so because the form may have been new on the national level, but it was, in something more than truly embryonic form, found in a number of state and local areas. Van Buren, for example, built on his own experience with the creation of the Albany Regency in the 1820s, which itself emerged more like the Whig Party, which is to say in an attempt to counter the success of the Tammany political organization in the state (and especially in New York City). The Jeffersonian and Hamiltonian organizations provided illustrations of the three parts of the mass-based party, but in decidedly underdeveloped forms nationally. Much more richly developed examples could be found scattered throughout the various states and locales. The original national parties provided more of a justification, based on the fact that the Founders themselves created and justified the early parties, than they did the nitty-gritty details of just how and what to create. State and local political organizations supplied those details.

As we have seen, the comparison of the North and South in these regards reveals that the South was later and slower to develop, and that the South was only beginning to catch up to the North in some of the major features of a full party system when the system collapsed. In this regard, the antebellum period is, as we will soon see, quite unlike the period after Reconstruction through the civil rights era, in which the party system in the South was dramatically stunted. We will build on this foundation in chapter 7 to show that the sluggish development of a southern party system resulted in somewhat less competitive elections in the region. The democratic consequences of this diminished competition are explored in chapters 8 and 9.

That the South had a party system that was slowly converging toward a fully competitive party system and, thus, converging to patterns similar to those found somewhat earlier in the North suggested that the South was at least nearing the "full flowering" of a mass-based party system that seemed to describe the nation as a whole as early as 1840. Being a part of a fully competitive national party system was fine to southern leaders when that system ensured them a veto within each party and a veto in the national government over fundamental changes to the status quo. But by the late 1840s, the South was becoming an ever-smaller minority in the nation, and the Wilmot Proviso demonstrated that the South could not count on even the standing two-party duopoly to ensure its ability to keep antislavery provisions off the agenda. And with the coming of new states and the failure to conjure a way to maintain the Balance Rule in the Senate after the Compromise of 1850, even the Jacksonian Democrat-Whig party system could not ensure the South a veto over antislavery provisions. With the consequent collapse of the Whig Party, the threat of a majority party forming without consideration of the South was made manifest with the rise of the Republican Party. Revelation of its ability to win majorities in House, Senate, and the presidency in 1860 left the southern white leadership with no veto over policy—Republicans could make law on their own. It left them with what they saw as no choice but to end any involvement in such a nation and thus tear the Union asunder rather than live under a Democrat-Republican two-party system.

In sum, the South could no longer imagine the creation of a two-party system in the region, at least one that mirrored the national two-party system. That the North was a majority of the nation and that the new Republican Party could become a majority without relying at all on the South meant that the South had two choices, risk giving up their socio-economic-cultural system built on slavery or leave the Union. Our next era will tell a very different story, but one that continued to require a southern sort of party system that contained no Republicans, or any other opposition party, to speak of.

4 PARTIES IN THE POST-RECONSTRUCTION ERA

The long sweep of dramatic events that transpired between the collapse of the Jacksonian Democrat-Whig party system and the end of the century, with the emergence of the Democratic-Republican two-party system in the nation and the emergence of the Jim Crow system in the South with its one party, merit a long introduction to this chapter. These include the collapse of the Whig Party and the emergence of the Republican Party in the 1850s, secession in light of the 1860 election and the Civil War, Reconstruction in the postwar South, what the white southern Democrats referred to as "Redemption" during and after the end of Reconstruction, the opening of what has been called the "Populist Moment," in the 1890s (Goodwyn 1978), and the transition to the "new South" (Woodward 1971) with its new social system, new economic system based on sharecropping, and the new political system of Jim Crow laws, all reinforced by violence and terror.

PREFACE: FROM THE COLLAPSE OF THE WHIGS TO THE CIVIL WAR

The Formation of the Republican Party on the Path to Civil War

The collapse of the Whig Party in the aftermath of the 1852 elections left open the question of whether a new party would emerge to forge a new two-party system. One could not even be sure of the basis for such a new, major party. Two possibilities arose in the 1850s for replacing the Whigs as a contestant to the Democrats, the Republican Party and the American Party.

The Republicans grew rapidly in reaction to the turmoil over the Kansas-Nebraska Act of 1854, and even won a plurality of House seats that year, carrying the speakership after a protracted battle (Jenkins and Nokken 2000; Jenkins and Stewart 2012). They ran John C. Frémont for president in 1856, although they fared less well in congressional elections that year and again in 1858 than they had in 1854.[1] Their rapid rise may have been due in part not just to the collapse of the Whigs or even the controversy over the Kansas-Nebraska Act, but also in part because they were born from a merger of former affiliates of the Liberty Party and the Free Soil Party (which had also benefited from some Liberty Party leaders joining them). These two parties had nominated such prominent politicians as Martin Van Buren for president (Free Soil, 1848), while others, such as Salmon Chase, were active in both parties. The Liberty Party presidential nominee (James Birney, OH) won sufficient votes in New York in 1844 that his candidacy may have cost Henry Clay the presidency that year, just as Van Buren's votes were sufficient to have made the difference in electing Zachary Taylor president in 1848 instead of Lewis Cass, particularly due to New York again. The Free Soil Party achieved noticeable representation in Congress (fourteen MCs, two senators), and they allied with Whigs, former Liberty Party members, and others in 1854 to create the Republican Party.

The Republican ideology leading into the election of 1860 and Lincoln's victory was well captured by the slogan "free soil, free labor, free men" (Foner 1971),[2] clarifying that the Republicans would be primarily a northern-based and mostly antislavery party (the former turning out to be exclusively so; the latter meaning antislavery but not abolitionist). Since the North had become considerably more populous than the South, compounded by the fact that a greater proportion of northerners than southerners could vote, it was now possible to win an outright majority with a very strong showing in the North and essentially nothing in the South.[3] This, of course, marked a dramatic change in the coalition opposing the Democrats in 1854—its location, makeup, and content—from what it had been even two years earlier.

The American Party, the potential alternative major party, was rather like the Republican Party in that it was centered in the North, but unlike the GOP, it managed to develop substantial appeal in the South, as seen by its winning a good number of congressional victories there (Gienapp 1987). It was based primarily on a single issue, nativism, or, that is, anti-immigrant appeals. There was indeed considerable immigration, mostly from Germany and Ireland in particular, but also from a number of European nations in the wake of the various losing attempts at revolution in 1848. Opposing immigration therefore had considerable appeal in places where these populations settled: in the big cities on the Atlantic coast; in emerging locations, such as Cincinnati in the Northwest Territories; and in additional places such as Baltimore in the South. The Americans' strategy was a bit dubious for building a major party. Early on they took a pledge of secrecy (giving them the nickname "Know Nothings," as that was what they were to say publicly about what they knew about the party), and they often formed joint or fusion tickets with Whigs, Republicans, Democrats, or any combination thereof that they could.[4] That is a good strategy for winning seats in the short term, less good for party building at the organizational and electoral levels over the long term.[5] In addition, most legislation of relevance to immigration was decided at the state or city level rather than in Washington, so they lacked as clear a national focus and message as the Republicans had.

The Republicans and Americans contested for supremacy in New York City and in other large urban centers (and recall from above the importance of New York in then recent presidential elections). The Republicans were willing to become sufficiently anti-immigrant to attract votes, but not as extremely so as the Americans. This was sufficient for them to carry New York City by the end of the decade, dealing the Americans a blow from which they could not recover. They captured control of a number of local American Party organizations, absorbing American Party voters but not its leaders into their party. This strategy enabled them to incorporate much of the American Party's electoral base into the Republican Party and thus to undermine the Americans. With that, they became the major alternative to the Democrats.

The Election of 1860 and Secession

The election of 1860 had two major consequences. First, the Republicans swept the presidency and Congress. This was the first time a purely northern Electoral College majority was put together, and demonstrated to the South that they could no longer count on having an effective veto to ensure balanced presidential and vice presidential tickets (see chapter 3), as they did not in this case. They thus lost the assurance of having the support of either the president with his actual veto or the vice president with his tie-breaking vote in the Senate, if the South were even able to achieve a tie in the Senate any longer. Obviously, either might support their personal interests, perhaps in opposition to the interests of the South, but the formalized, institutional check on northern power via the executive was lost. They also could be justifiably concerned that such a northern, winning coalition might well lead to action on the slavery issue, harmful to southern interests. And indeed upon the first opportunity to create a northern-based majority, the public voted for a party that ran on a call for free men. One other major consequence was that the erstwhile majority party, the Democrats, could not hold to their balanced intersectional alliance as effectively as they could against a competitor with a similarly balanced intersectional coalition, such as the Whigs. Indeed, while they nominated the most obvious of their leadership to the presidency, Stephen Douglas (Sen., IL), southerners walked out of the two conventions it took to nominate him. And the South ended up, in effect, nominating two candidates under different party labels in their rebellion from the Democratic Party.[6]

Southerners seceded from the Union before Lincoln took office and even before congressional elections were completed.[7] Seven southern and four border states attempted to secede, the final step before actual hostilities broke out as Lincoln sought to prevent the secession from being effective. And thus began the Civil War.

The Confederate Government Forms

Almost immediately upon secession, the eleven secessionist states formed a Provisional Congress and adopted a Permanent Constitution on March 12, 1861, to found the Confederacy (see Jenkins 1999, and sources cited therein). Their Constitution differed little from the one from which they had seceded, in part because they saw themselves as the true heirs of the founding. Their Permanent Constitution differed primarily with respect to the executive branch and, of course, directly enabled slavery. The Congress, however, was quite similar to the U.S. Congress, both in constitutional design and in terms of standing committees, and so on. Many of its members had also been members of the U.S. Congress—amounting to 42% of the Confederate House, 50% of its Senate, and nearly all of the Confederacy's executive leadership (see Jenkins 1999, 1150).

The most significant difference for our purposes is that no political parties were permitted in this period in the South. Of course, the Whig and American Parties were gone, there was no possibility of Republicans gaining any support in the Confederacy, and those third parties that had contested in the South in 1860 were essentially branches of the Democratic Party. That is, essentially everyone involved in those days either had been a Democrat before secession or was not a member of an existing party. Further, the Confederate government, as it turned out, lasted too briefly to have ever been able to get much in the way of new party development going, if any there ever were to be. And, of course, the overwhelmingly dominant issue of the war meant there was unity around the general goal of winning it, leaving room only for (considerable) disagreement over how to do so, that is, how to deal with conscription and taxation among other issues. Had the government lasted longer, it is certainly possible that parties might have formed around other disagreements, but there was no sign of such at all occurring over the duration of the Confederacy.

The lack of southern parties and the consequences of this fact are well reflected in the pattern of Confederate House votes. Jenkins (1999) compared roll call voting on the floors of the respective Union and Confederate Houses, and found that voting in the Confederate House was much less well structured than in the U.S. House. Party played a large and significant role in structuring votes in the Union, above and beyond the role of legislator ideology, but party affiliation had no effect, of course, in the Confederate House. Thus, Jenkins took advantage of this "natural experiment," holding institutional structure and experience fairly constant (and time fully constant), thereby varying primarily the presence of political parties. And he found they made the kind of difference in government that we would expect.

This also does mean, of course, that the Civil War ended and Reconstruction began with what would become a southern white leadership having experience either with no party at all or (in prewar days) with political loyalties only to the Democratic Party or to a long-defunct one. Thus, white southern political figures (excepting "scalawags") were either Democrats or were partisan novices upon reentry to the Union and to its politics at the national and state levels.

RECONSTRUCTION

The Origins of Reconstruction

On September 22, 1862, Abraham Lincoln announced that he would issue an emancipation proclamation, while offering states in rebellion (or having seceded, as seen from the southern point of view) the opportunity to end their rebellion (or to choose to rejoin the Union, from the southern perspective). None did, and so the Emancipation Proclamation was issued January 1, 1863, freeing all slaves in the eleven southern states that seceded. This action fundamentally changed the war, offering African Americans, whether slave or free, great hope, enrapturing abolitionists, and enraging white southerners. The proclamation essentially made the Civil War more formally fought over two goals, union and slavery, instead of just over union. In the North it sparked renewed enthusiasm for the war, which was important because 1862 was a difficult year for the Union, threatening support for the war effort and for the Republicans leading it. Issuing the proclamation can be understood as effectively committing the Union to some kind of action in the South, should the North be victorious. That is to say, it was in effect the first step toward what would become known as Reconstruction.

That the Civil War became a war about slavery as well as one about union was hardly novel to Lincoln or to the Emancipation Proclamation. Several of the states that seceded to form the Confederacy (Georgia, Mississippi, South Carolina, and Texas) included direct mentions of slavery in their declarations of secession.[8] Mississippi's, for example, reads in part,

> Our position is thoroughly identified with the institution of slavery—the greatest material interest of the world. . . . These products have become necessities of the world, and a blow at slavery is a blow at commerce and civilization. That blow has been long aimed at the institution, and was at the point of reaching its consummation. There was no choice left us but submission to the mandates of abolition, or a dissolution of the Union, whose principles had been subverted to work out our ruin.

In other words, while the primary emphasis of the federal government on justification for the war was union, it was certain—and it was understood on both sides—that the dissolution of the Union was, for much if not all of the South, for the purpose of preserving slavery. The Emancipation Proclamation simply shifted the focus directly onto slavery and made policy that the effect of the war (or at least of winning the war) would be freedom for those enslaved in the Confederate states. Just how to do that was left for the future, since nothing could be done until the war was won.

As northern victory neared, General William T. Sherman issued his Special Field Orders, no. 15, on January 16, 1865, merely a month after his March to the Sea. These orders were the first to address the question of what to do with respect to the newly freed slaves.[9] It became popularly known as "forty acres and a mule" (although it did not offer a mule). It included three parts: confiscating southern plantation land;[10] granting of that confiscated land at a rate of forty acres per family to the newly freed slaves; and giving the right of self-government to former slaves living in existing communities. It was, that is, not only the first formal plan at all, but it was the first plan worthy of the name "radical," as in "Radical Reconstruction." The order was issued after a meeting with Secretary of War Edwin Stanton (among others) four days earlier, so while the plan is correctly associated with Sherman, he did not take action without prior approval from his superiors in the chain of command. Sherman's plan was, however, also not implemented, being blocked by Sherman's immediately superior commanding officer and then overturned formally by President Andrew Johnson, who had succeeded Lincoln (Foner 2011).

With peace finally having arrived, it was time to develop an actual plan and implement it. The South needed to be reconstructed somehow from the devastation of a terrible war fought mainly on its soil. The emancipated slaves needed something, a great deal of something, by means of support, having been intentionally denied education and many of the basics of life by virtue of the way slavery was conducted in the antebellum South. The division that emerged between a Stanton and Sherman and other "Radical Reconstructionists," on the one hand, and a Johnson, essentially the entire Democratic Party, and the remaining parts of the Republican Party, on the other hand, indicates the nature of the division between Radical Reconstructionists and others. So deep were the divisions during Reconstruction that Johnson was impeached primarily for his efforts to block other proposals and appointments he saw as too radical, and he ended up but one vote short of conviction.[11] Thus, we enter the real period of Reconstruction, from peace (realistically from 1866) through the formal end of Reconstruction with the negotiated resolution of the contested electoral votes in the presidential election of 1876.

Reconstruction, Per Se

At war's end, the South was devastated. A significant percentage of young white males were dead or wounded (Huddleston 2002). The end of slavery and the years of fighting had wrought huge damage to the plantation economy. The political structure was gone, and not all former Confederates, especially the military and political leadership, were immediately repatriated. The U.S. government imposed a regime of Reconstruction that, from the southern, white perspective, was enforced by Union troops, and otherwise led by civilian "carpetbaggers."[12] Surviving former slaves had to adjust to something no one in virtually all of their families had experienced, freedom. But it was freedom for most without education, without much in the way of any obvious source of income, and even perhaps without a usable occupation, and with virtually no economic system in which to ply any such nonexistent trades anyway. As discussed above, the first concrete plan was Sherman's "forty acres and a mule." Needless to say, owners or heirs of such lands were less than thrilled at their erstwhile tracts being given to their former slaves.

The end of Reconstruction meant that it was possible for whites who had been a part of the Confederacy to return to full citizen status, and thus to imagine recapturing elective office as white southerners. While one could in principle imagine some other coalition, in point of fact, what happened was an attempt to return to something like the prewar plantation economy and to the middle-class and upper-middle-class dominance of that government. White southerners referred to this as "Redemption," a word that suggests not just reentering political life but returning to something as close to antebellum politics and society as possible (and with intentional religious overtones). The result was that Redemption took the form of a primarily white, southern Democratic Party coming back to power and eventually a Jim Crow political system and a sharecropping economic system to try to mimic antebellum life. One difference (perhaps the most important but only one of many) was that there was a well-defined opposition, consisting of the northerners now in the South and the former slaves who had spent ten years benefiting from Union support. And, from the white southern point of view, the desirable thing was that this was an opposition that a revived Democratic Party could easily defeat. It was not hard at all to win a majority of votes when the opposition party is the party of Lincoln, Union troops, and freed slaves, at least once whites were fully repatriated. Of course, failure to mobilize effectively could put even white majorities at risk. But "Redeemers" worked out solutions to this set of potential problems. As we will see, it became harder to assure winning majorities when the opposition was a different party, one that had a design that could imagine winning a majority consisting of the less well-off, the former slave population and poor whites, but one that was not associated with any taint of the party of Lincoln. Because it was an economically devastated region, the citizens who were relatively poor added up to a clear majority of the citizenry of the eleven states of the former Confederacy. The former plantation leadership or their successors thus could much more easily imagine being defeated at the hands of an effective Populist Party. And it was that imagination, among other things, that led from what was a possible "Populist Moment" to Jim Crow (Goodwyn 1978).

RECONSTRUCTION AND A
SOUTHERN REPUBLICAN PARTY?

Republicans and Reconstruction in the South. After the war, the Republicans quickly captured control of all southern state governorships and state legislatures, except for Virginia. Delegations from six southern states were not readmitted to the U.S. Congress until 1868, however, and four others not until 1870. The Republican coalition included the election of numerous African Americans to local, state, and national offices. At the beginning of 1867, no African American in the South held political office, but within three or four years "about 15 percent of the officeholders in the South were black—a larger proportion than in 1990" (McPherson 1992, 19).

One source of political and economic leadership of the Republicans in the South came from the numerous "carpetbaggers" who moved (often with major political appointments or other sorts of jobs) from the North to the South to aid in Reconstruction. They were typically those who brought the newly freed slaves into politics. Their motives for going south were diverse, of course. Foner, for example, wrote that (1988),

> most carpetbaggers probably combine the desire for personal gain with a commitment to taking part in an effort "to substitute the civilization of freedom for that of slavery." . . . Carpetbaggers generally supported measures aimed at democratizing and modernizing the South—civil rights legislation, aid to economic development, the establishment of public school systems. (296)

Carpetbaggers combined with African Americans and "scalawags" (southerners who supported the politics of northern carpetbaggers and freed slaves) to create the southern Republican Party and assume political leadership.

Political and racial tensions built up inside the southern Republican Party during Reconstruction, a tension exacerbated by virtue of Democratic attacks. This led to an opening for exploiting their divisions. As early as 1868, for example, Georgia Democrats in the state legislature won support from some Republicans to expel all twenty-eight black Republican members, arguing that blacks were eligible to vote but not to hold office. In several states, the more conservative scalawags fought for control with the more radical carpetbaggers and usually lost, even though they supported Reconstruction. Thus, in Mississippi, the conservative faction led by scalawag James Lusk Alcorn was decisively defeated by the radical faction led by carpetbagger Adelbert Ames. The party lost support steadily as many scalawags left it. Meanwhile, the freedmen (newly liberated blacks) were demanding a larger share of the offices and patronage, thus squeezing out their carpetbagger allies.

Was a southern Republican Party viable? These examples to the contrary notwithstanding, it might seem that the first years of Reconstruction provided a nearly unique opportunity for taking advantage of the diversity of people, experiences, and party affiliation in the newly revived state governments. Perhaps a long-term balance could be achieved between Republicans and Democrats in the South, as was being forged in the North. There would be a differing basis of these two proto-coalitions, of course. In the South the two parties, if ever such a system could be achieved, would be a GOP based primarily on freed slave votes and a Democratic core of the white plantation owners and the (relatively small) white middle class. These two core groups would contest their campaigns over the support of the rural, often poor, whites. Or so one might have imagined. And, indeed, were freedman able to vote over the long term and were poorer whites attracted to the Republicans for their economic opportunities and to the Democrats for their social positions, a two-party South contesting for poorer white support to determine who would win particular elections was logically possible.

By the mid-1870s, however, many Americans, even in the North, were beginning to tire of Reconstruction. So when another wave of antiblack and anti-Republican terrorism swept the South in 1875–76, President Grant and the federal government did not intervene. One by one, Republican governments in the South fell to the Democrat Redeemers, who were ready to use fraud and violence if necessary to seize power.

By autumn 1876, only three southern states retained Republican governments—South Carolina, Louisiana, and Florida. As a result of the disputed presidential election of that year and the resulting Compromise of 1877, President Hayes removed federal troops from these states and allowed the Redeemers to take complete control. The entire South was now under the sway of Democrats, and Reconstruction was over. As we will conclude more fully below, this mere decade was too short a time in which to establish a competitive party system. Even more, the electoral outcomes were so dynamic over even that ten-year period, there was nothing even close to a settling toward an "equilibrium" of a multi- (i.e., two-) party system.

"REDEMPTION" AND THE "NEW SOUTH"

How quickly had the partisan politics changed over this decade? In figure 4.1, we report the percentage of presidential electoral votes, senatorial seats, and House seats controlled by the Republicans in the eleven states of the now former Confederacy. With senators appointed by state legislatures, in most cases, the partisan affiliation of senators indicated which party held majorities in the state legislatures as well.

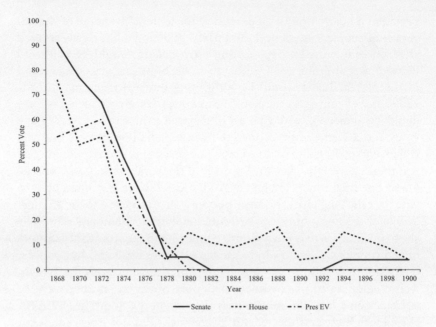

Figure 4.1 Electoral results, states of the former Confederacy, 1868–1900

As the states were readmitted and the Confederates regained voting
rights, the Republican victory totals declined dramatically. By 1880,
the Republicans no longer could count on winning even one electoral
vote from the South. From 1878 through the end of the century, the
South chose either zero or one Republican senator. Finally, the Democrats carried 85%–95% of the House seats in that period as well.
Over the decade of Reconstruction, Republicans went from winning
nearly every election (because former Confederates were not yet repatriated) in 1868 to an even balance in 1872, when elections were
close to competitive on the surface. But that balanced set of electoral
outcomes was true only for 1872. By 1876, Republicans had all but
lost any real chance at sustained electoral success, and by 1880, they
were all but eliminated from political life in the South entirely. The
idea of an electorally sustainable Republican Party in the South was
but a pipe dream.

The possibility of a sustainable two-party Democrat-Republican
Party in the South, mirroring in some fashion that of the North, was
not just a random thought, however. After all, African Americans were
a majority of the population in Louisiana and South Carolina and in
many parts of other states, and in others they were a large minority
and, therefore, a potentially significant coalition building block for any

party. At the very least, that was certainly enough of an electoral base on which to build a party. How, then, were white Democrats able to forge what appeared to be sustainable and overwhelming majority at the end of Reconstruction or even earlier?

The answer—"Redemption"—was a sort of first run at Jim Crow kinds of tactics. There were two major differences between what we might call the Redemption period and the Jim Crow era. One was that winning office as a member of the white southern minority was more nearly the dominant, if not the exclusive, goal of this earlier period. That is, reclaiming control of the political process was a first focus. The second difference was that the opposition—the party of Lincoln, Union, Reconstruction, and free blacks—made for a much more compelling target in elections than an opposition untainted by Lincoln, Union, and Reconstruction would have been. That is to say, a Populist sort of party, one that sought a coalition of freed slaves and poor southern whites without any of the Civil War, North, and Union baggage, could have plausibly been defeated, but not certainly and not without considerable effort. Indeed, in some places (such as where blacks were themselves already a majority) permanent control by white Democrats was a truly iffy prospect. But that is the story of the transition to Jim Crow, not to Redemption.

Table 4.1 lists in the first column the year in which Democrats regained control of the state. The first wave of "redeemed" states happened early, not long after readmission. But, as in the case of North Carolina (which is listed as 1870 because the legislature was controlled by Democrats that year), for example, it subsequently reverted to Republican control. The last Republican governor, Daniel Lindsay Russell, served until 1901 (he was a Republican running on a fusion ticket with Populists in the 1896 elections). Still North Carolina is more the exception than the rule, and most states reverted to Democratic control at the date listed and remained under their control continuously for a century. Note that all eleven former Confederate states were "redeemed" no later than at the end of Reconstruction, if not before.

Getting to that point was not necessarily simple. At one extreme, whites in principle had enough votes to elect Democrats back into office—and did. In others there was a black majority. These states, and some others with very large black minorities, tended to use the "Mississippi Plan" (so named because of its first use there). Sometimes, it involved vote buying, often of black votes. Sometimes it involved threats of violence. Often it included actual violence. These organizations were sometimes referred to as the "military arm" of the Democratic Party. The plan was put into effect in 1875 in Mississippi,

Table 4.1 Southern state provisions affecting turnout in the 1870–1921 period

State	"Redemption"	Poll taxes	Property relief	Literacy	Felon bar
Alabama	1874	1901[1]	1901	1901	1867, 1901
Arkansas	1874	1893	—	—	1868, '73
Florida	1877	1885,'89	—	1868[2]	1868
Georgia	1871	1866, '69, 1907	1907	1907	1868
Louisiana	1877	1898[3]	1898	1898[4]	1870, '79
Mississippi	1876	1890[5]	—	1890	1868,'76,'80, '90
N. Carolina	1870	1876	—	1876	1876[6]
S. Carolina	1877	1895	1895	1985, '98	1868, '95
Tennessee	1869	1870	—	—	1870, '71
Texas	1876, '83	1876	—	1869, '76	1902, '10
Virginia	1869	1876, 1902	1902	1902	1870, 1902

Source: Keyssar 2009. The columns are, from left to right, from Keyssar's tables A.10, A.11, A.13, and A.15, respectively.

[1] In 1875, passed law that banned poll taxes, overturned in 1901. The 1901 felony restriction law includes "tramps" and vagrancy.

[2] Literacy test allowed, never enacted by state legislature.

[3] Repealed literacy test, poll tax, and relief from poll tax for property owners in 1921.

[4] See previous note.

[5] The 1868 law banned literacy tests for voting, overturned in 1890.

[6] Passed law in 1868 permitting no felon restrictions in voting, over turned by later law.

where "Red Shirts" operated openly armed and threatening (and actually employing) violence not only against blacks but also against carpetbaggers and scalawags. The former often fled the state, the latter "converted" to become Democrats. Other states (Louisiana, North and South Carolina) had rifle clubs, the "white League," and even some remnants of the first Ku Klux Klan. This overt violence was paired with economic sanctions and other such means to reverse the black majority in the population into a black (and white Republican) minority at the voting booth. Consider one report: "During Mississippi's 1875 election, five counties with large black majorities polled 12, 7, 4, 2, and 0 votes, respectively. Indeed, what had been a Republican victory of 30,000 votes in 1874 became a Democrat majority of 30,000 in 1875."[13] Not only did winning back control of office rest on reduced Republican turnout, but, by driving away white Republicans, it also often effectively eliminated the political leadership of the party.

Once back in control, Democrats overturned a variety of Reconstruction legislation. For example, as noted above, Georgia ruled that while blacks could vote, they could not hold office, expelling all twenty-eight black Republicans in the legislature. Various other "black codes" were instituted—often a series of measures designed to regulate black labor through apprenticeship, contract labor, and vagrancy laws, but including restrictions on voting and other political opportunities. These, however, tended to be piecemeal efforts rather than a coherent attempt at the full scope of the social, economic, and political control that was to come under Jim Crow. The "Populist Moment," however, began to change that piecemeal plan into the more full-bodied, coherent suppression associated with the Jim Crow regime, which will be the subject of the next chapter.

RECONSTRUCTION, REDEMPTION, AND SOUTHERN REPUBLICANISM

The idea of a competitive two-party system in the South in the wake of the Civil War was clearly an idealistic fantasy. It had a logical basis. With freed slaves eligible to vote, they could serve as the backbone of a Republican opposition to the white southerners who one would expect to reformulate in their original Democratic Party. It was a disadvantage that the second southern party was to be the regional branch of the national Republican Party, but a fair Reconstruction and consistent application of the letter and the intent of the Civil War Amendments, combined with leadership from experienced and educated whites from the North should, the idealist would believe, have kept the southern Republican Party viable. In less than ten years, the idealist confronted the reality that the former Confederates were not going to play by the rules the carpetbaggers were trying to put into place in Reconstruction, nor were they likely to honor the spirit of Emancipation and of the Civil War Amendments. Indeed, before the federal troops enforcing Reconstruction were pulled within the decade, the first necessary condition of full southern, white Redemption, suppression of the Republican Party as an effective entity, was achieved. So effectively was it achieved that it would be a century before the GOP would reappear as an effective electoral force in the South. There was a very rapid and dramatic decline of Republican electoral success. Much too rapid and complete to imagine it otherwise remaining as even a weaker second party. While all of this was in the interest of returning the freedman to a status as close to slavery as the loss of a war would make possible, the necessary first step was for the Democrats to regain control of the political system and to bury the Republican Party as fully as possible.

The idealist imagining of a coalition of blacks and poor whites forming sufficiently to be a serious competitor to a white, middle-class, centric Democratic Party still had the logic of numbers on its side. Blacks and poorer whites made up solid majorities in lots of places. It was trying to achieve Reconstruction politically, by creating the same two-party system in the South as in the North that was the pipe dream. There was simply too much antagonism against the party of Lincoln, Union, and radical Reconstruction for that to be viable. But the numbers were still there, and perhaps an alternative second party could realize the political reformulation of the South into a competitive two-party system.

The Populists and Other Alternatives to Republicans

The Populists were that potential second major party, and they were the most important "third-party" movement in the post-Reconstruction South.[14] They were not, however, the only such movement. There were Grangers, Greenbacks, and Readjusters, among others. Democrats were divided into Alliance men (seeking to ally with party politicians from western states) contesting conservative Democrats (who wanted to ally with those from the northeast). There were thus a diversity of options in between the effective collapse of the Republicans and the short period we are calling (after Goodwyn 1978) the "Populist Moment," that is, between 1876 and 1890. Most had marginal effects on politics in any one state, let alone across the South.

One, perhaps the most important, exception was the Readjuster Party in Virginia (see Dailey 2000; Levine 2000; and Woodward 1971 [1951], especially chap. 7, "Procrustean Bedfellows," 75–106). To quote from Dailey (2000):

> The Readjuster Party—the party that "favored [n-word] voting"—was the most successful interracial political alliance in the postemancipation South. An independent coalition of black and white Republicans and white Democrats, the Readjusters governed Virginia from 1879 to 1883. During this period a Readjuster governor occupied the statehouse, two Readjusters represented the Old Dominion in the U.S. Senate, and Readjusters served six of Virginia's ten congressional districts. . . . A black-majority party, the Readjusters legitimated and promoted African American citizenship and political power by supporting black suffrage, office-holding, and jury service. (1)

She goes on to note that there were other such movements from the original Republican Party during Reconstruction through to the Populists, in every state. And, as we describe below, the Republicans continued to win elections in North Carolina up to the Wilmington race riot of 1898 and the beginning of Jim Crow in that state. And Republicans and others sometimes won as fusion candidates. As Woodward (1971) notes, only some of the time did these successes lead to major policy successes. On numerous occasions, including among those elected as Populists, victorious non-Democratic candidates ended up choosing to fail to or being unable to implement proposed reforms. At times, they even ended up repudiating their campaign pledges when in office and endorsing "Redeemer" policies.

The political changes of the late 1800s were rooted in the tremendous changes taking place in the nation's economy (see, e.g., Klepper 1974). During this era, America became the world's leading manufacturer, driven in large part by the opportunities that electrification of industry made possible. From 1860 to 1890, a half million U.S. patents were issued—over ten times the number issued in the previous seventy years. Not surprisingly, the population became increasingly urbanized such that while one in five Americans lived in a city in 1860, a majority of Americans lived in an urban area in 1920. The South lagged behind on this score with less than one in five residents living in an urban area by 1900, compared to two out of three in the Northeast. Within this era of tremendous economic growth there were also downturns—most notably "panics" in 1873, 1884, and 1893—which disproportionately hurt the nation's farmers.

The Populist political movement, according to Hicks (1931), grew out of a variety of factors, including deflation in agricultural prices (including especially a 50% drop in cotton prices) blamed on the gold standard, high interest rates, mortgage foreclosures, and high railroad rates, all of which threatened the livelihood of the American farmer (Hicks 1931). Lawrence Goodwyn (1978) added to this a special emphasis on the sharecropping (or crop lien) method that created a very large class of landless farmers caught in the cycle of indebtedness to landowners. This was a specifically southern phenomenon that provided a strong reason for alliance between white and black sharecroppers. Together, they amounted to a majority in a great many southern locales.

The Populist movement began in Texas and swept across the South before turning westward. Success was often obtained initially through electoral fusion, with the Democrats outside the South, and with alliances with the Republicans in southern states like Alabama, North Carolina, Tennessee, and Texas. For example, in the elections of 1894, a coalition of Populists and Republicans led by Populist Marion Butler swept state and local offices in North Carolina; the coalition would go on to elect Republican Daniel Lindsay Russell as governor in 1896. The very severe national economic Panic of 1893 provided considerable impetus for the elections in 1894 and 1896, which is why Goodwyn referred to it as the "Populist Moment" (1978).[15] However, the fusion strategy would be no kinder to the long-term success of the Populists than it had been to the Americans.

By 1896, the Democratic Party had taken up many of the Populists' causes at the national level. In that year's presidential election, the Democrats nominated William Jennings Bryan, who focused (as Populists rarely did) on free silver as a solution to the economic depression and to the lack of credit for "easy" money for farmers and others. The Populists had the choice of endorsing Bryan or running their own candidate. After great infighting at their St. Louis convention, they decided to endorse Bryan but with their own vice presidential nominee, Thomas E. Watson of Georgia. Bryan's strength was based on the traditional Democratic vote; he swept the old Populist strongholds in the West and South, and added the Silverite states in the West, but did poorly in the industrial heartland. He lost to Republican William McKinley by a margin of six hundred thousand votes.

The effects of fusion with the Democrats in the nation were disastrous to the Populist Party in the South. The Populist-Republican alliance that had been the basis of electoral success in the South, such as in their sweep in North Carolina, fell apart when nonsouthern Populists were aligning with Democrats, not Republicans. By 1898, only two years after Bryan ran for president both as a Populist and as a Democrat, the Democrats used a violently racist campaign to defeat the North Carolina Populists and Republicans, and in 1900 southern Democrats ushered in disfranchisement. In 1900, while many Populist voters supported Bryan again, the weakened party nominated a separate ticket of Wharton Barker and Ignatius L. Donnelly, and disbanded afterward.

On top of these political missteps, the Populists were being gradually stripped of their supporters. Between 1890 and 1910, ten of the eleven former Confederate states, starting with Mississippi, passed new constitutions or amendments that effectively disfranchised most blacks and tens of thousands of poor whites through a combination of poll taxes, literacy and comprehension tests, and residency and record-keeping requirements (see the discussion of Jim Crow laws below). Voter turnout dropped drastically throughout the South as a result of such measures. For example, in Louisiana black voters were reduced to just 5,320 by 1900, although they comprised the majority of the state's 1.4-million-person population. By 1910, only 730 blacks were registered, less than 0.5% of eligible black men. According to Pildes (2000, 12), "In 27 of the state's 60 parishes, not a single black voter was registered any longer; in 9 more parishes, only one black voter was." In North Carolina, black voters were completely eliminated from voter rolls during the period from 1896 to 1904. In Alabama, tens of thousands of poor whites were disenfranchised. The "Populist Moment" was over.

DEVELOPMENT OF THE PARTY SYSTEM AFTER RECONSTRUCTION

Next, paralleling our approach in chapter 3, we examine more carefully the trajectory of party development in the late 1800s, comparing across regions. How distinct and cohesive were the parties in office? How organized were they? And did they serve as a useful guide to voters in elections?

Party in Government

We begin with an indication of the degree to which the activities of elected officials in each region provided voters a clear signal of what the party stood for. These signals are once again measured using the concept of interparty difference, or what is often called partisan polarization, adopted from the idea of conditional party government. For most of this period, we compare the distinctiveness of Republicans and Democrats. We cannot do much over time measurement of the Populists; the "Populist Moment" was too short. We therefore draw from detailed historical analyses to supplement and enrich what is virtually cross-sectional data.

Our regional comparisons of interparty heterogeneity reveal a sharp difference between the antebellum and post-Reconstruction periods. Recall that, before the Civil War, there were both party and regional differences, of roughly similar magnitude, on the first ideological dimension in Congress. In figure 4.2, we see that, in the House after the War, northern and southern Republicans voted quite similarly on those issues, although southern Republican voting patterns varied more over time. Whether southern and northern Republicans should have been so closely aligned is another matter.[16] Northern Democrats differed only somewhat from southern Democrats, but much less than in the Jacksonian era. Figure 4.3 reports similar data for the Senate, but with so few and at times no southern Republican senators, we report only northern Republicans and the two regional groups of Democrats. Again, regional differences among Democrats were modest. Northern and southern Democrats differed little (albeit over the same times as did the comparable groupings in the House). These data suggest that post-Reconstruction national politics was more divided by party than by region, at least in the halls of Congress.

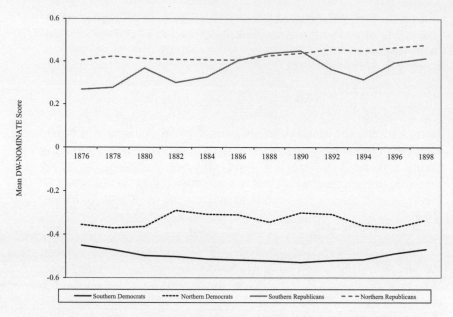

Figure 4.2 Mean House DW-NOMINATE score by party and region, 1876–1900

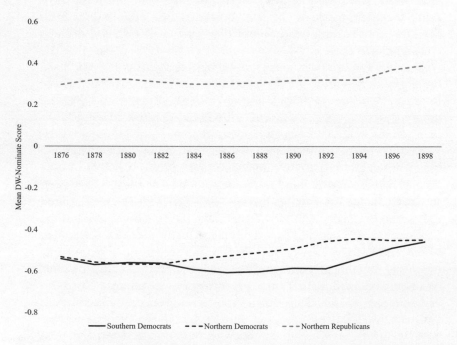

Figure 4.3 Mean Senate DW-NOMINATE score by party and region, 1876–1900

Overall, this was a period with small regional differences but with large party differences. After 1876, however, this distinction was of decreasing importance, as the Republican representation retreated to its roughly 10% level in the South, covering mostly mountain districts and, in figurative as well as these literal terms, being outside the mainstream of southern politics. This contrasts with the Democrat-Whig era, which had roughly equal and lasting partisan and regional differences between the two parties' national delegations. Regional differences were manifest, therefore, more by which party won seats in the region than by divisions within party delegations. For our purposes these regional differences are important because for voters to observe party differences it is necessary not only for the party's officeholders to take up distinct positions but also for each of the parties to hold a sufficient number of offices in the first place.

Thus far, our comparisons of party positions have taken place at a regional level. Voters may not always, or only, evaluate the parties' positions at such a high level of aggregation. Instead, or in addition, they might form their impressions of the parties by contrasting candidates put before them in actual races. At a more localized level, there appeared to be less policy differentiation of the parties in at least some regions of the South. As Moger described the situation in Virginia, "The Republican platform was very similar to that of the Democrats" (Moger 1942, 195). In addition, as we will see below it was often difficult for Democrats to differentiate themselves from Republicans because there often was no Republican candidate contending (see figure 4.5). So, it is not unreasonable to expect that party distinctiveness might have been less stark in southern localities than northern localities.

Party Organization

Party organizations appear to have been quite a bit more developed in the North than in the South during the post-Reconstruction period. As a general proposition, parties had never been as fully organized as they were in this era. As McCormick observed (1986):

> As organizations and as objects of loyalty, the major parties enjoyed their golden age during the last three decades of the nineteenth century. Although only loosely coordinated at the national level, the Democrats and Republicans each boasted awesome machines in localities where they were competitive, and on election days they shepherded enthusiastic and committed followers to the polls. (171)

As McCormick's "where they were competitive" caveat suggests, we might anticipate that southern parties lagged behind their northern counterparts when it came to organization. We adduce secondary evidence of this below. Before doing so, however, we note that for McCormick, the electoral function of parties was intimately tied to the accountability of parties once in office (1986):

> Correspondingly, the parties' virtuosity as electoral organizations strengthened their policy roles and influenced government decision-making. In close contact with the people, the party leaders who got out the vote also learned what the citizens wanted. Successful in electing candidates to office, the party organizations placed men in positions to procure the desired benefits. Party voters were confident in the men elected and gave officials relative freedom to determine the details of policy outcomes. It is not necessary to assume a complete identity of interests between party voters, party organizers, and party legislators to see that these connections—all deriving from the parties' electoral strength—helped shape the final form of public policy. (215)

To return to the point above, by comparison southern parties were much less organized: "Most injurious to the future of the Republican party in . . . southern states was the failure to redevelop the state party organizations" (Klingman and Lammers 1984, 68). In Georgia, after Republican candidates were thoroughly routed in 1874, "there was no Republican organization 'except enough to hold the offices of a Republican [national] administration within its grasp'" (Ward 1943, 198).[17] Two years later, no GOP candidates were put up for the state's offices, and in only one congressional district was there even the semblance of opposition to the Democratic nominee. In sum,

> After . . . the virtual collapse of the Republican organization, frustration and defeatism had taken their toll. With a passing of the years the party had settled down into a rut of inaction and disrepute. The continued predominance of the Negro, factional fights and the conflicts among party leaders, the greed for office and corruption in office, the questionable character of many of the leaders, the unsavory reputation of Southern delegates to national conventions, the failure to put up candidates for office, and the apparent lack of real desire among the leadership to expand the party and to win elections—all of these were factors which contributed to the deterioration of Republicanism in Georgia. (Shadgett 2010, 155)

In Florida, meanwhile, spoils were the only reason the Republicans were organized after Redemption (Klingman and Lammers 1984):

> Republicans were forced to deal with the immediate problem of surviving as a political organization. They responded by withdrawing almost

completely from state elections and concentrating instead on carrying Florida for Republican presidential aspirants and rewarding themselves with federal patronage positions. . . . Moreover, in 1920 the Florida Supreme Court refused to even recognize the existence of the Republican party in the state. (99–100)

In the end, "the condition of Florida's Republican party bordered on ineptitude" (Klingman and Lammers 1984, 77).

Given the disorganization that permeated the southern Republican Party during this period, it is perhaps not surprising that southern Democratic Party organizations also were less organized, compared to their northern counterparts. In the 1880 Georgia gubernatorial election, for instance, Democrats were unable to nominate a candidate for the office (Ward 1943, 200). The notable exception was Virginia, where competition from the Readjusters and Republicans encouraged greater organization by the Democrats (Moger 1942):

> Under Barbour's leadership the [Democratic] executive committee immediately laid detailed and specific plans to organize every district, county, and precinct within the state. Each local subdivision was to have a committee to list every voter on the registration books, with information concerning his political affiliation. Local canvassers were to find out who needed to be registered, and who should be transferred, and were to see that all was ready for election day. To make plans really effective, weekly reports were to be made by district, county, and precinct chairmen, and the precinct committeemen were given the particular duty of seeing that a full vote was polled. Prominent men in the party were appointed as speakers, and it was arranged to have a Democratic speaker on every court day in every county between then and the election. (189)

As for the manner of southern Democratic Party organization (Woodward 1971),

> Had the white man's party of conservatism been democratically organized, had the "party line" been determined and criticized democratically, the one-party system might not have been stultifying. But the organization and control of the party was anything but democratic. Issues, candidates, platforms—everything was the private business of a few politicians known by the discontented as the "ring" or the "courthouse clique." The extent of their domination and the nature of their machinery of control varied among the state rings, but the ring was always present. (52)

The southern Democratic Party of the late nineteenth century, that is, looked quite like that of the 1930s and 1940s documented by Key (1949).

There is little to say about the organization of the Populist Party. It lasted too briefly to be confident in any conclusions about organization, except to say that it struggled to achieve much of anything in this regard. The Populists began as a mass movement, perhaps the first in American history to achieve any significant degree of electoral success. As a mass movement, it had many meanings in different places, and bringing such a coalition together into a truly organized party is ever a substantial challenge. This was compounded in the South, especially, as any attempt to unite white and black citizens would face special difficulties on its own. But the Democratic Party strategy was to tear that coalition apart before it showed anything more than promise, whether that was by waving the bloody gray shirt, buying off emerging Populist leaders, or moving to intimidation and violence, such as in case of the Wilmington race riot. Their goal was precisely to undermine the movement before it became a truly organized entity.

Party in Elections

Again, we assess the vitality of parties in elections through voter turnout for this historical era. Historians regularly refer to the vigor of political parties as mobilizing forces, especially in this period, the period, after all, of the emergence of party machines (Kleppner 1979; Silbey 1991, 1994). When voters have a clear sense of what the parties stand for, they are more likely to identify with one of the parties, and not the other. When voters identify with a party, they are more likely to participate in elections, either due directly to this psychological attachment, or because parties are more likely to mobilize identifiers on election day. The "ethnocultural" explanation of post-Reconstruction era turnout in the nation is that of social identities (often among new or relatively recent immigrant groups) aligning with a party that referred to themselves as mobilizing their "armies" of supporters on election day, exploiting the social and cultural linkages between voters' identities and their partisan attachments as the key to mobilizing them.

There is broad agreement that electoral participation in the South was much more anemic than in the North during this period. As one observer put it, "Historians have long acknowledged a tradition of voter apathy in the Solid South of the late nineteenth and early twentieth centuries" (Schweiger 1991, 195). Figure 4.4 shows this more precisely by tracking electoral turnout among eligible citizens in the North and South from 1876 to 1900. According to the figure, the turnout rate was about the same in both regions in 1876, about 75% of eligible voters. By 1896, however, citizens in the North were still

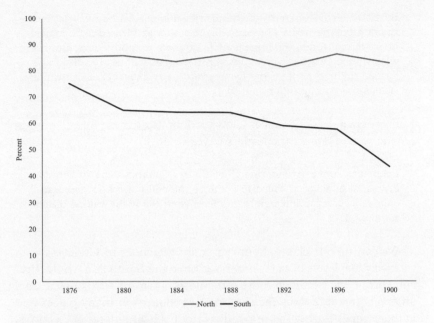

Figure 4.4 Regional difference in presidential turnout, 1876–1900

voting at a rate of about three in four, while the proportion of southerners had declined to less than one in two. We observed a very similar
pattern when we made the same comparison using estimated turnout
data from Clubb, Flanigan, and Zingale (1986).

Of course, African Americans who were de jure eligible to vote were
increasingly driven away from the polls by intimidation, the introduction of property, residency, and literacy requirements, and the lack
of competition in general elections produced by the white primary,
among other factors (Kousser 1974; see also Redding and James
2001). Redemption also depressed turnout among southern whites
in the 1890s. However, it would be a mistake to conclude that the
entire regional turnout gap evident in figure 4.4 is attributable to legal
barriers to the franchise. For one thing, there is substantial evidence
of a regional turnout gap prior to the adoption of Jim Crow laws, the
earliest of which appeared in the late 1880s (more on this below). In
addition, there is ample evidence of other mechanisms at work that
enervated the electorate. Across the South, "Many qualified voters
shunned politics . . . finding it even more obviously the tool of Democratic machines" (Ayers 1992, 410). As Woodward put it, "the absence
of any effective party of opposition was an additional invitation to laxity" (Woodward 1971, 66). In Virginia, for instance (Schweiger 1991):

> By the 1890s Democrats were faced with unprecedented rates of voter apathy across the state. The party might have been pleased if the majority of the nonvoters were undesirable poor whites and blacks. But the white businessmen, farmers, and professionals who had traditionally formed the backbone of the Democratic party exhibited a disturbing lack of interest in elections. (195)

Rather than a cause of concern, low turnout was a cause for celebration among some Democratic leaders (Ayers 1992):

> Politicians spoke "wonderingly" of the way politics were in the doldrums; of how voters failed to come to the polls; and how "ignorant" men showed an unintelligible indifference to the noble calling of citizenship. (410)

We can tie our claim about regional differences in Congress with relatively low levels of party organization in the South as a whole. Presumably, it will be much more difficult for a party to establish a label among voters if, as was the case for Republicans in many places and at many times during this era, it does not field candidates in elections. As one study put it, "It is a recognized fact that the easiest way to keep a political party small is to fail to put up candidates" (Shadgett 2010, 160). Even if candidates are not successful, and thus do not have an opportunity to take actual positions on roll call votes, presumably the positions that candidates take in a campaign affect voters' perceptions of the party label. The absence of an opposing party may also serve to erode, or stunt the development of, the dominant party's label, for without a real chance of losing their seats the members of the dominant party have little incentive to resolve their differences.

It is therefore important that during this period, the Republican Party often did not field anything like a reasonably competitive candidate for many congressional and gubernatorial races, and often fielded no candidate at all. This much is apparent from figure 4.5, which reports the proportion of southern gubernatorial and U.S. House races from 1880 to 1898 in which the Republican Party did not contest the race.[18]

The Republicans did not put up a gubernatorial candidate in any of the races in Georgia, Mississippi, or South Carolina, and skipped the election in a majority or near majority of races in three additional states (Alabama, Texas, and Virginia). Only in Tennessee and North Carolina, where mountain communities remained supportive of Republicanism, and in Louisiana, was a Republican candidate for governor entered in every election. In nine of eleven states the Republicans

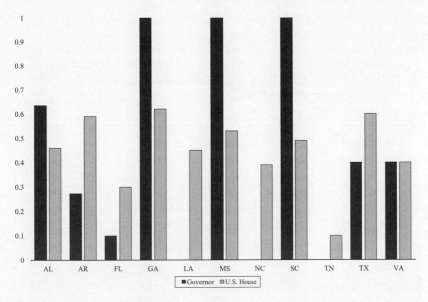

Figure 4.5 Proportion of gubernatorial and U.S. House seats not contested by Republicans, 1880–98

contested no more than 40% of House races over this period. Once again, Tennessee proved to be a notable exception with GOP House candidates appearing in nine of ten races.

Figure 4.6 compares the quality of U.S. House candidates by region from 1876 to 1900 using data provided by Jason Roberts and Jamie Carson (Carson and Roberts 2013). When the candidates fielded by both of the parties are of equal quality, this measure equals zero. When the Democrats hold a quality advantage this measure is positive, and when the Republicans do so this measure is negative. In the South, from the end of Reconstruction through the end of the century, the Republican Party failed to field quality candidates over half the time. In contrast, in the North both parties were able to field quality candidates (with a slight Republican advantage) until 1894. Thereafter, the Democrats ran somewhat weaker candidates, but compared to the South, candidate quality was much more balanced between the parties.

The Populist Party, especially in the South, was nearly a purely agrarian movement and thus not likely to reveal much in the way of organizational capabilities at the outset—and it survived for too short a period to have much life beyond that outset (Goodwyn 1978). To succeed, it had to unite black and white farmers, and Democrats sought

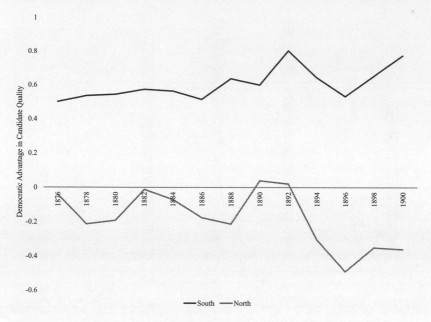

Figure 4.6 Candidate quality in elections by region, 1876–1900

to divide them by race, mostly, of course, by calls to the "Lost Cause," trying to pull whites back into the Democratic camp. Republicans, for their part, continued to appeal to blacks as the party of Emancipation. These pullings and tuggings had two consequences. First, it provided a mixed message to every potential part of the Populist coalition in the South (much as Republicans in the North "waved the bloody shirt" to keep farmers from defecting to the Populists). Doing so not only blunted the appeal to an agrarian and class-based party, but it blunted the enthusiasm of the appeal, reducing the motivation to risk much, or take any risk at all, in turning out. Second, to overcome that, the Populists would have liked to do what they did more successfully elsewhere, which is to organize as a movement and mobilize collective action in support of Populist principles, generating the needed enthusiasm to get supporters out to the polls (long wagon trains and various other examples of movement politics). But in the South, it was not wise for blacks to organize for collective political action at all, nor was it wise for whites to join with blacks in such demonstrations. As a result, the tactics of Populism nationwide worked only at best selectively in the South, and often not at all. And with that, the potential for high mobilization among those least likely to turnout ordinarily was lost, and thus, turnout, if anything, became harder to achieve.

CONCLUSION

In this chapter we have seen that, in the era after Reconstruction and compared to their counterparts in the North, southern parties were less organized, and less successful in mobilizing citizens to the voting booth. What Republican Party there was in the South post-Reconstruction, however, was more like its northern peers, at least in terms of roll call voting in Congress. That is, unlike the Democratic-Whig era, where party and region were both strong, consistent, and roughly equal bases for congressional voting, in the post-Reconstruction period, party was consequential but region was not. It was thus the movement from competitive to noncompetitive politics that made the South distinctive in this period. By the end, the one-party South was emerging with the Democrats being the only viable party in the region. But it was not just that there was no party to contest Democratic hegemony, because this was also the period in which the southern Democratic Party was asserting itself with a vengeance (rather literally with vengeance) to become the fully formed, lily-white Democratic Party in the one-party (or, as Key wrote, no-party) Jim Crow South, as we discuss next.

5 PARTIES IN THE JIM CROW SOUTH

With its black electoral base barred from the polls, the Republican party was virtually driven into extinction as an electoral competitor, and it survived largely on sufferance merely as a sham-patronage organization. Behind the Democratic party label, a very narrow, white, upper-status elite controlled politics in every southern state.—V. O. KEY JR. (1984 [1949], 32)

THE HISTORICAL CONTEXT

As we have just seen, the Populist challenge to the hegemony of the "redeemed" democracy in the South was short-lived. The motivation of white southerners to seek to ensure that the Populists were but a momentary challenge was owing to the fact that, whether we are considering the South in the nation or considering the planter aristocracy and the white middle- and upper-middle-class coalition (now often referred to as the "Bourbons") within each southern state, there was a general—and genuine—fear that failure to control their position even once could lead to utter disaster for them. In both cases, the core problem arises when the group seeking to achieve a well-defined set of outcomes in a majoritarian system is actually a minority. As such, it is always vulnerable to defeat. All the opposition need do is unite and their majority status will lead to victory.

This problem was "solved" in individual states in the wake of the "Populist Moment" in part by creating the Jim Crow laws that had the effect of disenfranchising nearly all African Americans and a good number of rural and poor whites—turning the majority of the population into a minority of voters. The Civil War Amendments effectively barred the South from writing laws directly to that effect, but they were able to do so indirectly, such as through passing laws creating poll taxes and literacy tests, and through the creation of whites-only primaries. There was much more to the complex of Jim Crow laws including the creation of separate lives, socially and economically, a separation achieved politically, at least partially, through formal laws. Here, we comment but briefly on these other dimensions (only some of which were encoded into law, rather than set as normative practices), but we do set the context for understanding how they could possibly have come about. There was a second side to the implementation of this multifaceted separation of the races for the purpose of political discrimination, and that was through intimidation and violence, and we illustrate that through lynchings, certainly its most decisive form of terror, and one example of a "riot," the Wilmington "race riot of 1898," which was essentially a coup, overthrowing a democratically elected government at rifle point.

We begin with a statement of these two related problems—how a minority in the nation could establish a framework, in spite of the Civil War Amendments, that made possible the enactment of Jim Crow laws, so that a minority within the South could hold power in a putatively majoritarian system of government, and do so continuously for generations. Then, we look at the motivations for why the Populists were the threat that appeared to set the legal-political part of Jim Crow into motion. We follow that by looking at the national setting, and how and why it turned out that the South could create a system of Jim Crow without interference from the federal government. We then look at the legal mechanisms enacted for effective disenfranchisement of African Americans and a goodly chunk of poor and/or rural whites and the two extralegal uses of violence, mentioned above. We conclude by enumerating some of the Jim Crow laws themselves, showing their overall effects on turnout and, in conclusion, examine the whites-only primary as one of the major mechanism for ensuring the durability of only one party in the region.

The problem. The white southern Bourbons, that is, the white planter and middle classes, were a minority of the total population in the South from the founding on, and the South was a minority of the nation from the founding on, as well. Thus, winning elections in a majoritarian system was a problem that this group faced repeatedly and at both state and national levels. The national problem was how a minority in the nation could create a system in apparent violation of the Constitution, and later of its Civil War Amendments (whether or not in violation of letter of the law, it was obviously so with respect to the spirit of the law). The parallel problem at the state level was how the Bourbons in the South could create an environment in which they could consistently win elections in spite of being a minority in a putatively majoritarian system.

The national solution, part I (1820–60). The three-fifths compromise in the Constitution officially recognized slavery and thus that this large and growing proportion of the southern population would not be citizens but "other persons," and thus not eligible for inclusion into the voting population. While the South received 60% of their count for purposes of representation, they gave up 100% of these "other persons" as citizens and therefore as part of the basis for seeking to form southern-centered majorities in national politics. In 1820, the direct effect of the Missouri Compromise was to limit slavery in the Louisiana Territory north of the parallel 36°30' except for Missouri. The practical effect was the "Balance Rule," in which it was tacitly agreed that there would be at least an equal number of slave as free states. As we discussed in chapter 3, with that, the South was effectively assured of a veto over any piece of legislation. That is, if the North tried to impose legislation threatening slavery, a united South could ensure its inability to become law, as with the Wilmot Proviso that passed the House in 1846 and in 1847 and was defeated in the Senate both times. This provided such an assurance, even as the South was losing in relative terms on population and economic success, as we saw above. And it was precisely the inability of even Clay, the Great Conciliator, to be able to conjure a way to maintain parity in the number of southern and northern states in 1850, after the Mexican War brought new territory toward statehood, which set in motion the chain of events that led to war within the decade. That is, as soon as those states were admitted, the southern equality in the Senate was lost—and lost for good in a virtual "one and done" way. The South would then, likely forever, be a minority in every part of the national government.

The state-level solution (1877–1900). The "one and done" philosophy was only a bit less true at the state level. If the southern planters, or middle- and upper-middle-class whites, were to win elections consistently, they had to face the question of how they would win office regularly, as a minority in a majority electoral system. Of course this was a problem only after Emancipation. Note that this differs in an important way from the position of the South in the nation. In our national republic, with separated but intermingled powers, there are numerous positions at which a minority might be able to exercise a check on the positive assertion of power, that is, where a minority might be able to "veto" new legislation, whether figuratively or actually (Tsebelis 2002). And, in this case, the South was able to exploit the national design of government to achieve their purposes. That is, all they had to do to achieve their goal was simply (at least as a base, necessary condition to their continued participation in the Union) to hold on to what they already had, slavery in the antebellum period, unchecked use of Jim Crowism after Reconstruction. Put in more general terms, the only true worry was that new law would change the status quo, since the status quo was already favorable to the South, recognizing slavery before the Civil War or being unable to overturn state-level Jim Crow laws after it. Hence, a single locus with a certain veto was sufficient power to at least hold on to their position, and thus to preserve the status quo. And that single locus typically needed only a minority to work, such as the one-third plus one to veto a nominee at Democratic conventions that used the two-thirds rule, or a fifty–fifty outcome in the Senate, which could be achieved by virtue of the South consisting of as many states as the North, but be an increasingly distinct minority of the nation's population.

The problem inside the South, especially once the South had lost its veto in the nation, was that what had once been a working majority was, in the wake of Emancipation, a minority in most states, at least as long as universal male suffrage was approximately true. Preserving the status quo was a much harder proposition. Thus the problem was that a minority coalition wanted to govern in the state, that is, to enact legislation, and for that to happen, they needed to win actual majorities—have a majority of their candidates win election to office and to be able to win passage of legislation on the floors of the various state chambers, which required a majority on roll call votes. And that is simply a different task, a transition from negative or blocking power to the necessity of positive power to win.

This new task, therefore, required different ways to achieve it. What they needed was a way to win voting majorities while being a minority of the population. There are two such ways. The "legal" way was to shape the electorate so that they were no longer a minority but they were actually or effectively an actual majority of the voting population. These made up some (but hardly anywhere nearly all) of what we call today the "Jim Crow" laws. Their purpose was to greatly reduce or eliminate the chances of victory by those who were most likely to oppose the relatively wealthy white minority, that is, the newly freed blacks and poor whites. The second way was to ensure that those who could and would vote against the upper-class whites would choose not to vote at all. That involved making the vote unusually costly for such folks, and that meant such devices as poll taxes or going completely outside the law to intimidation, violence, and even murder.

But there was a sense in which "one and done" applied here, too. The problem was not that the white plantation and middle- and upper-middle-class whites were that worried about the Republican Party. The GOP might win in certain places; in the mountains where resistance to the Confederacy and to its draft and taxes had been high, and in locations where freed slaves and carpetbaggers still made up something at least very close to a majority. After Reconstruction, these were small, scattered locales, not the basis for building a majority vote throughout the state. It was unlikely, to say the least, that a majority of whites in any state of the former Confederacy would vote for the party of Lincoln, Sherman, and the federal troops that had, not long ago, occupied their land.

The concern was that a viable opposition party would emerge that really could hope to forge a majority coalition, likely of the working, rural, and poor whites, along with whatever of the African American population was able to vote. It was the Populist Party that presented just such a plausible alternative way to create what might prove to be a durable majority. Indeed, as we saw, they did forge a majority coalition in a number of southern states, winning governorships and similar majorities across entire states. Its "one and done" aspect was that, should they truly hold full power in the state government, they would have in their hands the power to reshape state laws (e.g., to translate the principles of the Civil War Amendments into practice) that would create an electorate that reflected the true minority status of the Redeemers of the Democratic Party. That is, they could forge the institutional design that would make their chances of winning a majority, as a majority, relatively straightforward. From the perspective of the minority, something needed to be done to prevent this disaster. And the final disaster would be that not only could the opposition to the Bourbons forge an electoral majority, but also that they might organize into a political party to "institutionalize" their majority coalition, keep it active and vital.

Some things had already been done. Southern states had adopted "black codes" after the Civil War that restricted the rights of freed blacks, often making it at least very difficult if not outright impossible to vote. They were of dubious alignment with the Civil War Amendments. But then so were the true Jim Crow laws. In 1870, the federal government passed a "force" law (permitting the use of federal troops to enforce the newly enacted Fifteenth Amendment, barring discrimination in voting on the basis of race), and that, of course, threw the gauntlet down.

As we saw in the last chapter, most southern states had been "redeemed"—that is, a white Democratic Party had retaken majority control of the state government—by the time of the emergence of the Populist Party, and they were enacting at least some of the Jim Crow laws concerning voting.[1] Indeed, after "Redemption" few southern states changed their constitutions that were in force at readmission. By the 1880s, however, blacks were still winning elections, and indeed their electoral success was peaking in some locales. Reconstruction era "black codes" were gone or remaining pieces were relatively ineffective. The possibility of creating an organized party in opposition to conservative whites in the South, such as through the Populists perhaps, led ten of the eleven states of the former Confederacy to amend their constitutions, to adopt wholly new constitutions that included restrictions on suffrage, or to pass individual laws to that effect.

The national solution, part II (1877–1900). Here, the question of how the South could pass such laws in apparent contradiction of federal law and the Constitution must be raised, for this set of laws seems unusually contradictory. And, of course, the southern veto in the national government was effectively nullified by the time of Reconstruction, unable to be "redeemed." How then was the South stopping federal enforcement?

There was much more to the web of laws that discriminated between black and white southerners than voting and that therefore contributed to the Jim Crow system. But it was voting that matters most here. Not only did shaping the electorate provide the core basis by which a white minority could rule in a majority system over a long period of time, but it ensured control over all else within the legal system, most especially the ability to write new laws or defend old ones from being overturned. It is through this political base that the social, educational, and economic discrimination of Jim Crow laws was possible. According to Caro (2009), as Jim Crow neared its end, then Senate majority leader Lyndon Johnson defended taking out virtually everything else in the Civil Rights Bill of 1957 except voting. He argued that gaining the vote would make possible subsequent gains in many areas, including those he had just overseen being stripped from the bill.[2] Controlling who voted also made possible in this period the creation of a legal framework under which racial violence could go unpunished, the second prong of Jim Crow. For one example, being ineligible to vote also made one ineligible to serve on a jury. Thus, disenfranchising virtually all African Americans led to the creation of almost invariably "lily-white" juries, unlikely to convict whites of discrimination or even violence against African Americans, not even murder, no matter how clear the evidence (e.g., Packard 2003).

There came to be reason not to worry greatly about federal interference in this reshaping of the electorate. The "Compromise of 1890," as it was called, was a compromise in the Senate over three bills. Unable to forge majorities for any of the three bills individually, the Republican majority party chose to seek passage of the Sherman Silver Purchase Act and the McKinley Tariff Bill, in exchange for the Senate putting aside the Federal Elections Bill. This last bill was called the Lodge Force Bill in the South (after Henry Cabot Lodge, its sponsor) and would have provided federal supervision of U.S. congressional elections. While designed to apply everywhere, it was only in the South that it was expected to have major effect. And thus, only thirteen years after the end of Reconstruction, Lodge's bill would have brought federal troops back to the South. While the Silver Act rewarded western states in particular as a way to get western state support for Republican proposals, the killing of Lodge's bill added support for the compromise from the South. The passing of the Sherman Act and the withdrawal of the Lodge Bill served to help undermine the core basis of support for the Populist Party by the GOP rewarding the West and the South, respectively. More immediately, the compromise enabled the Republicans to pass a tariff that neither the South nor the West wanted. When the Federal Election Bill was withdrawn from the Senate floor, the last major attempt to force the South to adhere to the Civil Rights Amendments was over, and the South could move forward on at least the electoral side with the Jim Crow legislation.

While this 1890 "compromise" was critical, it was not the first sign that the national government might not interfere in the southern plans. Seven years earlier, the Supreme Court in *Civil Rights Cases*, 109 U.S. 3 (1883; five related cases that were united in one compound decision), set the stage for support for racial segregation, in spite of the Civil War Amendments. It did so by making it explicit that even the Court believed that the newly amended Constitution supported separation of the races in the private sector. In 1896, the truly landmark case of *Plessy v. Ferguson* extended that view and held that separation by races was lawful even in government actions, provided the separation preserved "equality."[3] One consequence of this decision was to permit separation of races into black and white public schools, provided children of both races had equal opportunity to attend a school, no matter how unequal the facilities and training offered.[4] And, thus, in the midst of the Populist period, the South had a legal framework to pass Jim Crow laws.[5]

State Solutions, Enacting of Jim Crow Laws

Such laws with respect to electoral participation did not say that African Americans could not vote. Instead they mandated means by which the state could impose high costs for turning out, and it made it possible, sometimes via providing actual mechanisms within the law, to apply the law differently by race (or, if desired, by class). Thus, for example, literacy tests and poll taxes could in principle apply to everyone, but they could also be applied discriminatorily. One way to avoid making such discrimination quite as vividly apparent was to enact a "grandfather" clause, whereby one would be exempted from, say, taking the literacy test or paying the poll tax if one could prove a grandfather had been eligible to vote, provisions of which no former slave could meet. In fairly short order, all eleven states of the former Confederacy had enacted some version of these, as we saw in table 4.1.

A second prong of this attempt to control the size of the electorate was to reduce the chances of an opposition party forming. Of course, eliminating a very large part of the potential opposition support in the electorate due to disenfranchisement is certainly a big part of the story—poor whites had very few former slave, carpetbagger, or scalawag voters to join. A second indirect way to reduce the chances of any opposition from being able to organize is to deny them access to most of the young, ambitious politicians who could serve as the current and future leadership of such an organization. As it happened, in equally short order as the passing of the voting-related planks of Jim Crow, each southern state also had passed into law the principle for a whites-only primary. By declaring a political party not formally a part of the government, but a private organization, it exempted the party from the requirements of the Constitution in these matters. It was therefore perfectly legal for the Democratic Party to hold a primary for whites only. And since the defeat of the Populists meant that there was no serious opposition in the general election most of the time, the nominee was virtually or actually uncontested for most major and statewide offices. And thus, whites effectively chose most officeholders through their whites-only primary elections. Table 5.1 illustrates the spread of the use of the white primary, something essentially accomplished by 1902. One possibly unintended long-term consequence of the controlled primary elections was to make it much harder for a second party to get established in the region. Recall that the first presidential

Table 5.1 Laws or constitutions permitting "white primaries" in former Confederacy in 1900

	African Americans	% of population	Year
Alabama	827,545	45.26	1901
Arkansas	366,984	27.98	1891
Florida	231,209	43.74	1885–89
Georgia	1,035,037	46.70	1908
Louisiana	652,013	47.19	1898
Mississippi	910,060	58.66	1890
North Carolina	630,207	33.28	1900
South Carolina	782,509	58.38	1895
Tennessee	480,430	23.77	1889 laws
Texas	622,041	20.40	1901/1923 laws
Virginia	661,329	35.69	1902
Total	7,199,364	37.94	—

Source: Beckel 2010, 590–91. Beckel reports (590n3), "Table is posted on Wikipedia, under Disfranchisement After Reconstruction Era. Created from the Historical Census Browser, 1900 Federal Census, University of Virginia (last accessed Aug. 14, 2012); Julien C. Monnet, The Latest Phase of Negro Disenfranchisement, 26 HARVARD LAW REVIEW 42 (1912). Data obtained from existing data in table. Number of African Americans total obtained by 827,545 + 366,984 + 231,209 + . . . + 661,329 = 7,199,364. Percentage data: 827,545/45.26% = 1,828,425 (rounded to nearest whole) for total population of Alabama, 366,984/27.98% = 1,311,594 (nearest whole) for Arkansas, etc. Total of all state populations = 18,975,448. 7,199,364/18,975,448 = 37.94%."

primary was not held until 1900 (and was held in Florida, indicative that the southern Democrats were particularly enthusiastic about this Progressive Era reform, unlike most other such Progressive proposals).

That these acts worked in terms of reshaping the electorate can easily be seen. Figure 5.9 below shows the large sweep of disenfranchisement, comparing the North and the South in presidential election years. Figure 5.1 shows the same point in the relevant period here, using midterm election turnout from 1870 to 1914. There is no certain measure of turnout by race, but figure 5.2 reports estimated turnout by race in the South over the period of enactment of Jim Crow laws (see also Redding and James 2001). Both show that there were dramatic declines in turnout by race and across the region generally. That is to say, the Jim Crow disenfranchisement affected rural and poor whites—in Alabama it is estimated that disenfranchisement affected about a third more whites than blacks. In either case the effect was substantial—and determinative for the Bourbon class.

State Solutions, Violence: The Wilmington Race Riot of 1898

The second weapon for shaping the electorate was the use of terror and violence. In the 1890s, North Carolina was the last deeply contested two-party state in the South, with Democrats facing a Fusion

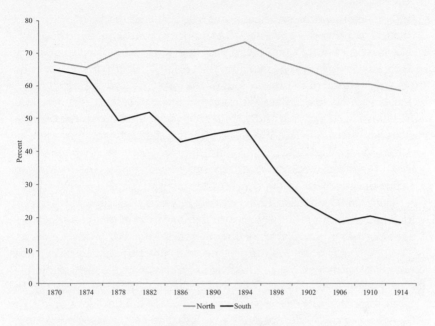

Figure 5.1 Turnout by region, midterm elections, 1870–1914

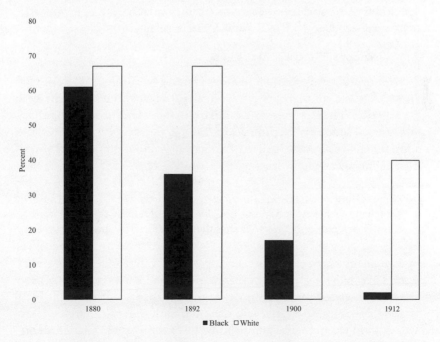

Figure 5.2 Estimated percent turnout by race, Confederate states, 1880, 1892, 1900, and 1912 presidential races

party consisting of Republicans and Populists that had won statewide offices including the governor and majority control of the legislature. The Fusionists were thus able to pass laws increasing black turnout by decreasing property requirements for voting. In 1898, the Democrats regained control of the state (both of the governor and the legislature). The largest city in the state, Wilmington, retained a black majority, and Fusionists won the mayoralty and other citywide offices. After those elections, "Red Shirts" (mostly former Confederate soldiers), led by Alfred Moore Waddell, a losing candidate for governor as a Democrat, took over the city by armed might and forced the elected leadership to flee the city, barring the way for the (black) MC of the local area to return from Washington to his district. In doing so, they killed many and injured even more through direct application of brutal force. They appointed a new (white) city council, which "elected" Waddell mayor. The new Democratic majority in the state government reacted to this bloody coup by passing the first Jim Crow laws in North Carolina: a poll tax, a literacy test, and two years later a whites-only primary. In many ways, this act of terrorism was the start of the Jim Crow era, even though electorally relevant Jim Crow laws had been passed elsewhere. But the Wilmington race riot set a precedent for mixing violence with legal discrimination, and the disenfranchisement laws typically were in place before the social and economic discriminatory laws of Jim Crow were enacted (Cecelski and Tyson 1998; Unfleet 2009).

State Solutions, Violence: Lynchings

Violent overthrow of democratically elected governments was one way in which white southerners used extralegal means to enforce the new social order. There were many others ranging from threats of and actual use of economic discrimination through murder. Quite often these were publicly acknowledged. At the extreme of that point, "Pitchfork" Ben Tillman was quoted as saying (Logan 1965):

> We have done our level best [to prevent blacks from voting] . . . we have scratched our heads to find out how we could eliminate the last one of them. We stuffed ballot boxes. We shot them. We are not ashamed of it. (91)

Lynchings were a common tactic designed to terrorize blacks and of course eliminate particularly outspoken opponents to Jim Crow. Often these were related more to the economic and especially social aspects of Jim Crowism, but blacks who tried too hard to register and vote or, worse, engaged in politics more fully, were sometimes lynched themselves.[6] And lynching is not only the most extreme form of the use of

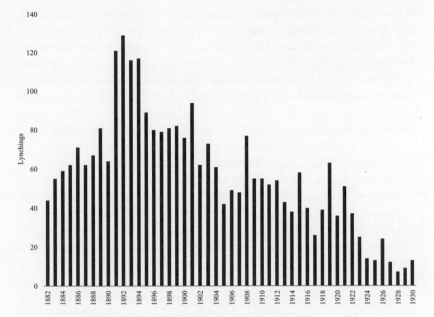

Figure 5.3 Lynchings in the southern states, 1882–1930

violence, it happens also to be among the most carefully documented, and so we consider it in a bit more detail.

Lynching, often in broad daylight with cheering crowds, which all too often included law enforcement officers as part of the mob (or as nonreacting onlookers to mob violence), was used to ensure that opposition to Jim Crow and related practices would not organize. Figure 5.3 shows the number of lynchings by year across the South. These actions were not limited to the eleven states of the former Confederacy but included Kentucky, Missouri, and Oklahoma, and lynchings in these states are included in the figure. That lynchings peaked in the 1890s set the stage for the Jim Crow era.

Ending Jim Crow Required Federal Action

The era of Jim Crow lasted from the 1890s to 1965 with passage of the Civil Rights (1964) and Voting Rights (1965) Acts. These laws, at long last, made the Civil War Amendments effective within the South. Of course, there had been numerous federal interventions that had chipped away at the legal framework of Jim Crow even before the 1954 *Brown v. Board* decision and the Civil Rights Bill of 1957, let alone before the Civil and Voting Rights Acts in the mid-1960s. One important decision of relevance here (*Smith v. Allwright*, 1944) ruled that a Texas law creating a whites-only primary was unconstitutional. The whites-only primary rather quickly faded into disuse, leaving the South to rely on poll taxes, literacy tests, and the like to maintain white dominance in voting, but also easing the way in the coming decades for the Republicans to begin serious state-level party building. Other developments included:

- 1938: In *Missouri ex rel. Gaines v. Canada*, the Supreme Court ruled that Missouri could not satisfy its obligation to provide equal protection by sending an African American resident to an out-of-state law school and that Lionel Gaines must thus be admitted to the all-white University of Missouri School of Law. This case was the beginning of the NAACP Legal Defense Fund's effort to eliminate the separate-but-equal doctrine.
- 1948: Truman integrated the military by executive order 9981, thereby bypassing the Congress, against which the Senate would have undoubtedly resisted.
- 1948: In July, Hubert Humphrey passionately called for the Democratic Party, at its national convention, to move forward on civil rights, to "get out of the shadow of states' rights and walk forthrightly into the bright sunshine of human rights." Southern Democrats walked out of the convention, some forming a "States' Rights Democratic Party" (aka "Dixiecrat Party") and nominating Governor J. Strom Thurmond (SC) as presidential candidate and Fielding L. Wright (MS) as vice presidential nominee, eventually carrying four states (Louisiana, South Carolina, Alabama, and Mississippi) and thirty-nine electoral votes.
- 1950: In the *Sweatt v. Painter* and *McLaurin v. Oklahoma State Regents* decisions, the Court struck down segregation of African American students in law and graduate schools. The Justice Department, in its brief to the Court, said it believed *Plessey* was unconstitutional and should be overturned. NAACP Legal Defense Fund lawyers, led by Thurgood Marshall, began to devise a strategy that would force the Court to reexamine the constitutionality of the separate-but-equal doctrine in its entirety.

But these predecessors were either relatively small, albeit important, weakenings of the legal framework of Jim Crow, or were, like *Brown v. Board*, resisted in the South. Thus, it is fair to say that the legal aspects of Jim Crow, enacted in the 1890s and into the first few years of the twentieth century, created the system that lasted for over half a century. It created, that is, the South that V. O. Key Jr. (1949) so brilliantly studied.

Of course, we observe the beginning of all of this by watching the destruction of any truly viable southern Republican Party. Its coalition of northerners and freed slaves disintegrated. It did so first as Reconstruction ended, Union troops left, and many carpetbaggers returned home or sought to fit into their new surroundings. Disenfranchisement of African Americans quickly commenced. African Americans made up a very large minority of the vote in most of these states and an absolute majority in Mississippi and South Carolina. Eliminating all but a tiny proportion of those who made up anywhere from one in five (in Texas) to three in five members of the population from being able to vote was a radical transformation of the effective electorate. This was even truer when as many as another one in five or even more were poor white southerners who also were removed from the electorate. That is how one can transform a minority of the population into a majority of the electorate. Further, just in case some resisted disenfranchisement, lynchings (see figure 5.3) peaked in the 1890s, as Jim Crow laws went fully into place. Just to be even surer, once opposition was no longer organized at all, with the end of competitiveness of both the Republican and the Populist Parties by 1900, whites-only primaries went into effect throughout the former Confederacy, assuring that competitive elections would be fought there rather than in the general elections and, by law, African Americans could not participate.

THE "PARTY SYSTEM" UNDER JIM CROW

After the "Populist Moment," there was really no organized, coordinated, or even consistent opposition to southern Democrats in elections, in office, and hence in governance. The Republicans had been defeated in almost every former Confederate state before the Populist surge, while in North Carolina alone, the Republicans survived in alliance with the Populists, but this alliance was defeated in the wake of the Wilmington race riot. By about 1900, the institutional mechanisms were in place to ensure neither of these opposition parties resurfaced in any serious way, outside the few mountain districts, with a real Republican presence. And certainly, nothing like the Progressive movement that swept parts of the northern Republican Party or surfaced as a party in its own right appeared at even trace levels in the South. The Progressives' politics assured that, but the institutional mechanisms that undergirded southern Democratic dominance also would have assured that, as well. Together, these developments left the lily-white Democratic Party secure in its one-party dominance throughout the South. Outside of the limited mountain areas, a Republican Party existed almost solely as a basis for receiving whatever modest pork the national Republican Party would send its way when it was in power (which all but ended in 1932). It was the effects that this absence of regularized competition had on the Democratic Party that led Key to refer to the Democrats as secure in "no-party" dominance within the South (presenting themselves as a one-party regional unit in national politics). That is, in the absence of organized opposition, the Democrats declined into relative disorganization themselves, into, that is, the factional, friends-and-neighbors, courthouse-gang regime Key described.

For our immediate purposes, this means we need to ask slightly different questions about the political parties during Jim Crow. It will be a story not about development of one or two political parties in the South, but a story of how the southern Democrats fit into the national two-party system. Particularly with respect to the party in government, which is where we begin, we first look at the shape of the national parties in Congress from where we stopped, in 1900, by extending it from the post-Reconstruction period through the twentieth century and into the twenty-first century. This macroview will provide the basic outlines of the full account left to come, which illustrates what Democratic politics was like in the nation, given the peculiar status of the southern wing of the party and the absence of a competitor in the South, and then how that changed with emergence of a real southern Republican Party. Then we will look more precisely at the Jim Crow period until that emergence. That occurs not in 1965 at the end of Jim Crow laws, but it ends when Republicans begin to contest regionwide, which dates to about 1980. The analogy is that, like when looking at southern schooling, separate but equal may have formally ended in 1954 with *Brown v. Board*, but actual integration was resisted, so that actual separate schools dated from the nineteenth century fully until resistance was defeated, until 1970 (Clotfelter 2011). In a similar (if less violent) way, the emergence of the Republican Party took time, once the main legal and institutional obstacles were removed, and that, like school desegregation, its emergence began about fifteen years later.

The Civil Rights Movement

Resistance to and protests against slavery, the many and various anti-black laws, such as those known as Jim Crow laws, the sharecropping and tenancy agricultural systems, and many other aspects of southern life came early in American history and were more or less continual throughout it. In 1831, Nat Turner led perhaps the most famous slave rebellion in American history, for example, one that resulted in fifty-five deaths among whites. Two factors made the protests of the 1950s and 1960s different than all that preceded: first, their ability to grow into a widespread and systematic movement, one that deserves capital letters—the Civil Rights Movement (CRM)—and, second, their ability to reach a national audience, to move the citizens of the North, and to receive widespread attention and support among white citizens nationwide. Racial discrimination and civil rights, for example, were, together, the "single most important problem facing the country," in the Gallup Poll of March 27–April 2, 1964.[7]

The CRM emerged from the grass roots, but, of course, its success was made possible by a changed institutional context. As we have seen, the southern Democratic congressional delegation began to separate more consistently from their northern counterparts in Roosevelt's second term, following the 1936 elections. The result was a voting strategy in which southern Democrats would sometimes vote with the northern Democrats to create a party unity vote, and sometimes they would vote with Republicans to form a conservative coalition, that is, one based on ideological rather than party lines (Brady and Bullock 1980). The unreliability of Democratic unity when it came to civil rights votes meant that advancements would come about by other means, such as Truman's executive order, Humphrey's convention speech, and the creation of the "Dixiecrat" Party, all in 1948. We have reviewed briefly a series of Supreme Court decisions that also whittled away at the legal underpinnings of Jim Crow laws (see also Valelly 2004). These offered increasing degrees of success for the strategy of the NAACP (established in 1909, at the very beginning of Jim Crow), which, among other aims, sought to use civil suits in the courts to overturn the effects of the "separate but equal" ruling in *Plessy v. Ferguson* (1896). Their efforts culminated in the landmark case *Brown v. Board* (1954) simply ending the legality of "separate but equal."

Three further features were particularly important for setting a context in which a civil rights campaign could be successful. Returning African American veterans from World War II and the Korean conflict provided a base for activism of those unwilling to give up the relative freedom and, in some cases, an integrated setting for a return to life under Jim Crow. The economic boom of the 1950s and 1960s made views of southern poverty all the more striking and disharmonious with the then current views of America. And such views were made much more readily and vividly close at hand due to the rapid spread of television from which to view not only southern poverty (both white and black, sharecropper and Appalachian miner) but also the dogs, fire hoses, and other instruments (batons, guns, and bombs) of suppression of the CRM marches.

The CRM is generally seen as emerging out of the 381-day bus boycott in Montgomery, Alabama (1955–56) and extending through the 1960s. A slightly earlier beginning might be attributed to the decision by Emmett Till's mother, Mamie Till Bradley, to hold an open coffin funeral (he died August 28, 1955), exposing just how badly southern whites had mutilated her son's face and body. The pictures were published in such black news outlets as the *Chicago Defender* and *Jet* magazine and brought international attention to the American South and undoubtedly reminded many blacks of just how little the South had changed since they or their parents had emigrated from it.

Rosa Parks refused to give up her seat and move to the back of the bus in Montgomery. She was arrested on December 1, 1955, for her trouble. She was not a lone actor and not the first to refuse to give up her seat. Nor was she unprepared, having been trained as an activist. Indeed, without a supportive structure and nascent organization, it might have been just one more lonely and quickly forgotten protest, isolated unto itself. But the mix of existing leadership and organization set the lengthy boycott into motion and led to the development of further organizing, including spurring the formation of the Southern Christian Leadership Conference, the emergence of the Reverend Martin Luther King Jr. as an international leader, and the attraction of national media to the South to cover the boycott. The spark of Parks's courage, that is, had a prepared base of kindling from which to grow into the CRM's firestorm.

Similarly, the next major event in the CRM, the sit-in protest at the Woolworth store's lunch counter in Greensboro, North Carolina (February 1, 1960) was not the first such sit-in.[8] It was, however, the first that drew sustained national attention, in part because of the success of the bus boycott earlier, in part because of the ability of television (now in a majority of U.S. homes for the first time) and other news media to attract attention, and in part because it also attracted a new generation of civil rights leaders from the college students such as those who participated in the sit-ins around the South. The Student Nonviolent Coordinating Committee (SNCC) was founded at Shaw University in Raleigh, North Carolina, earlier that year, and worked with, and was inspired by, the sit-ins. SNCC attracted many important civil rights leaders (e.g., Stokely Carmichael, Julian Bond, John Lewis, and Ella Baker). SNCC went on (with other civil rights organizations) to play central roles in the Freedom Rides in 1961 (riding on buses throughout the south in racially integrated groups) and voter registration drives including the Mississippi Summer Project (where three civil rights workers were killed). They also played a major role in the March on Washington in the summer of 1963, and the march to Selma, with its "Bloody Sunday," in 1965.

Timing also mattered. Setting the summer of 1963 as the time for the March on Washington proved timely not only for pulling together the increasingly rich and diverse strands of the CRM but also for now President Johnson to use its force later in the year to build a legacy of support and goodwill around the nation in support of his efforts to get the Civil Rights Act of 1964 passed in tribute to the assassinated President Kennedy. This act followed up, and in many ways instantiated, much that Johnson, as Senate majority leader, had stricken out of the Civil Rights Act of 1957. And, following his landslide victory in 1964, when he won everywhere in the nation but his own, once solid, South and his opponent Barry Goldwater's (R, AZ) home state, Johnson was able to form a congressional majority in both houses based solely on northern Democrats. He used this majority to pass much of the Great Society legislation, including the Voting Rights Act of 1965. This act put real strength into enforcement of voting rights, unlike its weak, mostly symbolic, predecessor in 1957. The passage of the Voting Rights Act is often used to mark the formal end of the Jim Crow South. It took, of course, concerted action, including the remaining strength of the CRM, to transform the promise of the Voting Rights and Civil Rights Acts and the *Brown* and related decisions from the Supreme Court into genuine action on the ground.

Party in Government

Regional divisions in the Jacksonian era remained substantial, even on the first or "liberal-conservative" dimension of the Poole-Rosenthal voting scales (see chapter 3). Regional polarization within each party was approximately as large as the polarization between the two parties. As we saw in chapter 4, this had been reversed in the post-Reconstruction South, such that northern and southern Republicans voted largely alike, as did northern and southern Democrats. That is to say, at least on the issues that compose the first dimension of DW-NOMINATE scores, there was great party polarization but virtually no regional divisions within either party. In this way, the last decades of the nineteenth century look much like those at the end of the twentieth century and the beginning of the twenty-first.

What made the North and South different, then, was not how MCs voted in Congress (at least on this principal axis) but how the public voted in elections. The South differed from the North after 1877 largely because they elected Democrats to Congress, nearly exclusively, while the Republicans, but a trace in the South, were the majority party in the North, but not an overwhelmingly dominant majority. Democrats were remarkably successful in House elections in the post-Reconstruction period. Whereas they held only 40% of the South's delegation to the House after the 1872 elections, that climbed to 70% in the 1874 elections, and they then held between 85% and 95% of the delegation from there through the end of the nineteenth century and into the twentieth century, with but the single exception of 1882. There were no exceptions through the remainder of the Jim Crow era.

The southern Democrats made up a large fraction, often a majority, of the Democratic delegation in the U.S. House in most of this period. Their dominance in their region meant that this continued into the twentieth century. In figure 5.4, we report the percentage of the total Democratic delegation in the U.S. House constituted by Democrats from the former Confederate states in various years of the Jim Crow era. We provide this percentage for the first year after each census-induced reapportionment (i.e., 1903, 1913, . . . , 1953) as well as 1901, the first reelection of FDR in 1936, and the election of the Republican majority in the "Do Nothing" Congress in 1946. As the Jim Crow era got underway, southern Democrats were a majority of their party's delegation, even though (or perhaps because) Democrats were the minority party in the state. They fell sharply into minority status within their own party after the 1912 elections, in which Wilson

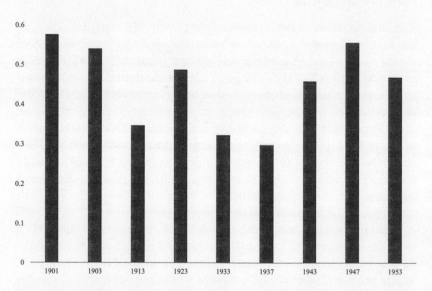

Figure 5.4 Southern proportion of Democrats in U.S. House, various years, 1901–53

won the presidency with a relatively small plurality but helped his party carry majorities in Congress. Except in the two New Deal elections, they made up 40% and occasionally (as in 1947–48) a majority of the Democrats in Congress.

The party's congressional politics was, of course, greatly shaped by the size of the southern delegation. The general point was that, since the South made up a very large fraction of Democratic votes in Congress, their support was very important and they thus had a great role in shaping policy choices. Obviously, in years in which they were a majority, they shaped those choices, at least as they played out in the House, but their electoral strength in the South was critical to the party in presidential as well as congressional elections and thus politics.[9] In that regard, their strength was magnified in the House due to the use of seniority (which became virtually an ironclad rule in the 1920s through the 1970s) and the growing advantage the South held over the North in their ability to return incumbents to office for very long periods of time. In the Senate, the twenty-two Democrats from the states of the former Confederacy had to be supplemented by only a very few additional votes (often from southern, if not formerly Confederate, states) to be able to threaten seriously the use of the filibuster. Thus their numbers were magnified by the internal structure of the Congress. In either event, they were able to exert significant if not dominant influence over Democratic congressional politics.

THE BIG PICTURE: PARTY POLARIZATION, 1900–2012

Figure 5.5 reports the degree of partisan polarization in the national Congress from the end of Reconstruction through 2012. These data provide a view of national partisan politics that informs the rest of the history of southern politics and its role in the nation. The congressional partisan divide was large at the turn of the twentieth century, declined over the course of that century, settling to a low degree of polarization in the post–World War II era, and then began a slow ascent to return to a high degree of partisan polarization, at the same level as, if not perhaps even exceeding, that of the late nineteenth and early twentieth centuries.

Figure 5.5 tells us how divided the two parties have been in roll call voting. We extend this comparison to include region in figure 5.6, in which we report the average DW-NOMINATE score for the four party and regional groupings from 1900 to 2012 (that is, roll call voting through the One Hundred Twelfth Congress). As the figure makes clear, Republicans (at least on average) voted quite similarly on the issues that define the major axis of choice over this full period, waxing

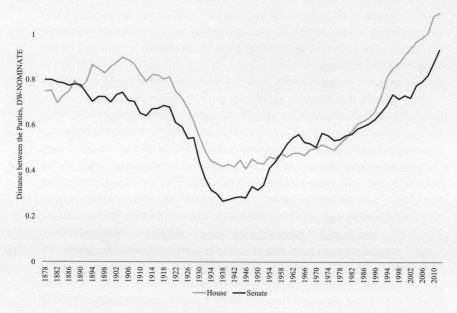

Figure 5.5 Party polarization, 1878–2012

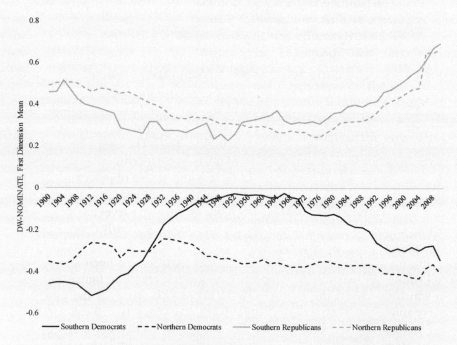

Figure 5.6 Mean U.S. House DW-NOMINATE score by party and region, 1900–2012

and waning slightly, but basically varying around a similar national pattern. This might be expected, regardless of regional differences, if the very few southern Republicans had, as a primary objective, maintaining close relations with the national GOP to ensure that they could receive whatever largess from the national party they could get.

The Democratic story is quite different. Southern Democrats were initially the most liberal of the four groupings (or at least voted least like the Republicans). From about the time of the return of a Republican majority in 1920 through the second New Deal election, southern Democrats began to vote more and more conservatively, and a large gap emerged between the two regions in the Democratic Party in the late 1930s. With first a short but sharp decline in conservative voting after 1972 and then a continuous move toward more liberal voting patterns starting in 1980 or so, the classic regional divide within the Democratic Party shrank dramatically. Figure 5.7 shows essentially the same thing (if anything, perhaps slightly more exaggerated) for the U.S. Senate; except of course, there were no Republican senators from the South at all until Senator John Tower was elected from Texas in 1960. We therefore focus on the House for the most part in the remainder of this chapter.

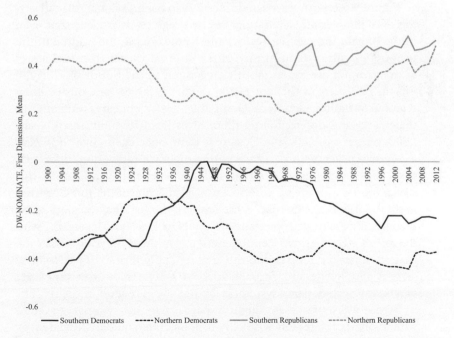

Figure 5.7 Mean U.S. Senate DW-NOMINATE score by party and region, 1900–2012

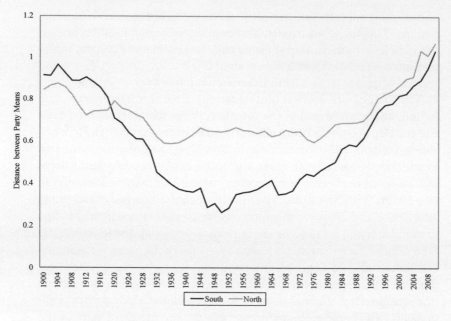

Figure 5.8 Partisan differentiation in the U.S. House, by region, 1900–2010

Figure 5.8 reports partisan differences in congressional roll call voting over this period, separating the two regions. It is clear that even
in the North, the two parties were less polarized in the middle of the
twentieth century than at any other time. However, those changes
in polarization are much more exaggerated in the South than in the
North. The story of the late 1960s to date is largely one of declining
regional variation. Southern Democrats are, it appears, returning to
their party and differentiating themselves from Republicans. By, say,
2000, patterns of voting in Congress were, once again, like they were
a century earlier, with partisans voting together and voting differently
from the competing party, regardless of where they reside. In this
sense, the story of the twentieth century, and thus of the Jim Crow era
in the South and its demise, is the story of the regional division in the
Democratic Party, its appearance in the New Deal, and its ending with
the rise of a competitive Republican Party in the South. With that, the
United States has returned to the apparent equilibrium of a two-party
system nationwide and, in particular, of a polarized, or at very least
of a neatly sorted, party system at least at the elite level in the nation.

Figure 5.8 looks as we might expect a national two-party system
with a one-party region within it to look. The standard division by
party on policy in a two-party system is modified with a one-party

South in which the southern Democrat seeks to appeal to the more moderate center to ensure the ability maximally to ward off any new party seeking to break into this one-party system, whether from left or from right (Palfrey 1984; Aldrich and Lee, 2016).

Parties as Organizations and in Elections

In the absence of a second party, there is no party organization to speak of in this period. It is, of course, Key's contention (1949) that his evidence points strongly to a declining vigor of Democratic Party organization in the South, state after state, due to the absence of regularized and organized competition to challenge the Democrats and to provide any advantage to paying the costs of creating and maintaining a well-organized Democratic Party. Instead, the organization, like the rest of the party, consisted mostly of a locus for competition within it for political gain, the sort of competition meant to be regulated by an organized two-party system campaigning for the votes of the public. The final empirical look here is turnout by region. The political laws of Jim Crow were intended, of course, to shape the electorate, such that the more well-to-do white political elite could win elections consistently. And continued application of that principle was key to maintaining its lily-white and majority status. But the dramatic gap between northern and southern turnout in figure 5.9 also reflects the lack of effort needed by the state Democratic organization to win elections in the fall. Any action occurred in the whites-only primaries. And without competitive motivation, why organize?

CONCLUSION

While Jim Crow laws had many consequences, one of particular relevance to this account is that they made possible the ascension of the Democratic Party to become essentially the only game in town for aspiring politicians and thus for the ability to shape politics and policy in the southern states for half a century. They were, in many ways, akin to the one party in a one-party authoritarian state. This chapter illustrates their ascension to that status. One view of this is the dramatic decline in turnout as seen in figure 5.9. Those data demonstrate the success of the Democratic Party's attempt to reshape the effective electorate from one in which they would be a minority into one in which they could expect to win majorities. They did this by (selective) application of law and by (also selective) application of violence (note, e.g., the gradual decline in lynchings, in figure 5.2, as the reshaping of the electorate led to declining turnout early in the twentieth century). Middle- and

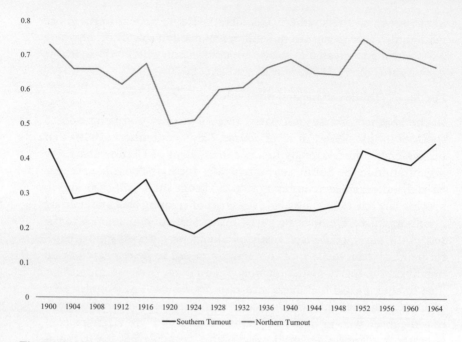

Figure 5.9 Presidential year turnout by region, 1900–1964

upper-middle-class whites were a minority in the South, but when only 30% of the electorate votes (and when the middle-class whites got to select which 30% that was), this group could win majorities in elections repeatedly.

In the national picture, northern and southern Democrats did not act much differently in Congress until the second Roosevelt election, and, of course, they made up a large proportion of the Democratic delegation then. Republicans held a majority in Congress much of the time, and indeed became the effective majority party in the nation at the turn of the twentieth century through to the Depression, and so could obviously win national majorities with precious little support from the South. They simply did not need them to govern.

It was only when the Democrats became the majority party in the 1930s that differences between the two wings of the party began to matter in national politics. In the 1930s and 1940s, southern Democrats began to vote differently from their northern partisans, and they perceived threats to their position (i.e., to the ability to sustain a Jim Crow South) both from within the party and from the Supreme Court. While they might defect from the (northern) party line and indeed from the Truman presidential coalition in 1948, those threats were nonetheless manageable. But the directive from *Brown v. Board* (1954, 1955), the emergence of an increasingly organized movement, on its way to becoming the CRM, and the movement's success in touching the conscience of the public in the North changed that threat from one that appeared to be manageable into a true crisis in their ability to maintain a system built on Jim Crow. And, indeed, Jim Crow was defeated within a decade.

6 THE SOUTHERN TURN TO REPUBLICANISM

HISTORICAL SETTING (1937–2012)

The coming of regularized two-party competition to the South in the last half of the twentieth century stands as one of the singular advances of democratic development in the United States.[1] The demise of the one-party South had ramifications not only for the South, whether Democrat or Republican, white or black, but also for the nation. By the end of the century, the Republican Party not only was arguably the larger party in the South, but southern Republicanism had also become the primary source of leadership in the national Congress after the 1994 elections (Aldrich 1999) and, in 2001 (if not 1989), a southern Republican was elected president.

This emergence of party competition ended one of the last vestiges of the old, one-party, solid South that we associate with Jim Crowism, and that Key (1949) understood to be antidemocratic. Key's theoretical argument was that sustained and regularized electoral competition was necessary for the development of a strong, organized party system, and that such an organized system of bi- or multiparty competition was necessary for effective democracy. The ability of the southern Democrats at the turn of the twentieth century to thwart sustained electoral competition meant that the South also failed to develop organized political parties.[2] As a result of that failure, the South, in turn, was a failed democracy. The history of southern politics in the fifty years since Key wrote is the story (occurring precisely as he theorized would happen) of how regularized electoral competition, and therefore how organized parties, and consequently how an effective democracy, appeared in the South.

**The End of the Solid South (1937–79) and
the Rise of the Republican Party (1980–2012)**

In this chapter we divide this lengthy era into two periods, the period starting with the origin of the durable cleavage in the Democratic Party, dividing North and South, through the Civil Rights Movement and the passage of the Civil Rights and Voting Rights Acts (which marks the accepted end of Jim Crow in the South) to the emergence of the Republican Party as a major party in the South, starting in 1980. Thus, the first period we will discuss runs from 1937, at the first appearance of the lasting split between northern and southern Democrats and the creation of the conservative coalition, and it ends with the Congress elected in 1978.

The second period we will discuss is the era in which the Republican Party emerged as a fully competitive, major party throughout the South, yielding a fully competitive two-party system in the region, integrated into the same fully competitive two-party system in the nation. In that sense, the period starting in 1980 was the first time that a nationwide two-party system was in place everywhere and was fully integrated into a cohesive two-party system in state and nation since the 1840s and the "first full flowering" of the mass-based parties in the Jacksonian-Whig system, and in some important ways, it was even more complete and fully converged toward equilibrium than then.[3] The first part of this period starts in 1980, with the election of Reagan as president with substantial support from the South and with the election of a sufficient number of southern Republicans to the Senate to create a Republican majority there (at least until they stood for reelection in 1986). And it can be argued that this period of growth culminated in 1994, with the election of a majority of Republicans to both the House and the Senate, and in which the new Republican majorities had a very large component of its leadership from the South. While many things have changed since 1994, the competitiveness of the two parties nationally has not. This is a period that has not yet ended, and so it ends for our purposes in 2012, which is to say at the current moment, or at least the most current moment the availability of data makes possible.

THE END OF THE SOLID SOUTH AND DIVISION
IN THE DEMOCRATIC PARTY (1937–79)

In national politics, the South remained a critical component of the Democratic Party in the New Deal Democratic majority. While it was always a critical component, it made up an actual majority of the Democratic House delegation only in the 1947–48 "Do Nothing" Congress, when the GOP held the overall majority. This was so because southern Democrats held every Senate seat and all but the same few mountain Republican House seats in their region. Thus, with the South always reliably Democratic (and doing so without real competition in the general election), the party's relative size depended upon what happened in northern elections.

The 1936 election, however, was such a vast landslide for FDR and the Democrats that, for the first time in party history, the northern Democratic contingent was so large that it composed an absolute majority of the whole House on its own. The last time that had been true for any party was in the era of the Civil War and Reconstruction when Lincoln and the Republicans could win passage of legislation with only northern votes, as in 1861. In Reconstruction they added the votes of northern transplants and the freed southern slaves. This winning combination ended, virtually completely, with the close of Reconstruction, as we showed in chapter 4, due to the return of the white southerner to the electorate, disenfranchising freed slaves and many of the poor whites, and then to its institutionalization via the passage of the Jim Crow laws.

In the 1937–38 Congress, the South needed allies to ensure that their central concerns would hold as the ongoing status quo. To achieve this, the southern Democrats did not care if votes came from moderate Republicans or from northern Democrats. And thus, for nearly the first time, circumstances dictated that they look broadly for support in the committees and on the floor. The southern Democrats were motivated in this regard by two of Roosevelt's moves with his unusually large majority. One was the amplification of the second New Deal, which, if enacted as parts of it were, would move the federal government more strongly into the economic and social affairs of the nation, and thus into the South.[4]

The Supreme Court's overturning of the "second" New Deal legislation led FDR to propose as well what came to be known as the "Court packing plan," which would have given FDR sufficient new seats to create a majority on the Court, presumably creating, that is, a Court with a northern Democratic majority. Such a Court majority could have overturned precedents that Jim Crow laws in the South depended upon. Rather like under Jackson in the 1830s, the threats to the South in the 1930s were not a direct threat (to slavery in the 1830s or to Jim Crow laws in the 1930s) but a warning, through tariff and Nullification and through New Deal policies, respectively, that the North could change the status quo in the South if they so wished.

Southerners might well have surmised (correctly) that the northern Democratic House majority would be lost fairly quickly, as it was in the wake of the 1938 elections. Even so, the high level of government intervention envisaged by the second New Deal, and the threat of an FDR-packed Court put the South's hold on the status quo at risk. So threatened, they created an informal "conservative coalition" by no later than 1937 to seek to ally with the Republicans on the floor, if necessary. And, increasingly, they found it necessary to do so.

The conservative coalition remained a congressional mainstay long after the second New Deal and the Court packing plan were distant memories. Early on, relatively few votes met the criteria for being a conservative coalition vote, under 10% until the 1940s. This percentage climbed slowly but steadily in the House and Senate over the 1940s and 1950s when it reached 20% and then nearing the 30% mark in the late 1950s in the House. In the Senate, it was closer to 30% in the 1940s and just at 20% during the 1950s. Over this first quarter century, when the coalition did appear, it typically won—in the House in the 80% to 90%, and even 100%, range over various Congresses, until declining to "only" about 55% as the Eisenhower era ended. There was a somewhat slower buildup in the Senate, but one that lasted at high levels a bit longer, before it too fell to about 50% in 1959–60.[5]

As the percentage of roll calls in which the conservative coalition formed on the floor continued to increase into the 1970s, their success rate declined, especially through the Great Society Congress, before regathering strength and reaching a success rate of about three votes in four as Nixon's first term ended. It emerged as a major voting pattern in Congress in the 1970s, nearly reaching the same magnitude in sheer numbers of votes as party affiliation as the basis for forming a coalition on the floor, but its success rate again declined. It began to wane as a voting structure in the 1980s, and most observers quit counting up such votes in the 1990s, its decline tracking very closely (if in the opposite direction) the growth of partisan polarization in Congress. These trends can be seen in figure 6.1 for the post–World War II era. There, we contrast the two major voting coalitions in the House. Party unity votes are those in which a majority of Democrats voted one way, while a majority of Republicans voted the other way. Conservative coalition votes are those in which a majority of northern Democrats voted one way and a majority of southern Democrats and a majority of Republicans voted the other way. What should be most evident is that the 1960s and 1970s stand out in that the incidence of the conservative coalition forming was relatively high, while party unity was at a low ebb. Indeed, the votes that defined a conservative coalition vote appeared in 1973–74 about as often as party unity in structuring

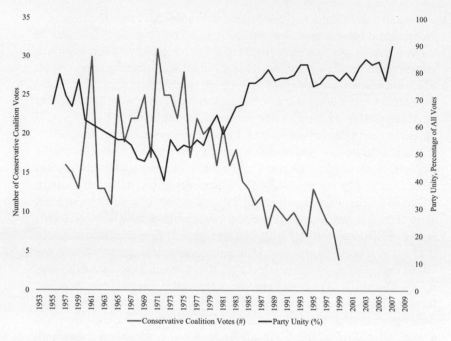

Figure 6.1 Party unity and conservative coalition votes, U.S. House, 1953–2009

votes in the preceding few Congresses (especially the Great Society Congress of 1967–68).

The dates of relevance for the conservative coalition also encompass a vast array of changes relevant here. These changes cleared the way not only for the end of Jim Crowism but also for the rise of the Republican Party in the South. These include changes in the national Democratic Party (and, eventually, to the appearance of the "southern strategy" in the national Republican Party), in Court rulings, in movement politics, and, in the South, to demographic, economic, and social changes that fed into the politics of the rise of the Republican Party.

THE RISE OF THE REPUBLICAN
PARTY IN THE SOUTH (1965–2012)

What few African American voters there were before the New Deal presumably identified with the party of Lincoln, if they identified with any party, and, more certainly, they voted for its candidates. The northern migration following World War I increased the numbers of African Americans who could vote, and FDR attracted a significant base of support in the burgeoning African American communities in northern cities such as Chicago and New York. The 1936 election marked their addition to the New Deal coalition, although it was rather a slim majority by contemporary standards.

The events surrounding Emmett Till's murder, the Montgomery bus boycott, Little Rock High School's desegregation, and the other dramatic moments of the Civil Rights Movement in the 1950s brought African Americans' struggle to the nation and especially to the white northern public, enhanced due to that new medium, television. These occurred during a period in which there were pro- and anti-integration forces prominent in both political parties, and while John Kennedy's call to Coretta Scott King in support of the Reverend Martin Luther King Jr. while in jail in October 1960 might have signaled the ascendance of the pro–civil rights wing in the Democratic Party, it was the actions of his vice president, upon assuming the presidency, that led to the Civil Rights and Voting Rights Acts. That a leading southern Democrat would take such action sent a clear message to the public about where the national Democratic Party was going. Combine that with the leading Republican conservative and 1964 presidential nominee, Senator Barry Goldwater (AZ), voting against the Civil Rights Act, and these actions sent signals about each party. The 1964 election results demonstrated the consequence. Goldwater carried much of the South (and nothing else except his home state), while Johnson's landslide also marked as dramatic a change in the voting of African Americans. Thenceforth, their political loyalties and votes have been overwhelmingly Democratic.

As rapid as that change was, an even more immediate consequence was the increasing relevance of electoral politics to African Americans. When a group is barred from political participation, they are likely to be estranged from politics, seeing it as largely indifferent to their beliefs and actions. As we noted earlier, while he was Senate majority leader, Lyndon Johnson had reduced the content of the 1957 Civil Rights Bill, the first since Jim Crow laws were enacted, to be strictly about voting, and even that part was largely ineffective. It was the promise of the 1964 Civil Rights Bill and the much stricter provisions of the 1965 Voting Rights Act, compared to his 1957 bill, under then President Lyndon Johnson that made electoral politics relevant to the daily lives of African Americans in ways that had long been true for white Americans.

The American National Election Study (ANES) provides a dramatic illustration of this point. In figure 6.2, we report by region the percentage of black and white Americans, over the first fifty years of ANES studies, who found questions about party identification so foreign that they were recorded as "apolitical" in the sense of being unable to comprehend the party questions. Only trace levels of "apoliticals" were recorded for white respondents, hovering in the 1%–3% range.

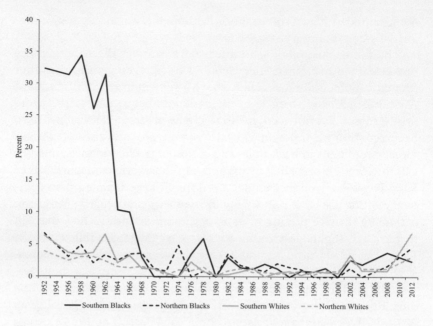

Figure 6.2 Apoliticals by region and race, 1952–2012

Northern blacks mirrored whites in this regard. In contrast, before the mid-1960s, between 25% and 35% of the (few) southern African American respondents asked these questions were unable to respond. In the year the Civil Rights Act was passed, the percentage of black apoliticals plunged from 31% in 1962 to 10%, then to 4% in the next presidential election year. That is, as soon as there was a Civil Rights Act of consequence, southern blacks came to look exactly like whites in this regard. A more dramatic, step change response can hardly be imagined.

While one might imagine that southern conservative loyalties might shift to the Republicans just as dramatically, that is not what happened. Johnson expected them to, at least according to Bill Moyers (2005):

> When he signed the act he was euphoric, but late that very night I found him in a melancholy mood as he lay in bed reading the bulldog edition of the *Washington Post* with headlines celebrating the day. I asked him what was troubling him. "I think we just delivered the South to the Republican Party for a long time to come," he said. (167)

The lengthy buildup of the Republican Party in the South from thereon was not for want of national party leaders trying to—and sometimes succeeding in—winning support for their own campaign. Richard Nixon did devise a southern strategy for appealing for southern votes, typically using phrases like "states' rights"[6] and "law and order" to signal his interest in and, in 1972, opposition to the use of school busing to achieve desegregation in schools—whether in the North or the South. He was reasonably successful in winning southern support in 1968, but the likely full effect was blunted by Alabama governor George Wallace's third-party candidacy that year on an even more explicitly pro-southern campaign. Nixon was very successful in the South in 1972, but then, he was very successful everywhere in his massive landslide reelection. To be sure, Republicans began to make some gains in the South in voting for other offices, but progress was slow. While 1972 was a good year for Republicans in the South generally, voting for GOP candidates averaged no more than about 30% for the national legislative and gubernatorial elections. That was much more than earlier, but it was not yet enough for winning very many victories. And voting for state legislative seats was still under 20% on average. The 1972 election was pretty much a peak in that period. Republican votes in the South dropped off by 1976 with the election of a moderate southern Democrat (and born-again Baptist) as president.

It was not until 1980 that voting for southern GOP candidates began a slow, continuous buildup through the end of the century for offices other than the presidency. We will present evidence of this in the next chapter. The 1994 elections were a watershed in this regard, as they were the first in which southern voting for governor, MC, and U.S. senator averaged 50% or more. The buildup continued such that by 2000 state legislative seats were competitive in many parts of the South, as the averages for the two state chambers crossed the 40% mark. And it was the continuous building of support over time that is most prominent. Of course, that trend has continued beyond 2000, such that, for example, the North Carolina house, senate, and governorship were captured by Republicans in 2012—for the first time since the nineteenth century.

Our account of the emergence of southern Republicanism has emphasized the key role of the Civil Rights and Voting Rights Acts, and thereafter the Republican Party's southern strategy. We would be remiss, however, if we did not acknowledge additional factors that others have emphasized in the party realignment of the region. One take is that the New Deal was a key driver of southern party change, and that it was just delayed in the region (Shafer and Johnston 2009). Other accounts stress the role of northern migration to the South (Polsby 2003; see also Lublin 2004).

Before we turn to tracking movement of the three spheres of the southern party system toward equilibrium, we briefly engage a debate regarding why the Republican Party advanced in some parts of the South more rapidly than in others. Why did the Republican Party advance more rapidly in Tennessee and Georgia than in Mississippi, Louisiana, and eastern North Carolina? Why did the party never entirely lose its toehold on the mountain regions of Tennessee and North Carolina?

To explain these patterns, some point to the historical legacy of slavery (Acharya, Blackwell, and Sen 2014) or racism (McVeigh, Cunningham, and Farrell 2014) as a key determinant for the growth in GOP support. For instance, Acharya et al. show that southern counties with large slave populations in 1860 were more supportive of the Republican Party in 2010. Their argument is that the historical persistence of racial attitudes together with the Republican Party's stance on civil rights contributes to our understanding of where GOP support and thus party competition emerged after the Voting Rights Act. In a closely related study, McVeigh et al. (2014) show that the Republican Party in the modern era has been more successful in southern counties where there was greater Ku Klux Klan activity in the 1960s.

The most comprehensive analysis to date, by Robert Mickey (2015), demonstrates convincingly that Deep South "authoritarian rulers," who varied in terms of the internal racial conflict and political institutions in their jurisdictions, differed in predictable ways in their responses to the challenges to their control. Namely, authoritarian southern "enclaves" differed in predictable ways in their degree of violence, incorporation of African Americans, and reconciliation of Democrats with the national party.

We see these studies as building on our investigation. That is, where we describe how a system of parties developed across the South in government, as an organization, and in elections, these studies disaggregate the emergence of party systems from the regional to the state level to ask what local factors accelerated or hindered the pace of this development.

PARTY SYSTEM DEVELOPMENT TO EQUILIBRIUM

Party in Government

In this chapter, we begin each section with an analysis that parallels as closely as possible the analyses found in chapters 3–5. We follow that with new evidence that we can gather for this more contemporary pe-

Figure 6.3 Difference in House mean party ideology by region, 1938–80

riod but which was unavailable for the nineteenth century (and often for the pre–World War II era). As noted above, we name the two post–World War II eras "The End of Jim Crow" (1937–79) and "The Rise of Southern Republicans" (1980–present), respectively.

The end of Jim Crow. Figure 6.3 reports the absolute difference in the average party DW-NOMINATE scores of U.S. House of Representatives by region from 1938 to 1980 (through the Ninety-Sixth Congress) (this is a subset of the period shown in figure 5.2). A larger difference indicates greater ideological differentiation of the region's representatives. The year 1937 denotes the beginning of the period in which southern Democrats began to vote less often with their northern partisans and more often with the Republicans. The result is visible in figure 6.3, in which one can see much greater partisan differentiation in the North, where Democrats and Republicans voted together less frequently than in the South. This pattern of regional differences in partisan polarization lasted through the 1970s. Figure 6.4 demonstrates that this regional disparity is due almost entirely to the regional differences within the Democratic Party, as the few southern Republicans voted much like their northern counterparts. Because there were no southern Republicans in the Senate until 1965, when

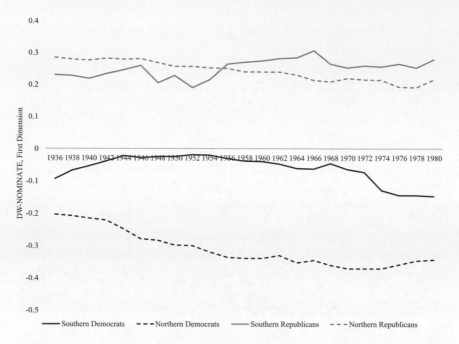

Figure 6.4 Mean House DW-NOMINATE scores by party and region, 1936–80

Thurmond switched affiliation, there are no comparable figures for that chamber. However, the regional differences among Democratic senators appeared at the same time in the Senate as in the House and otherwise tracked their lower-chamber patterns all the way to 1980 (see figure 6.8 below).

The rise of southern Republicans. Starting in 1980, matters on the floor of Congress began to turn. Figure 6.1, above, demonstrates a sharp rise in party unity votes in 1981, with a continued decline in the percentage of conservative coalition votes. That also shows up in figures 6.5 and 6.6, the two comparable figures for the period starting in 1980, as patterns that are dramatically different from their counterparts, figures 6.3 and 6.4. We can see the decline in regional differences in partisan polarization in figure 6.5. Indeed, while the North is slightly more polarized than the South, the differences are relatively slight throughout, and certainly so in comparison to figure 6.3, which ends just as figure 6.5 begins. The bigger difference is over time, in which we can see the sharp and continuous increase in partisan polarization in each region from 1980 onward. And figure 6.6 illustrates that this change was mostly due to the increasing liberal voting of southern Democrats.

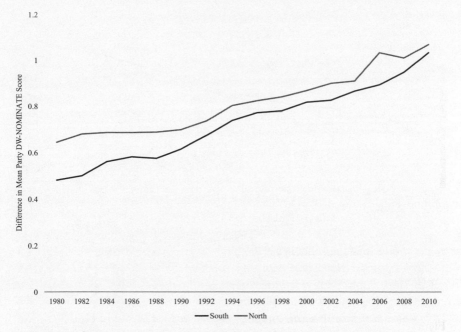

Figure 6.5 Difference in House mean party ideology by region, 1980–2012

To be sure, this figure provides a visible reminder that the South was, overall, voting more conservatively than the North, but this was true in both parties, so the picture is more one of intraparty convergence and interparty differentiation than it is one of regional variation. That is, once Republicans began to win significant numbers of seats from the South, the northern and southern branches of each party began to resemble one another more and more.

Figures 6.7 and 6.8 report similar data for the full range of time and in the U.S. Senate. Republicans appear first in the mid-1960s (and it is a single senator for a while). Even so, the figures are, while certainly not identical to those for the House, still dominantly a story about partisan polarization. However, not only is there more party differentiation in both parties in the Senate, but the level of party differentiation also stalls in the South, so that the North once again becomes more polarized than the South in the Senate.

Overall, due to the power of incumbency and the importance of the position to ambitious politicians, replacement of conservative southern Democrats in the Congress took time. This slow change was reinforced by the time it takes to get sufficient numbers of ambitious politicians with enough political experience, particularly in holding such penul-

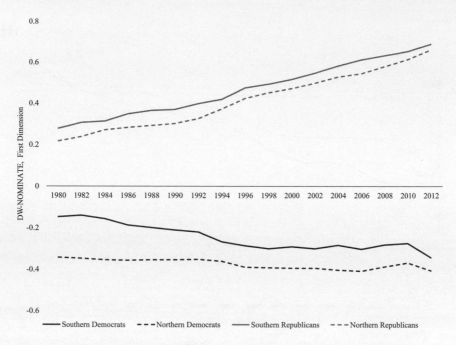

Figure 6.6 Mean DW-NOMINATE scores by party and region, 1980–2012

timate positions as a seat in a chamber in the state legislature, to be ready to challenge the career-ambitious incumbents. We will discuss this process further in chapter 7. Meanwhile, the result was a slow transformation at the top. The end result, accomplished by about the turn of the twenty-first century, was that the regional delegations of a party were not identical, but they were much more nearly so than had been true since before World War I.

In this regard, the contemporary partisan Congress is in some ways the historically first period of full equilibration of the two parties in government. In the Jacksonian era, parties were moderately polarized from each other, but the regional delegations within each party were also moderately polarized. In the Reconstruction and post-Reconstruction South, there were few regional divisions; Democrats voted alike, North and South, and so did Republicans—it was just that there were few Democrats from the South during Reconstruction and few Republicans from the South after Reconstruction. Only in the last forty years, then, have we seen, first, significant numbers of representatives from both regions in both parties and have we seen, second, relatively little regional difference in voting within either party. It is a fully developed, competitive two-party system in state and nation.

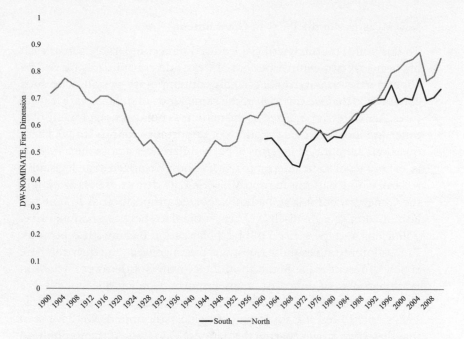

Figure 6.7 Difference in Senate mean party ideology by region, 1900–2012

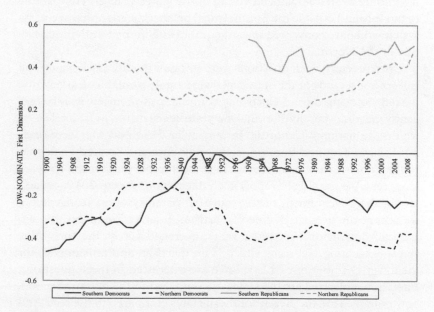

Figure 6.8 Mean Senate DW-NOMINATE scores by party and region, 1900–2012

New Measures of the Party in Government

To this point, the analyses have featured data comparable across each of our nearly two-century periods. We can add considerably more data about parties in government in this contemporary period. One such extension is that we can look at the same kinds of data in state legislatures. Are states as polarized as the nation? Is polarization growing over time? Are there regional variations of importance for our study? These questions are phrased in terms of party differences across the nation. It is, of course, of some interest to observe how polarized state legislative roll call voting patterns may be. We see a high degree of polarization in the Congress, but it is still a hotly debated proposition as to how polarized voters are themselves. Thus, someplace between national level politicians and the general public, polarization becomes less obvious. But, as interesting as those questions are in general, the question here is how different is the South from the North? Southern politicians in Washington were united on many important policy questions in the Jim Crow era. With a two-party South emerging in full bloom in the 1980s and 1990s, are southern politicians still united? We have seen that they have grown apart in the national Congress. If the Republican Party is vital in the South, we might well expect that the South will have come to share polarized voting in the states at levels comparable to those found outside the South. It will be an indication that the party system will have converged toward equilibrium in the South much like that in the North.

Until recently, such questions were difficult to address, because roll call voting records at the state level were rarely available. Largely due to states moving toward electronic compilations themselves, it has recently become possible to analyze state legislatures more or less as we do the national Congress. In particular Shor and McCarty (e.g., 2011) have acquired state roll call voting data and created analogues to the Poole-Rosenthal scores we have been reporting for the national Congress. We are able to report such data from 1996 to 2010, or fairy late in the development of the southern party system.[7] In figure 6.9 we report the average degree of partisan polarization along the first roll call dimension over those years, averaged across the forty-nine states (excepting Nebraska which is nonpartisan and unicameral) for the lower chamber of each state. We are interested in three questions. First, how polarized are the states as compared to the nation? Second, how polarized are the eleven southern states compared to the rest? And finally, how have these patterns changed over the 1996–2010 period? We cannot make precise comparisons among states and between a

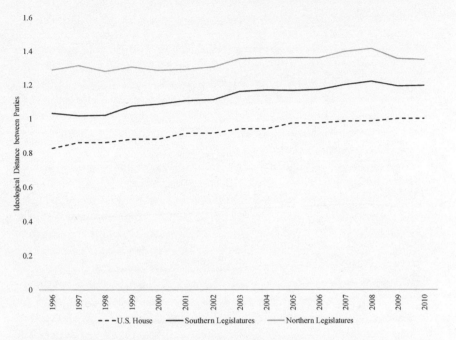

Figure 6.9 Party differentiation within state legislative lower houses, by region, and in Congress, 1996–2010

state and the nation. Each needs to be kept separate. But we can get a sense of how internally polarized each legislature is and we can ask whether the Republicans and Democrats are more differentiated from each other in that legislature than they are in other states or in the national Congress.[8]

By these measures, the typical state has even more polarized voting than the U.S. House.[9] Second, the North is more polarized by party than is the South. However, the South is almost exactly halfway between the somewhat lesser polarization of the U.S. House and the greater polarization among northern states. Finally, polarization has grown in all three cases; it has grown most sharply in the South, although these differences are not great.

As figure 6.10 shows, the South (the solid lines) votes in their state legislatures more conservatively than does the North (the dotted lines), at least within each party, and the southern Democratic Party appears to be relatively more conservative than its northern peers. The main story, however, is that Republicans, whether from North or South, are substantially more conservative than either northern or southern Democrats. To the extent that there is any change over time, it is that

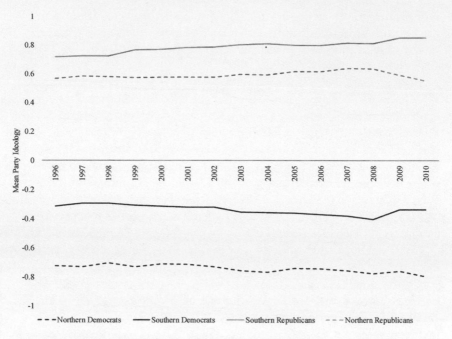

Figure 6.10 Party differentiation within state legislative lower houses by party and region, 1996–2010

Democrats are drifting slightly more liberally in both regions, with just a little more drift left in the South. Overall, we conclude that state legislatures are polarized in their voting behavior quite like that found in the national Congress, and indeed, if anything, even a bit more so. This polarization holds both in the North and in the South. Given that almost exactly half of MCs were elected earlier to their respective state legislatures, this fact of polarization across federal levels means that many of the most effective MCs arrive in Washington used to the politics of a legislature polarized by parties. Even more, as Aldrich and Thomsen recently showed (2017), given that there is polarization, this tendency is reinforcing and thus actually is pushed toward equilibrium. They show that those whose policy stances fit better with the party in Washington than in their state capitol are much more likely to run for higher office, reinforcing those partisan divisions.

Party Organization

In this section we move directly to the systematic measures of partisan organizational capacities that are available for this era, but not earlier. We do so because the reliance on secondary analyses of the rich historiography necessary for trying to assess the quality of party organizations in earlier periods has been all but replaced by systematic observations and measurements in the post–World War II era.

The end of Jim Crow. We wish to know how southern party organizations have compared to those in other parts of the country. To gain some perspective on this, we use data from Gibson, Cotter, Bibby, and Huckshorn's 1983 study of party organizational strength.[10] That study surveyed state party chairs who served between 1960 and 1980, asking about the characteristics and activities of their state party organization when they served as chair. With Brad Gomez, we conducted a new survey of state party chairs in 1999, replicating the collection of much of the Gibson et al. data.[11] The 2011 data were collected in a survey by researcher Rebecca Hatch.

Next, we conducted a factor analysis for the 1960–80, 1999, and 2011 survey data using party organization variables in order to compare party organizational strength across time. In order to make comparisons across time, the factor analysis needs to include the same variables for each period. In their original factor analysis, Gibson et al. included some variables that are not available in the 1999 and 2011 survey data. Therefore, new factor scores were generated for Gibson et al.'s 1960–80 survey data, as well as the 1999 and 2011 survey data, using only the variables that were common to all surveys. The following variables were included in the factor analysis for the 1960–80, 1999, and 2011 periods: Publishes newspaper/magazine, operates voter ID program, commissions public opinion surveys, involved in recruiting candidates, runs campaign seminars, headquarters located in separate building, number of nonelection year full-time staff, nonelection year budget, salaried state party chair, employs a comptroller, employs an executive director. Two factors emerged.[12] Factors were retained after considering the Kaiser criterion (Kaiser 1958), as well as Thurstone's "very simple structure" criterion (Thurstone 1947).

Using the overall measure of party organization, figure 6.11 reports scores for the South and for the remainder of the country in four periods—1960–69, 1970–80, 1999, and 2011.[13] Larger values indicate more organization than average, smaller scores less. The most striking thing about figure 6.11 is the huge regional gap in state party organization in the 1960s. Southern party organizations were more than a standard deviation less organized than were northern party organizations during this period. This gap became smaller in the 1970s; still, southern parties were less organized than their northern peers. By the turn of the century, southern party organization had overtaken and

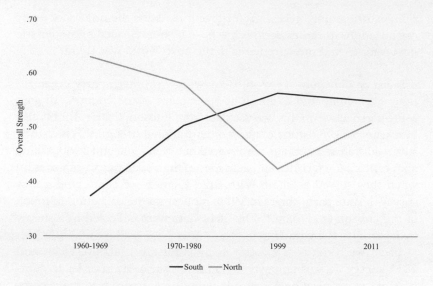

Figure 6.11 Party organizational strength by region, 1960–2011

surpassed organization in the North, and currently organization in the two regions appears to be very much at the same level.

A few examples serve to illustrate the substantive size of the regional gap in the 1960s. In this period, outside the South 23% of state chairpersons were salaried; in the South 9% were. Outside the South 50% of state parties employed a comptroller; in the South just 18% did. Outside the South 80% of parties published a newspaper; in the South just 27% did. Outside the South 46% of parties conducted voter identification programs; in the South just 18% did. Outside the South 30% of parties commissioned polls; in the South 9% did. Outside the South 98% of parties recruited a full slate of candidates; in the South 55% did. Outside the South 63% of parties conducted candidate campaign seminars; in the South 36% did.

One question is how much of the growth of organizational capacity in the South was due to the development of a regionally strengthening Republican Party and how much was due, perhaps in response to Republicans beginning to emerge as competitors, to greater organization in southern state Democratic parties. Figure 6.12 reports overall party organizational strength by region and party. As the figure shows, both Republican and Democratic state parties contributed to the South's improvement in organization in the 1970s, both in absolute terms and relative to the North. However, organizational gains in the South came earlier and more strongly among the state Republican

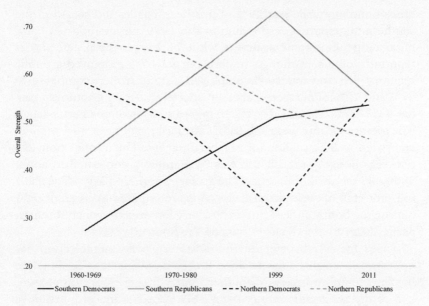

Figure 6.12 Party organizational strength by region and party, 1960–2011

parties. Southern Republican parties began this decade with a level of organization about one and one-half standard deviations below the mean, and ended it almost half a standard deviation above the mean, allowing them to surpass the level of organization among northern Republican state parties by 1980. When we combine the southern parties' improvement with the slow but steady decline in Republican Party organizations elsewhere, the GOP in the South is today more organized than in the North. Southern Democratic parties began the 1970s in the same predicament as the southern Republicans, and ended it somewhat better, but still nearly a standard deviation below the mean. This upward trend in southern Democrats' organizational strength has continued steadily until the present day. Because northern Democratic parties barely improved their organizational strength over this period at all, the regional difference in the organizational capacity of Democratic parties is almost completely indistinguishable. So, both parties contributed to closing the South/North organization gap, but the Republicans contributed somewhat more, and southern parties were aided by relatively stagnant improvement in party organization outside the South.

To provide some illustrations of the relative strength of the regional parties, in 1999 53% of southern state parties maintained a separate office building, while just 29% of northern parties did so. All of the southern state parties responding to the 1999 survey reported commissioning public opinion surveys, while 71% of northern state parties reported doing so. Among southern parties 67% employed a public relations director and 100% employed a comptroller, compared to 47% and 78% of northern parties, respectively. Among southern parties 93% employed a field staff, compared to 67% of northern parties. The average election year budget of southern parties was $4.1 million, compared to $2.4 million for northern parties. The average nonelection year budget in the South was $1.2 million, compared to about $800,000 for northern parties. The average southern party office had a full-time staff of twelve in an election year, compared to a staff of eight outside the South. Indeed, there were very few areas in which southern parties lagged behind parties outside the South.[14]

These figures also suggest that southern party organization has improved in absolute terms since the 1960–80 period. To illustrate further the improvement of southern party organization in the latter half of the twentieth century, figure 6.13 reports the proportion of southern state parties that possessed certain characteristics or were engaged in various activities in four periods. In sum, in virtually every area we compared, southern parties were more organized in 2011 than they were in the 1960s and 1970s (the exception being publishing a

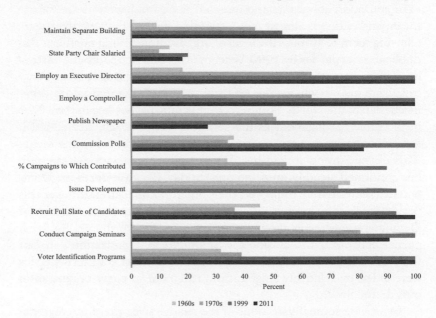

Figure 6.13 Southern party organization, 1960–2011

newspaper). Some organizational improvements were very significant (such as conducting voter identification programs and recruiting a full slate of candidates), while others were more modest (salaried state party chair).

We conclude this section by measuring the party organizations not using the activities of the parties as reported by their chairs but using the activities of parties as reported by citizens. Specifically, we describe the prevalence of party contacting in each region. From 1956 to 2012, the ANES has asked its postelection respondents whether either or both of the major political parties contacted them during the campaign, and whether the contact concerned the election. Figure 6.14 reports the proportion of respondents in each region indicating that they were contacted specifically for electoral purposes. These data include both those who reported voting in the election as well as those who did not. Prior to 1980, southern parties almost always lagged behind their northern counterparts in the frequency with which they mobilized potential voters. Southern parties quickly caught up in about 1980, and the regions were then at parity until about 1994, contacting voters at rates not much different than in the preceding few decades (about 25% of all respondents). After 1994, parties in both regions substantially stepped up their efforts to contact voters such that by 2004 more than 40% of voters reported being contacted by a party. A

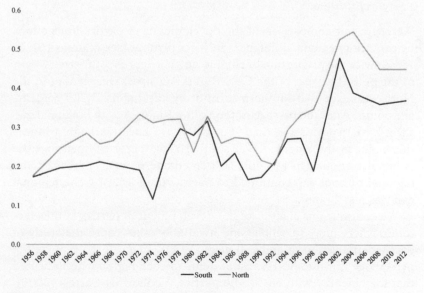

Figure 6.14 Party contacting, 1956–2012

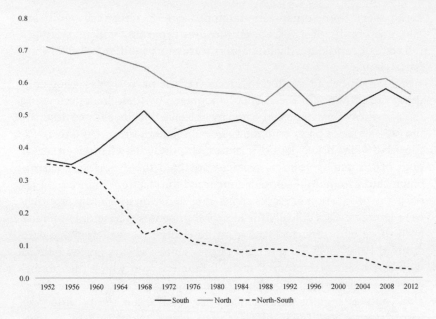

Figure 6.15 Turnout of voting age population by region, 1952–2012

regional difference has reemerged, though, with southern voters about 7% less likely to be contacted.

Party in Elections

We begin our comparison of the development of parties in elections by exploring regional differences in voter turnout (see figure 6.15). In 1952, twice the proportion of eligible northerners as southerners went to the polls. The year of the Civil Rights Act's passage, turnout in the North still exceeded southern turnout by approximately 20 percentage points. After the passage of the Voting Rights Act, the regional gap shrunk to 15% in 1968. In 1980, where we have marked an inflection point in the emergence of southern two-party competition, the regional turnout gap was still 10 percentage points. Thereafter, the regional turnout gap continued to narrow until in 2012, the regional gap was just 2 points.

We continue our analysis of the development of parties in the electorate where modern scholarship invariably takes us: to the study of party identification (Campbell et al. 1960). Figure 6.16 reports the percentage of white ANES respondents in each region who indicated that they identify with one of the parties.[15] Following Bartels (2000), we exclude nonvoters. We exclude blacks from these comparisons due

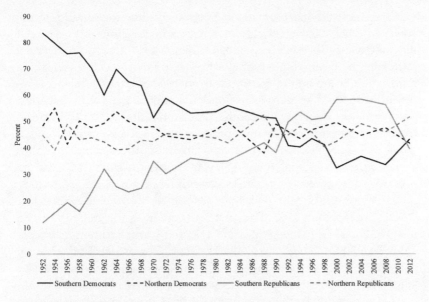

Figure 6.16 Regional comparison of white partisans, 1952–2012

to the dramatic difference that the Voting Rights Act made for blacks in this period, and to be certain that any differences we find are not attributable to the different racial makeup of the regions.

By summing the percentage of respondents who identify as Democrats or Republicans we can observe the remaining share who identify as so-called pure Independents. Today, virtually all southern whites are at least leaning in the direction of one of the major parties. Indeed, for most of this period there does not appear to be much of a regional difference in the share of residents who are pure Independents. In the 1970s and 1980s, by contrast, there was generally a greater share of Independents in the South than outside the South, to varying degrees. Others have described this as the dealignment of partisanship in the South (Stanley 1988). One explanation for this is that white Democrats were on the way to becoming Republican identifiers. In the 1990s, neither region was clearly less partisan.

Of course, there also has been a dramatic shift among southern whites from the Democratic to the Republican Party (Stanley 1988; Black and Black 2003). In 1992, for the first time in the modern era roughly equal proportions of southerners identified with the two parties and in a way that very much mirrored the situation in the North. From 1992 to 2008, there was a leaning toward the Republicans in the South, and in 2012 partisan balance was restored.

A third way that partisanship in elections is often measured is to ask voters whether they perceive there to be any major differences between the political parties (Weisberg 2002).[16] Figure 6.17 reports the regional difference between voting whites who did perceive such a difference outside the South and in the South from 1952 to 2012.[17] Positive values indicate that more ANES respondents outside the South perceived party differences than did southern respondents. According to the trend line superimposed in the figure, in the 1950s we would predict about 5% more northern white voters than southern white voters to perceive a party difference; this gap was greatest in 1968 (8.5%) when only 50% of southern white voters saw a difference between the parties, quite low for a presidential election year. In only one presidential year (1972) did less than 55% of northerners perceive a difference between the parties (when many Democrats defected from their nominee). Beginning in 2004, though, we would predict no regional gap in perceived party differences at all. Today, there are, if anything, somewhat greater perceived party differences in the South than in the North. This suggests that party strength in southern elections now rivals its strength in northern elections, something that was not always the case.

It is also notable that in both regions, the proportion of voters perceiving differences between the parties increased dramatically over this

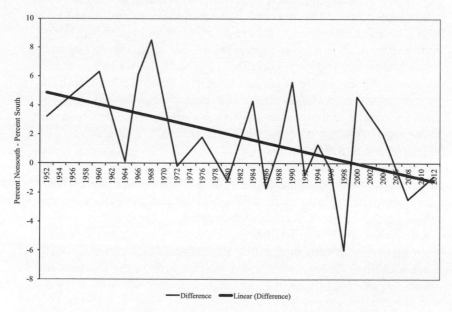

Figure 6.17 Regional difference in perceived party differences among voters, 1952–2012

period. In other words, the regional gap did not close due to declining perceived differences in the North but increasing perceived party differences in the South. For instance, in the South 54.1% of white voters perceived there to be a party difference in 1952, while fully 85.5% perceived such a difference in 2012. Virtually all of the increase in recognizing party differences took place in the 1990s, suggesting that voters' perceptions of party differences stem from the quite visible election of a cohort of southern Republicans to Congress, or what some have termed the end of "Southern realignment" (Stanley 1988).

Related to voters' perceiving a real difference between the parties is voters' tendency to favor one of the parties over the other beyond mere identification. From 1964 to 2012 the ANES has asked its respondents to indicate how warmly they felt toward each of the parties. We calculated the absolute difference in these ratings by year for Democrats and Republicans in each region and report the results in figure 6.18. Focusing first on southern Democrats, up until 1970 this group was more enthusiastic about their party in a manner that very much mirrored partisans of both stripes in the North. However, beginning in 1972 and continuing thereafter southern Democrats' favorability toward their party as compared to the alternative lagged behind northern

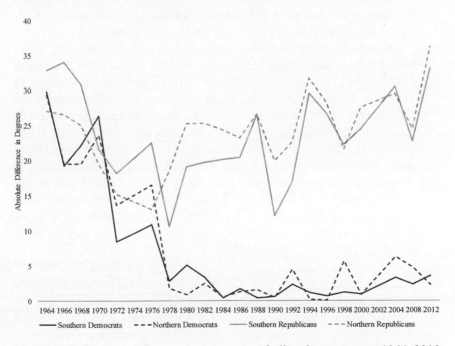

Figure 6.18 Absolute difference between party feeling thermometers, 1964–2012

Figure 6.19 Party loyalty in presidential voting, 1952–2012

Democrats and southern Republicans. In this period, southern Democrats were similar to northern Republicans in this regard.

Identification with and favorability toward a political party is less meaningful if it does not lead to support for the party's candidates (Miller 1991; Bartels 2000). Figure 6.19 reports the proportion of Democratic (Republican) identifiers who also reported voting for the Democratic (Republican) candidate in the most recent presidential election. Following Stimson (1975), we term these voters party loyalists. In 1952, 64% of southern whites were party loyalists in presidential races. With the exception of the 1972 election, in which Democratic voters defected from their party's nominee in droves, the proportion of party loyalists climbed virtually every year until 90% of southern whites were party loyalists in 1996 (and thereafter). The proportion of partisan loyalists grew somewhat outside the South as well, from 83.5% in 1952 to 87.3% in 2012.

Virtually all of the increase in southern party loyalty is attributable to southern whites' party identification falling in line with their increasingly Republican presidential voting behavior. There was no increase in the likelihood that southern Republican identifiers would vote for Republican nominees, only in the likelihood that Democratic identifiers would vote for Democrats.

Comparing the regions, the proportion of partisan loyalists outside the South exceeded the proportion of loyalists in the South by about 20 percentage points in 1952, a gap that steadily narrowed until it was closed completely in 1996. While a small gap in party loyalty emerged in the 2004 elections, the size of this gap is substantively and statistically insignificant, and it disappeared again shortly thereafter. In sum, party loyalty among southern whites has increased substantially since the 1950s, and the difference in party loyalty between southern and northern whites has disappeared altogether.

These results build on those of Bartels (2000), who estimated the impact of party identification on presidential vote propensity for white southerners and northerners using a different approach. That study estimated separately the effect of being a strong Republican rather than being a strong Democrat on Republican candidate support, the effect of being a weak Republican rather than being a weak Democrat on Republican candidate support, and the effect of being a leaning Republican rather than being a leaning Democrat on Republican candidate support, and then weighting these estimates by the proportion of the sample comprised of each group before combining them into a summary measure. In contrast to our findings, that approach uncovered little regional difference in the effect of partisanship on white southern and northern vote choice (Bartels 2000, 41).

Figure 6.20 reports the loyalty results for congressional voting where we separate the respondents by party identification and region. Here, a different pattern emerges from that observed in the presidential loyalty data. First, in contrast to the steady increase in party loyalty at the presidential level, in congressional voting party loyalty in both regions declined from around 80%–90% in the 1950s to about 80% today. Comparing the regions and pooling the partisans, in the 1950s and 1960s, southern white voters were somewhat more loyal to their parties than were northern whites. However, beginning in 1970 southerners have usually been less loyal than northerners, with 1994 and 1998 (both midterm elections) the exceptions where there is no gap. In 2012 there are few regional or party differences in congressional loyalty to be seen.

This is mostly attributable to southern Democratic identifiers' rapidly growing support for Republican congressional candidates—98% of Democratic identifiers voted for the Democratic congressional candidate in 1952, but just 78% did so in 2012. Party loyalty among the much smaller sample of southern Republican identifiers actually increased somewhat over this period, from 68% in 1972 (the first year that the ANES sample included more than fifty white southern Republicans), to 81% in 2012. So loyalty in congressional races, like presidential races, was lower in the South historically, but only among

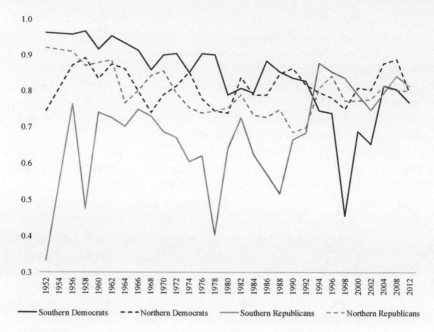

Figure 6.20 Party loyalty in congressional voting, 1952–2012

the small number of Republican identifiers who often supported Democratic congressional candidates prior to 1994.

A final way to measure the strength of parties in elections is to see if citizens' party affiliations neatly divide them into two groups with different ideological orientations (Aldrich 1995). Figure 6.21 reports the proportion of Democrats (Republicans) who identified themselves as ideologically liberal (conservative) over the period 1972 (when the ANES began to measure ideological orientation) to 2012. These data include both voters and nonvoters because the number of southern respondents who both voted and identified an ideology is quite small (less than one hundred) in some years. In the South, and pooling across parties, the share of respondents whose ideologies are consistent with their party's reputation and platform grew from a bare majority in 1972 (53%) to 88% in 2012. This gain was chiefly attributable to dramatically improved ideological consistency among southern Democrats. Outside the South, ideological consistency increased from a little more than 70% in 1972 to 95% in 2012. Again, the Democrats were the prime movers. The combined effect of these trends is that the regional gap in ideological consistency dropped from about 20 percentage points in 1972 to very little gap today.

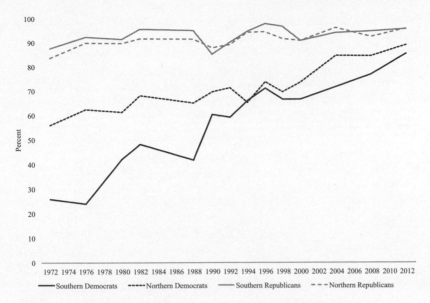

Figure 6.21 Ideological consistency among partisans, 1972–2012

CONCLUSION

In this, the final chapter of our recounting of party development in the American South since 1832, we have at last observed the full emergence of two-party competition in the region. In government, we have seen that southern legislators, be they U.S. House members or state legislators, are today (just about) as divided, or polarized, in the South as they are in the North. Southern state parties are today substantially more organized than their northern counterparts by almost any available metric. Finally, there has been a convergence in the attitudes and behaviors of northern and southern voters, indicating that the regions' parties are equally vibrant in the electoral sphere. The parties of the South have reached equilibrium, matching that in the North.

This evidence establishes a foundation upon which to test the theoretical claims we laid out in chapter 2. Namely, we have established that the American South has for virtually its entire history experienced a party system that has been out of equilibrium as compared to the party system in the North, and certainly as compared to the southern party system today. The next step in our theory is to argue that a party system out of equilibrium will fail to generate consistently competitive elections and in turn will lead to a less effective democratic politics. In part 3 we analyze these claims.

PART THREE

THE DEMOCRATIC FRUITS

OF PARTY COMPETITION

This book makes the argument that a competitive party system is necessary for effective democratic governance. This basic idea is rather simple. Competition between or among political parties in elections, which is to say, in their quest to win political office, leads the parties, once in office, to respect the concerns, needs, and aspirations of the public who elected them.[1] Or, perhaps one might say it leads politicians to respond to the concerns of those who can toss them out of office the next time around.[2] In this way, competitive political parties yield political outcomes that seek to give benefits to all.[3] No other political system can be counted on to reward the mass public as consistently.[4] An absence of incentives to reward the full electorate is not only true for all nondemocratic systems, but it is also true for putatively democratic systems over which there is no genuine competition for office. When there is no (or manufactured)[5] competition, the incentive for officeholders to reward the public lessens. It is the desire for office—and more importantly, the consistent risk of losing office—that provides the steady motivation for political elites to pay attention to the public (Schlesinger 1966; Mayhew 1974; Sartori 1977). In this sense, political parties are a device that James Madison would find fitting smoothly with separation of powers and checks and balances in serving to ameliorate the likelihood of tyranny.

In the following chapters, we examine this claim by looking to see if the emergence of a competitive party system in the American South was, in fact, associated with better political and social outcomes for the general public. Here, we will consider whether the presence or absence of party competition is related to the delivery of the fruits of democracy reaching the public. This inquiry has two components. First, as we saw above, the two nineteenth-century periods of party competition in the South were real but relatively brief, much briefer than in the North, and often less competitive even at their "height" of interparty competition in the South than in the North. As we saw above, for example, turnout in the antebellum period was higher in the North than the South as Democratic-Whig competition opened, and it was only at the end of that period of competition that southern turnout approximated that in the North. Looked at on average, therefore, turnout was lower in this period in the South than the North, although it appeared to have reached comparable levels in "equilibrium." The second component is that, in the post–World War II period, roughly the first half of it consisted of a one-party South and a two-party North, while the second half saw the emergence of two-party competition in the South at comparable levels to the North, which is to say as a fully competitive two-party system. This handy division means that we are able to make a comparison not only between North and South but also between a noncompetitive and competitive South. As a matter of understanding, this is especially helpful because the postwar era is so much more data rich than the earlier two, so that we can use these features to make a fuller and richer set of examinations, assuming that, were we able to do so in the nineteenth century, we would have observed predictable outcomes.

7 PARTY SYSTEMS AND ELECTORAL COMPETITION

In the last several chapters, we assessed the two major parties in each of three eras (and the one party of the Jim Crow era). In the next few chapters, we turn the direction of division around, so that we look at three aspects of party development and accountability in a more directly historically comparative way. The argument in this chapter builds a case for how a well-developed party system is a reliable way to yield consistently competitive elections. The first step is to study how the party pipeline worked in each era. The general story is that a party becomes a serious, major party when it attracts an initial, and then increasingly large, share of individuals who have long-term political ambitions, and they display the key marks of ambition in democratic politics, seeking office not just in the short term but also in a long-term perspective. That is, they at least anticipate the possibility of making politics a career. They do so in large part by responding to their constituency who have and potentially will continue to elect them to office. This chapter focuses mainly on the first marker, while chapter 8 examines the second marker.

We thus ask, first, whether both of the two parties in each region showed enough promise so as to be able to attract ambitious young politicians. One of the major strengths of the Democratic Party in the "no-party" South was that, no matter how closely an aspiring politician's beliefs fit with the Republican Party, he would not join it, because he would surely lose in any local or even state-level office and thus would never see his career get started.[1] Hence, demonstrating an ability to win many kinds of offices was a necessary first step to becoming a major party. So, we first evaluate the competitiveness of elections by region, and how this competitiveness changed over time. In doing so, we are particularly interested in whether states and regions with a more developed party system also experienced more consistently competitive elections. Indeed, we will (at last) test this critical linkage, developed in our theory presented in chapter 2.

Second, we can observe whether a party, such as the Republicans in the South in the post–civil rights era, has become not only a sufficiently competitive party but also a major party by looking to ensure that it has widely attracted the ambitious strivers seeking a long-term career in office in the name of that party. Recall that in chapter 2 we defined a major party to be one that contests, repeatedly, for a wide variety of offices and has some realistic possibility of success. We assess whether a given party has attracted the necessary long-term aspirants to merit the label of a major party in two ways.

Given that a party is competitive, we then ask whether it is filling the pipeline. That is to say, we assess how ambitious office seekers launch a career in elective politics and then climb what Schlesinger (1966) called "the opportunity structure" (the somewhat looser political equivalent of the career path), one office at a time. A party that attracts young ambitious office seekers and sees them attempt to climb to ever higher office is a party that is becoming a truly major party with every prospect of maintaining its position over the long haul. Were it not, those serious about a career in politics would look elsewhere.

This point is, therefore, a crucial transition. A party may have reached a stage where it can compete strongly for any given elective office. That is a necessary step, but it is insufficient for a fully developed, mature party to be "fully developed," that is, in a rough sort of "equilibrium." It is necessary not only that the party *can* compete strongly, but it is also necessary that it actually *does* compete strongly for most offices, most of the time. To achieve that next critical step, the party must be able to attract a large corps of attractive, ambitious politicians who choose that party as the vehicle through which they will seek to realize their career ambitions. At that point, the party, as one of the two major parties, is in the happy position of being in a self-reinforcing equilibrium in which more and more ambitious young politicians join their ranks, up to the point of having sufficient numbers to be able to count on there being a nearly complete slate of attractive candidates for office, election after election. They may not win those offices, but they run, they threaten to win election, and they demonstrate the seriousness of their threat by winning elections from time to time.

Our third empirical question, then, is whether the party is not only competitive and offering up candidates for office, but whether it is attracting the sort of candidates typical of the ambitious office seeker in a major party. That is, a second factor to consider when weighing whether a party has attained the status of a major party is whether its candidates are strong candidates. We cannot, of course, gather much systematic data about those who failed to win office, at least not all the way back to antebellum America. We can, however, look closely at the attributes of those who win.

These three aspects of party success obviously go together. A party is competitive by virtue of winning an increasing number and diversity of elective offices. That is possible when it has attracted sufficiently large numbers of politicians who connect well enough with the public to defeat their major party (and other) opponents. And then, there will be growing numbers of strong and effective winners in the party.

These three questions—can the party win, does it attract apparently ambitious people, and do they fill the pipeline of the opportunity structure sufficiently to win in competition regularly—beg the question of whether all this matters. In particular, does party competition produce truly ambitious office seekers in the sense of Schlesinger, and once in office do they respond as he argued ambitious careerists would in a republican democracy? Schlesinger wrote (1966),

> A political system unable to kindle ambition for office is as much in danger of breaking down as one unable to restrain ambition. Representative government, above all, depends on a supply of men so driven; the desire for election and, more important, reelection becomes the restrain upon its public officials. No more irresponsible government is imaginable than one of high-minded men unconcerned for their political future. (2)

Are they responsive to public sentiment? Do they shape their political ambitions around the winning of office and thus reflect the views of those who can choose them—or do voters throw such rascals as them out? And, thus, is democratic responsiveness and accountability lodged within the personages of the core of the political party, its ambitious office seekers and officeholders? These are the questions we consider in the two chapters that follow. Before turning to those questions, however, we offer a note on the nature of party development.

A Note on "Top-Down" and "Bottom-Up" Party Building

The view that a party is a major party only if it is able to attract a large enough number of attractive, ambitious politicians into the pipeline is a view of party building, at least with respect to these critical aspects, from the "bottom up." That is, the young strivers enter politics at some relatively low level of office (hierarchically low, not low in importance to the people who might benefit greatly from a well-run local political office or school) and climb the opportunity structure, one rung after another. The pipeline of candidates, that is, fills at the bottom and gradually fills the pipeline at higher and higher levels. This is the view Aldrich emphasized (2011) in discussing how Martin Van Buren was able to build the national (Jacksonian) Democratic Party by piecing together a coalition of already existing state and local party-like organizations. It is obviously quite possible to imagine the reverse, "top-down" construction. This view is what Aldrich (2011) emphasized in describing how Hamilton, Jefferson, and Madison built the Federalist and Democratic-Republican Parties at the end of the eighteenth century.

In truth, both "directions" are not just possible but extremely likely to be true simultaneously. This appears to be the case for the building of the Republican Party in the South in the last thirty or forty years. The core principle is that a party is not "fully developed" until and unless it has a large enough corps of ambitious, attractive politicians, so that it can regularly fill the ballot with competitive races. Attracting candidates in sufficiently large numbers is therefore a necessary component for becoming a fully developed, major party, and this is a bottom-up process, for the most part, as we will see. At the same time, the hopeful party leadership needs a way to attract those ambitious politicians. This, too, is a necessary component, one that invariably must come before the pipeline can fill. While, in principle, there may be many ways one might imagine attracting strong candidates to affiliate with a party, the most obvious way is to demonstrate that they can win by having candidates that compete strongly and win already. This is especially important as they anticipate climbing the opportunity structure, when any reasonable individual anticipates increasingly fierce competition as they move up. It so happened that the long barrier to entry of the Republican Party into the South was broken in an essentially top-down way. This made it possible for the party to attract the ambitious politicians needed to fill the pipeline and for the party therefore to become increasingly fully developed. We will develop the specifics of this story once we answer our first question, and as we turn to our second one.

How Competitive Were the Parties?

Our first question, then, is how competitive were the two parties in the South in our three periods of at least minimal competition, and how did that compare to elsewhere in the nation?

1832–52. The sharp rise of the Whig Party in the mid-1830s and its equally dramatic decline (e.g., Sacher 1999) are illustrated in fig-

ures 7.1(a) and 7.1(b), for the North and the South, respectively. As
can be seen there, the Whigs quickly became a major competitor at the
national and state levels in both regions. The party was not particularly strong at the gubernatorial level in either region, but it regularly
carried essentially half the electoral vote for president in both regions.
Its real strength was in the Congress—and since that included the
Senate, which required winning elections within the state legislatures,
by implication the party was strong in the states as well.

The Whigs were, however, clearly more competitive in the North
than the South in these regards. The southern U.S. House delegation was never comprised of a majority of Whigs, as it was for several
congresses in the North. More than 40% of the northern U.S. House
delegation hailed from the Whig Party from 1836 to 1854, while Whig
support in the South for congressional candidates only reached this
level from 1836 to 1842. In the Senate, Whigs were able to secure
approximately two in five northern seats from 1836 to 1854, but only
reached this level of support in the South from 1840 to 1844. That is,
not only were Whigs winning fewer seats in the South, but it appears
that they were also declining in strength in those contests sooner in the
South than in the North.

Another tool to assess the relative competitiveness of the South
and the North is to compare their swing ratios (Niemi and Fett 1986;
Brady and Grofman 1991; Engstrom and Kernell 2005). A swing ratio
is defined as the percentage change in legislative seats associated with a
1% change in aggregated legislative votes. It reflects the responsiveness
of the composition of government to changes in popular sentiment as
expressed via elections, with larger ratios indicating greater responsiveness. The widespread (and after 1842 required)[2] state adoption of
single-member districts for U.S. House offices created a nonpropor-
tional relationship between the ratio of votes won and seats held by
parties. When a party is competitive in a state, region, or the nation,
its losses and gains are amplified by the electoral system turning small
declines and increases in vote share into larger declines and increases
in seat share. When a party is not competitive, or when a party has no
considerable rival, its seat share will only sluggishly respond to change
in its vote share. We can also learn about electoral competitiveness
from the swing ratio. When individual races are not competitive, the
dominant party can suffer a decline in electoral support without losing
office, and this will coincide with a low swing ratio.

Swing ratio data calculated by Brady and Grofman (1991) are available beginning in 1850, as the second party system is drawing to a
close and as the South is beginning to catch up with the North in

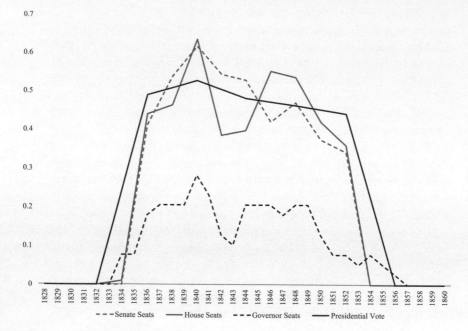

Figure 7.1(a) Northern Whig electoral support, 1828–60

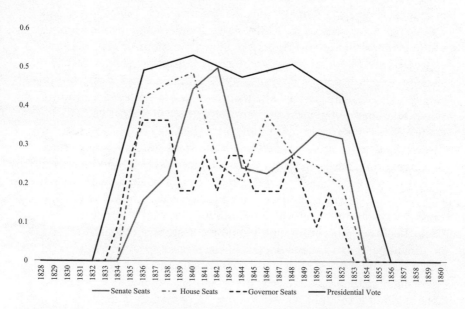

Figure 7.1(b) Southern Whig electoral support, 1828–60

terms of party development and electoral competition. In 1850 (see figure 7.2), the swing ratio in all states (5.2) was only slightly smaller than the ratio among northern states (5.5). In 1852, the regional gap grew, likely due to redistricting, as the swing ratio nationally dropped to 4.1 while the ratio in northern states remained 5.5. In 1854, the regional gap returned to approximately the same size as in 1850, but then grew until 1860 when the ratio in the North (4.9) was nearly a full point higher than in the country as a whole (4.0). This is as we would expect due to the earlier collapse of the Whig Party in the South.

Why were southern parties less fully developed (see chapter 3) and less competitive in the Whig period? One possibility is that this was a legacy of the politics that led into that of the Democrat-Whig period. Key (1949) emphasized the importance of the opportunity for competition for promoting party development in the "no-party" South in the 1940s. As Aldrich (2000, 643) paraphrased Key, "if only there was regularized competition, there would be organized parties." By that he meant not that competitive outcomes create organized parties but that the opportunity to compete on something like a level playing field creates an incentive for parties to organize, and this organization produces competitive candidates. In other words, the opportunity for electoral competition is critical because it motivates parties to improve their organizational capacities; electoral competition encourages and reinforces the development of the regional party systems.

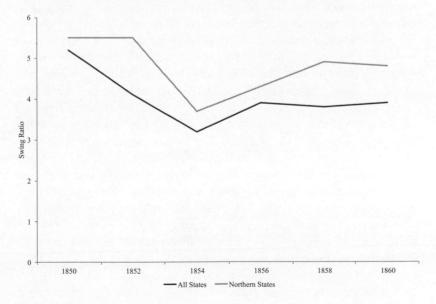

Figure 7.2 Swing ratio, 1850–60

So, if southern elections were less competitive than elections in the remainder of the country in the late 1820s and early 1830s, this argument goes, as the Democrat-Whig mass parties era opened there would be less reason for the southern parties to believe that elections would be competitive, and thus less reason to organize. And it does appear that 1820s elections were less competitive in the South. For instance, the mean proportion of the U.S. House vote obtained by the winning candidate in each congressional district from 1828 to 1832, that is, leading into the Jacksonian Democrat–Whig era, was about 59%, compared to 72% in southern contests. That is to say, southern House districts averaged being about 13 percentage points less competitive than in the rest of the nation. From 1840 to 1848, at the peak of two-party competition, the regional gap in competitiveness remained but was much smaller. The South was about 6 percentage points less competitive. Elections in the South were considerably less competitive than they were in the North as mass parties were forming for the first time, and it appears that this regional difference, while narrowing, never fully disappeared, even at the height of Whig strength. Thus, it appears that the South was closing in on the North, but perhaps because they started so very far behind northern levels of competition, they never quite caught up. Whether they would have done so had the Whig Party survived another decade is mere speculation.

Another perspective on this possibility of entrenched lack of competitiveness in the South, as well as a potential explanation for why southern elections were already less competitive prior to the Democratic-Whig period, emphasizes the relative agreement among enfranchised persons in the region, which resulted in a modestly stunted two-party system (Berkowitz and Clay 2011). If there is a consensus among citizens (or at least voting citizens) on the chief issues of the day, we should observe less competition in elections. The reason is that in the presence of consensus, there is less at stake in removing the "ins" and replacing them with the "outs." In the South there was a consensus among eligible voters on matters related to slavery and civil rights, and there was less urbanization. This greater unity was reflected in the southern veto in the national legislature, required to protect the South's "peculiar institution." More generally, as we have shown, southern congressmen were more likely than nonsouthern congressmen to form cross-party coalitions within their region. This relatively higher regional unity in the South is reflective of the strict unity on matters related to slavery and civil rights. It is possible, therefore, that the lower barriers to cross-party voting among southerners in the federal Congress might have led, like its counterpart a century later that Key studied (1949), to increased factionalism and thereby decreased party strength within the southern states, at least relative to their northern counterparts.

1872–1908. As one study of this period drily noted, "It is a recognized fact that the easiest way to keep a political party small is to fail to put up candidates" (Shadgett 2010, 160). And, after the Compromise of 1877, the Republicans often did just that in the South. The Republicans did not put up a gubernatorial candidate in any of the races between 1877 and 1900 in Georgia, Mississippi, or South Carolina, and skipped the election in a majority or near majority of races in three additional states (Alabama, Texas, and Virginia). Only in Tennessee and North Carolina, where mountain communities remained supportive of Republicanism, and in Louisiana was a Republican candidate for governor entered in every election. In nine of eleven states, the Republicans contested no more than 40% of U.S. House races over this period. Once again, Tennessee proved to be a notable exception with GOP House candidates appearing in nine of ten races. All told, however, of the 1,708 House races that took place in the South between 1868 and 1908, the Republicans failed to put up a candidate in 467 (27%) of them. Between 1876 and 1908, the Republicans did not put up a candidate in 412 of 1,403 House races, or 29% of the time.

In contrast, the Democratic Party failed to field a U.S. House candidate in the eleven southern states only nineteen times between 1868 and 1908 over the same 1,403 contests (1.3%). Eleven of the nineteen instances occurred prior to 1876, leaving just eight races in which the Democrats failed to field a candidate after the end of Reconstruction.[3] Finally, four of the eight races in which a Republican ran unopposed took place in Tennessee's Second District, which has not elected a Democrat since 1855, and a fifth in the state's First Congressional District.

Two-party competition was keen in the rest of the nation. Outside the South, between 1876 and 1908 the Republican Party did not field a candidate in fifty-nine of 4,038 races, just 1.4%. Over the same period, the Democratic Party outside the South did not field a candidate in 306 of the 4,038 races, or 7.5%. Thus, the Republican experience in the South was unique; only there and only with that party was failure to nominate a candidate at all common. Of course, unlike what one might infer from Shadgett's observation, the failure of the Republican Party was not because they could not get anyone to run for office; instead, they could not get anyone to run for office because such races were hopeless most everywhere in the South.

Did the pattern of party development we have described map onto the pattern of electoral competition in the South? Figure 7.3(a) reports the trend in southern Democratic Party strength from 1868 to 1908, the period the white, Democratic, planter aristocracy referred to as "Redemption." The Democratic Party entered this period representing just one-third of state legislative seats and governor's offices and capturing about the same proportion of congressional seats. The party was somewhat more successful in securing congressional votes, winning two in five, and presidential votes, obtaining roughly half.

Following the Panic of 1873, the Republican Party was crushed in the 1874 elections, losing their majority in the U.S. House and almost half of their seats to the Democratic Party. In the South, specifically, the Democrats continued their systematic destruction of the Republican coalition. The Democratic landslide signaled the imminent end of Reconstruction. After Reconstruction, Democratic strength in the South continued to grow, particularly in the state legislatures and in Congress. Gains also took place in gubernatorial and presidential contests, but they were not as great. The rather sharp but short-lived decline in Democratic victories reflects the gains of the Populists in the early to mid-1890s. This dip reflects the potential threat of this emerging party to southern Democrats and the speed with which the

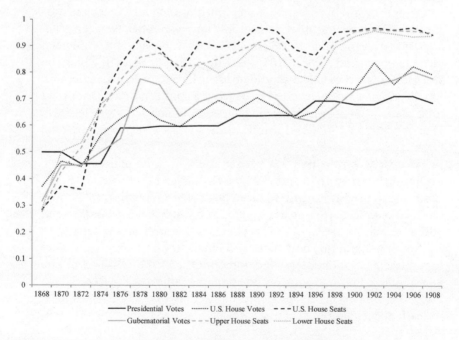

Figure 7.3(a) Democratic Party strength in the South, 1868–1908

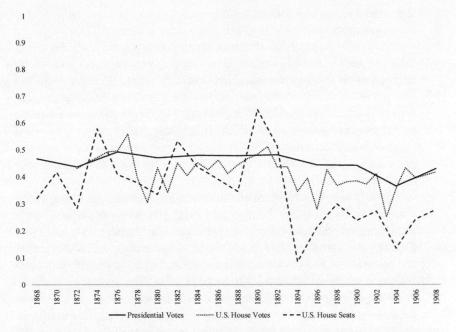

Figure 7.3(b) Democratic Party strength in the North (federal offices), 1868–1908

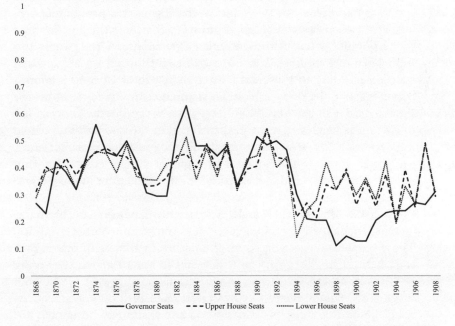

Figure 7.3(c) Democratic Party strength in the North (state offices), 1868–1908

southern Democrats moved to extinguish it before it cut too deeply into their otherwise ironfisted grip on electoral office.

Nonetheless, this "Populist Moment" proved to be but a bump in the road, and there was a continuing buildup in southern Democratic success, such that, as the twentieth century opened, they controlled about 95% of the electoral votes and a similarly overwhelming proportion of the U.S. House and Senate seats. That is, at the national level, it had become a one-party South. Inside the region, they controlled eight in ten governorships and a similar share of the seats in the two chambers of the state legislatures. That is, at worst, they were simply dominant.

Outside the South, in contrast, elections were more consistently competitive (see figures 7.3[b] and 7.3[c], where we separate the offices into federal and state level for ease of presentation). After the Democratic gains in 1874, and continuing through to 1892, neither Democrats nor Republicans held a convincing upper hand, although Republicans usually had a slight edge. This is especially true if we focus on vote shares, rather than seat shares, which are inherently more volatile (at least with respect to House seats and governor's offices). In 1894, support for Democratic candidates collapsed, but then recovered substantially over the next decade.

Recall that another way to assess the competitiveness of the electoral system is to measure the swing ratio—the change in a party's seat percentage in a legislature resulting from a 1% change in the party's share of the popular vote. Figure 7.4 reports the congressional swing ratio from 1876 to 1908 for all states as well as for the subset of northern states. According to these data, after the close of Reconstruction a regional gap in the swing ratio quickly emerged and persisted through the remainder of the period. While a 1% change in vote support led to a 4%–5% change in seats in the North, in the country as a whole it led to just a 3%–4% change, implying of course that responsiveness was much worse in the South. The regional difference in the swing ratio would persist (and indeed grow) for the remainder of this period.

1948–2012. After World War II, a series of maneuvers occurring at an elite level aimed to realign voters and transform southern politics. These maneuvers were based on the parties' reactions to the enfranchisement of southern African Americans in the 1960s via the Voting Rights Act (42 U.S.C. § 1971). As we discussed above, buoyed by the success of Senator Barry Goldwater (R, AZ) in the 1964 presidential election, Republicans created a "southern strategy," originally for the 1968 presidential campaign of Richard M. Nixon (Lamis 1988;

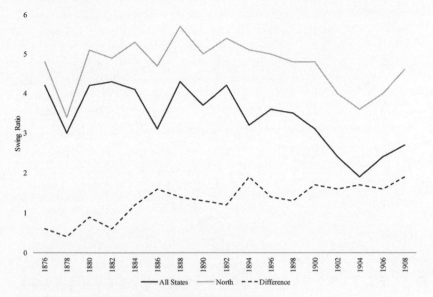

Figure 7.4 Swing ratio by region, 1876–1908

Aistrup 1996). This strategy was designed to attract white, southern voters resistant to integration through the use of racially motivated appeals by the GOP presidential campaign. On the Democratic side, President Lyndon B. Johnson made direct appeals to southern blacks via the 1964 Civil Rights Bill and the 1965 Voting Rights Bill, which drove whites to embrace the regionally nascent party—at least at the presidential level (Carmines and Stimson 1989). This combination of party strategies apparently succeeded from the perspective of the GOP, as evidenced by their newfound electoral success at the presidential level among southern voters. Thereafter, southern GOP gains were registered in U.S. Senate, state governor, U.S. House, and finally state legislative elections. This pattern has led commentators to conclude that the GOP became competitive in the South from the "top down" (Bullock 1988a, 1988b; Aistrup 1996). Figure 7.5 documents this gradual emergence of Republican voting in the eleven former states of the Confederacy from 1948 to 2012.

Adopting counties as his unit of analysis, Aistrup (1996) found that white voter support for the GOP presidential nominee led to white support for GOP senatorial, gubernatorial, and state legislative candidates in the subsequent four-year election cycle.[4] Moreover, white support for GOP gubernatorial candidates (but not U.S. Senate candidates) positively impacted white voting for GOP state legislative candidates in

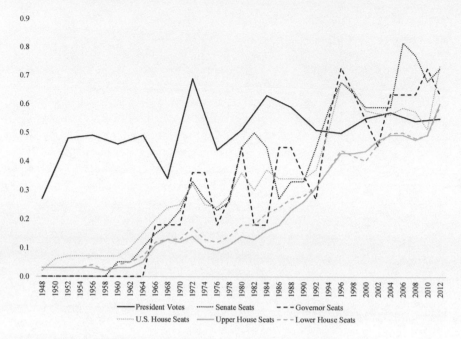

Figure 7.5 Republican competition in the South, 1948–2012

the following election cycle.[5] Theoretically, Aistrup attributed the success of the GOP to the development of GOP organization and, at the
level of the voter, to changes in party identification.[6] As we saw in chapter 6 (see especially figure 6.12), both parties' organizational capacities
in southern states were well below those of their northern counterparts
in the 1960s but were dramatically catching up in the 1980s. (Indeed,
southern Republican parties exceeded northern Democratic parties by
these measures in the 1980s.) Both southern parties peaked in these
measures in the 1999 survey. Thus, at least in the few available and
widely spaced surveys, the GOP organizations appeared to lag behind
the creation of the southern strategy. Similarly, as figure 6.16 shows,
rates of southern Republican Party identification increased rapidly
from the 1950s (going from 10% in 1952 to 30% in 1960) and then
climbed steadily but gradually to about 40% in 1988. It exceeded
Democratic identification rates in the early 1990s. It thus seems that,
while there was movement in these measures, Republican presidential
candidates could win southern electoral votes well before the southern
electorate or state organizations grew to comparable levels.

Thus, we argue here that, while prominent Republican individuals
at high levels of office were able to win support, perhaps repeatedly,

from southern voters, they were not able to pass on their political organization and resources to develop a Republican Party in the South from the top down. Rather, the success of Republicans in the South at the presidential level made it possible in the late 1960s through the Reagan administration to argue there was potential for success in building a Republican Party in the South. The development of an organized and sustained Republican Party in a given state, however, required voters potentially available for the wooing and a sufficiently large number of sufficiently strong candidates to turn that voting potentiality into actuality. In turn, that required a party attractive to a large number of ambitious, potentially strong candidates. That is, we anticipate that the critical step between attracting the attention and occasional support of the southern voter to a Republican candidate and attracting the sustained voting loyalty of that voter to the party, in general, was the development of a cadre of ambitious, office-seeking politicians to the Republican rather than to the Democratic Party. In turn this should mean that we will observe the development of a *sustained and systematic* Republican Party in the South moving from the bottom upward, even if there were candidates for high office who could, on occasion, demonstrate that Republican contenders could, in principle, run well in the South.[7] So, while figure 7.5 illustrates voting *potential* moving from top down, highlighting the opportunity for the Republican Party to compete widely, party development to translate that potential into sustained success on behalf of the party's candidates should develop from bottom up. We will return to this question below, but for now we focus on the clear rise of southern party competition in the modern era, as reflected in a variety of measures.

First, in figure 7.5 we can see that in 1948, the Republican Party was ineffective in contesting many offices in the South. The party did fairly well in its search for presidential electoral votes in the 1950s and 1960s. Outside of McGovern's dismal showing in 1972, however, the next breakthrough happened in the Reagan era. The GOP competed increasingly well for House and Senate (and gubernatorial) offices in the 1980s, but it was really not until the 1990s that they first won a majority of such races in the South. It was then, also, that the party picked up steam in state legislative races, reaching the 40% or so mark in the mid-1990s. Thus, before 1980, the GOP was effectively a limited party in the South, but over the 1980s and into the 1990s it began to build the kind of strength typical of today. That is, it was finally competitive over a broad range of offices only as the twentieth century ended. With that, the GOP was prepared to build an effective electoral arm in the South.

Next, the South was historically less competitive than it is today, but has it become more competitive relative to the rest of the country? In figure 7.6 we compare the South's competitiveness in presidential races with the five border states where slavery was prevalent but that did not secede—Maryland, Missouri, Kentucky, West Virginia, and Delaware—from 1948 to 2012.[8] Beginning in 1948 and continuing through 1988 in every presidential election save 1964 the southern states were less competitive than the border states. In some elections (1948, 1972, 1984, and 1988) the competitive difference between the two regions was dramatic. The average yearly difference between the two regions between 1948 and 1988 was about 8.5%. Beginning in 1992, however the South has been *more* competitive in four of the six elections that have since been held and was equally competitive in one of the two remaining (2000). In sum, the South used to be less competitive than the border states in presidential contests, but clearly this is no longer the case.

A similar picture emerges when we compare the division of U.S. House seats by region over the same period (see figure 7.7). In the 1950s virtually all southern U.S. House seats were occupied by Democrats, while the party's advantage in the border states was not nearly as large. With some variability this difference in regional competitiveness

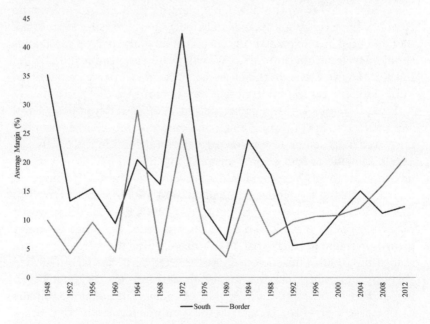

Figure 7.6 Average margin of victory for winning presidential candidate in southern and border states, 1948–2012

continued until the 1980s when the Democrats' fortunes improved temporarily in the border states while remaining stable in the South. In 1992, the two regions converged on this measure and in both regions were thereafter much more competitive than they had been historically. In both absolute and relative terms, the South has become more competitive as reflected in the partisan division of congressional seats.

The South also became more competitive during the twentieth century (again in absolute and relative terms) as measured by the swing ratio (see figure 7.8).[9] In the early 1900s and continuing through the period that Key (1949) studied, the swing ratio in the northern states was substantially higher than in the nation as a whole (and by implication the ratio in the southern states was much less). Coinciding with the Voting Rights Act of 1965, however, northern and national swing ratios became much more alike, and since 1980 they have been virtually identical.

Finally, in chapters 3–6, we documented the history of political party development in the South and its convergence with the North in the last two decades of the twentieth century. In this chapter we have thus far documented the growing electoral competition in the South over the same postwar period. Together, these two trends tend

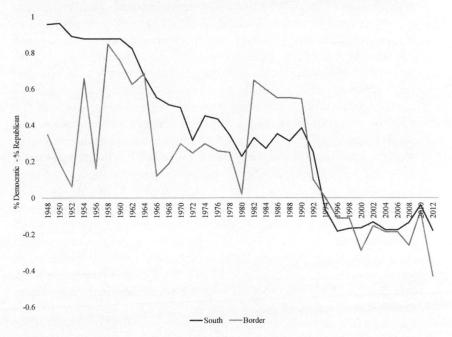

Figure 7.7 Division of U.S. House seats (% Democratic less % Republican) by region, 1948–2012

Figure 7.8 Swing ratio by region, 1908–2004

to support our claim in chapter 2 that the movement of a party system toward an equilibrium in which both parties are mature leads to more competitive elections. However, our test of this claim could be more rigorous. It is possible, for example, that the states in which parties have most rapidly and forcefully moved toward equilibrium are not the same states in which elections have become most reliably and completely competitive. If this were true, we might observe some of the patterns seen above even if a party system were not a precursor to competitive elections. Thus, we test this claim by nesting measures of electoral competitiveness and party development within individual states. Specifically, we model presidential election competitiveness at the state level (where larger values reflect greater competitiveness) from 1948 to 2012 as a function of three measures of party development—the distance between the DW-NOMINATE scores of the state's median Republican and Democrat U.S. House member for each Congress (reflecting party in government), the average level of party mobilization reported among ANES respondents in each state/year (reflecting party organization), and the proportion of ANES respondents that report that they see a difference between the parties in each state/year (reflecting party in elections). We anticipate that for each of these measures the estimated effect will be positive, or that as party systems are closer to equilibrium elections will be more competitive.

Table 7.1 Effect of party development on electoral competition, 1948–2012

	Competitiveness
Party in government	0.061*
	[0.027]
Party as organization	0.041
	[0.039]
Party in elections	0.100**
	[0.030]
Constant	−0.228**
	[0.019]
R^2	.07
N	401

* $p < .05$; ** $p < .01$.

The results of this model, reported in table 7.1, lend considerable support to the theoretical argument we laid out in chapter 2. First, the results show that in states where the elected officials are more distinct ideologically, elections are more competitive and there is little uncertainty about this conclusion ($p = .02$). Next, in states where a greater share of residents report being contacted by one of the parties, elections also tend to be more competitive, although we are less certain about this conclusion based on this model alone.[10] Finally, the models also confirm that where citizens observe a difference between the parties, elections are more competitive, and again we can be very confident in this conclusion ($p < .01$). In sum, the maturation of party development in all three areas—elections, organization, and government—leads to more a more competitive electoral environment.

Ambition and Party Development

As we argued in chapter 2, the development of a second major party, and thus the creation of a "mature" (or "in-equilibrium") multiparty system is necessary for the establishment and maintenance of a well-functioning republican democracy. Three integrated components of the theory of political parties and of party systems imply testable hypotheses about candidates and officeholders in the maturation of a second major party in each era. The first is that a party system, one with at least two fully developed parties competing broadly cross the range of elective offices, is a necessary component of an effective democracy. This is the claim of Key in *Southern Politics* (1949), among others. The second component is that most ambitious politicians are attracted to engage in elective politics (and holding the offices so selected) through the agency of one or the other major party. This is the claim of, inter alia, Aldrich (2011). The third is that the typical member of the set of ambitious politicians is essentially defined as one who chooses (elective) politics with the intent, should all go well, of it being a lifelong career ambition. As a result the typical such ambitious politician enters partisan elective politics at entry levels of office and climbs from those "base offices" up the rough, informal hierarchy of offices, what Schlesinger (1966) called the "opportunity structure," from lower to higher levels.

The primary observable consequences of this set of claims are that we can trace the development of a regularized set of office careers over time. Of course, people will enter elective office at every level of the opportunity structure. The Whigs, for example, were most successful with presidential nominees who were, like Andrew Jackson, military leaders, real or concocted war heroes, perhaps even, as in the case of Zachary Taylor, candidates whose first elective office was the presidency. But we can tell that a political party has begun to develop systematically as a locus for ambitious politicians when we find that they attract substantial numbers of people who choose to run for lower-level offices as their entry, remain in politics for substantial portions of their careers, and climb offices up the opportunity structure, from lower to higher levels. What we can observe from this upward flow, if that is indeed how the party develops, is that voters will respond systematically to being presented with a group of attractive, ambitious, career-seeking politicians, such that their votes follow the rise of these young politicians up the opportunity structure.

The Whig Party, 1836–52. A test of this account is that the pattern of voting regularly for a new party, in this case the Whig Party, should reflect that systematic climbing up the opportunity structure. That is, support for Whig candidates should occur first at the lower levels of office and move systematically up the opportunity structure, step-by-step, in response to the flow of ambitious politicians up that same set of steps.

We report the details for voting for the Whig Party, 1836–52, the return of the Democratic Party in the post-Reconstruction South, and the rise of the Republican Party in the South over the last few decades. Here, we summarize these findings with the use of a single figure in each period (e.g., figure 7.9 for the Democrat-Whig period). One of

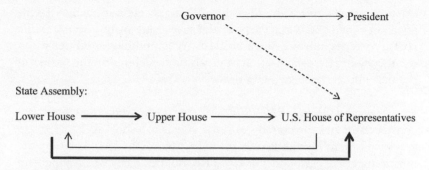

Figure 7.9 Party building for the Whig Party in the South, 1836–52

the injustices this presentation does to the data is that it reflects only the positive and clear findings. The period here is relatively short for this sort of analysis, and so the "power" of the test is not high. That is to say, the relatively few years of data for this inquiry here leave a fair amount of uncertainty, reflected in relatively large standard errors of estimates. As a result, we draw connections over time cautiously, reporting in the figure, with unbroken, dark arrows, only those relationships that appear strongly and consistently. The lighter solid lines, and especially the light, dotted lines, indicate patterns that are suggested by the data but that have a fairly high degree of uncertainty about them. And patterns that might well actually be there, but not break through even this more generously high degree of uncertainty, cannot be known, of course.[11]

Even given those caveats, there is clearly much stronger evidence for the "bottom-up" account of Whig Party development than the reverse. Thus, for example, Whig seats in the lower state chamber systematically precede more upper-chamber seats. Even more clearly, state lower-chamber Whig seats lead systematically to seats for Whigs in the U.S. House, and only slightly less clearly do state upper-chamber seats lead to U.S. House seats. There is modest evidence of House voting influencing the support for Whigs to the lower state chamber (consistent with the norm of rotation in office), and no other "top-down" voting. Nothing, but a hint at the gubernatorial level, appears to influence presidential voting, perhaps because there were so few presidential elections in this short period of multiparty competition in the South, and there is only a similarly suggestive but isolated hint of gubernatorial voting influencing subsequent voting patterns for the U.S. House. In short, the legislative data seem to present clear evidence of the flow of ambitious, popularly attractive candidates up the opportunity structure, and there is little evidence to suggest the reverse flow of voting. We, therefore, at least tentatively, reject the idea that Whig success nationally systematically shaped the Whig Party in the electorate in the South, while voting patterns indicate that ambitious Whig politicians did behave as the theory implies—vote-attracting candidates climbing the ladder of political success, one step at a time.

The Democratic Party, 1876–1900. The period between the end of Reconstruction and the coming of Jim Crow is too short to do a full accounting of party building over time. Further, it is complicated by the beginning of the period in which the Republican Party was competitive with the Democratic Party during Reconstruction, and then the Populist Party emerged to challenge the Democrats seriously, if briefly, at the end of the period. What we can do is look at the dynamic of two-party competition among Democrats.[12] The results are presented in figure 7.10.

While thus less than a full analysis, we find that there is, with only a very small exception, evidence only for "bottom-up" dynamics. Voting for both chambers of the state legislatures in this period influenced subsequent voting for governor, but not the reverse, and state upper-house votes affected votes for the U.S. House and not the reverse. There is, as the one exception, a very modest two-way relationship between voting for governor and for president. In sum, we can nearly rule out any "top-down" model and conclude that evidence does support the account of ambitious politicians playing a central role in party-building efforts during this period in which Democrats faced real chances of defeat in general elections in the South, short though that period is. It was so short, of course, because the South turned "Redemption" into "Jim Crow" just as the Populist threat appeared strongly.

The Republican Party, 1948–2008. In 1948, the Democrats were riven by debate over civil rights and the position of the South in the party. Truman integrated the armed forces that year, and then Mayor Hu-

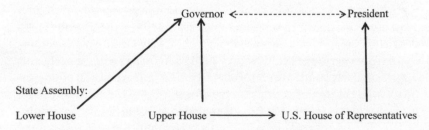

Figure 7.10 Return of the Democratic Party in the South, 1876–1900

bert Humphrey (Minneapolis) gave a stirring speech in favor of civil rights at the party's national convention. In response, the southerners walked out of the convention, and then Governor J. Strom Thurmond (SC) served as presidential candidate for the "Dixiecrat" Party that year, carrying a good number of southern electoral votes. The stage was thus set. In 1952, Eisenhower began to win considerably greater voting support in the South than his party had yet attained, and this fact of early development held throughout this period. It thus makes sense to begin to assess the development of the Republican Party in the South starting at its electoral beginning. Our task here is to compare the two subperiods of this era. One is this early period, which we end in 1978, just before the Reagan version of the southern strategy and the breakthrough for Republicans outside of the presidential level. That breakthrough thus marks our second period, 1980–2010. A high mark occurred, of course, in 1994, as the Republicans won a majority of seats in both the House and Senate that year, for the first time in forty years, and they selected primarily southerners to lead their party with its first national congressional leadership in more than a generation.

What we can see is actually a richer story in both subperiods than we saw earlier (see figures 7.11 and 7.12). The earlier period is, as we should expect, more limited in its systematic, effects over time, as there was considerably less development of voting for Republicans over this time. But, whereas there is a clear upward flow, there are also balancing downward flows. The most recent period, by contrast, is more richly developed, and it includes a considerable amount of flow in both directions (although it is not quite obvious how best to characterize the relationship between the U.S. House and the governor's office). At a minimum, we would conclude from figure 7.12 that there is as much or more evidence of a bottom-up pattern of citizen voting as there is a pattern of top-down voting.

In addition to evaluating the directionality of party development

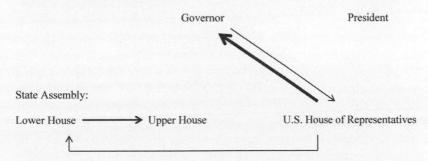

Figure 7.11 Party building for the Republican Party in the South, 1948–78

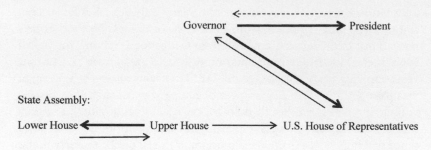

Figure 7.12 Party building for the Republican Party in the South, 1980–2010

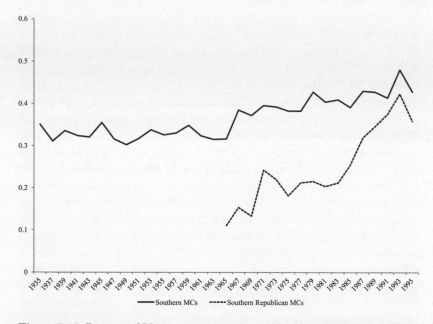

Figure 7.13 Percent of House representatives with prior service in state legislature, 1937–95

using trends in voter support across a variety of offices, we can also do this using the biographies of elected officials. Specifically, we examine whether southern elected officials at higher levels of office holding were increasingly likely to have arrived in these positions through the traditional political opportunity structure that Schlesinger (1986) identified. In figure 7.13 we track the proportion of all southern and southern Republican U.S. House members who previously served in their state's legislature. Looking first at all southern congresspersons, from 1935 to 1964—when virtually all southern MCs were Democrats—

approximately one in three House members previously served in their state's legislature with no upward or downward trend. However, beginning in 1964 and continuing through the close of the data in 1995, this proportion modestly but steadily increased, approaching one in two House members. When we narrow our focus to southern Republicans, in 1964 (when sufficient numbers are present to make a meaningful comparison for the first time) just 11% of members had previously served in their state's legislature. This share increased robustly to more than two in five by the 1990s. The growth in the number of southern Republicans in the House was achieved in part by the progressive ambition of its officeholders.

The Emergence of Ambitious Politicians in the South

Our final view on this process is of the nature of the kinds of candidates who win election. That is, we have seen the "second" major party in each southern party system (the Whigs forming to contest the Jacksonian Democrats; the return of the Democrats to elections and then to power after Reconstruction; and the Republicans in the two periods of the post–World War II era) becoming more competitive with the first major party in elections. We then saw that, not only were they becoming more competitive, but also they were building the party's electoral arm systematically through the rise of substantial numbers of ambitious politicians up the opportunity structure. Here, we will look at the nature of the winning candidates. What we would like to ask is whether the two emerging major parties were attracting the kinds of politicians we take to be careerists in mature party systems. We cannot do that for the early periods, but we can look at those who emerged successfully from the electoral system. That is, we will look at the people elected to the U.S. House (giving us the largest number of officeholders rather far up the opportunity structure) in each of the periods to see if there are significant differences between North and South. In particular, we have seen traces of southern party systems approaching the level of professionalism characteristic of the North, but it was not until the period beginning in 1980 that the two major parties in the South were fully developed and thus should be fully approaching the ability to attract professionally oriented young politicos.

In the contemporary period, the measurement of "serious" challengers has a rich history. The first and simplest measure, whether someone had run for elective office in the past, has long stood the test of "best efficient measure," since Jacobson originally proposed it (1989).[13] But, of course, that is endogenous to what we are doing here. The idea of the "bottom-up" results is precisely that many are moving sequentially up the opportunity structure, such that by the time we look at the U.S. House, there will be many challengers running for it who have already held elective office. Thus we are led to look at alternative measures of attributes of victors that would indicate they are more rather than less "professional" in their political careerism. And, of course, we are limited by what might be able to be collected in the early nineteenth century.

Given that there is no one direct measure, we have chosen to examine three different variables that could be expected to show traces of a more professionalized versus more amateur character. Informal electoral politics tends to favor those already well known, as voters look for cues to guide them in this less well-structured electoral environment. As a result, there is a tendency for families to form multigenerational dynasties in less professionalized environments. To be sure, the very names Bush, Clinton, and Kennedy, among others, illustrate that there are "royal" families even in the most mature party systems. Still, the incidence of such should be lower, if young, ambitious strivers are better able to make their own careers on the basis of high levels of skilled campaigning. And, of course, we would be saying that this is a tendency that should mark the South more than the North, if the South has been less professional in its electoral politics.[14]

Similarly, with stronger candidates running at all levels, one would imagine that the age of entry into high levels of office, such as the U.S. House, would be older than in a less professionalized setting, because to compete in such systems one needs to have established a personal reputation and following, rather than joining the party to help provide such credibility.

Finally, and perhaps most directly, if ambitious politicians start their careers at entry level offices and climb the opportunity structure systematically, the more professionalized polities would be expected to have incoming officeholders having held a larger number of prior political offices. In figure 7.14, we report the difference between North and South in each of these three variables in each of the four periods. These are oriented such that a positive number indicates the North was more professionalized than the South. Thus, the "dynasty" variable looks at the difference in the percentage of southern MCs who had a relative who had served in Congress before them less the similar percentage from other states. "Age" subtracts the average age of entering MCs from the South from the similar age of those from the North. And, "prior offices" subtracts the average number of offices held by incoming MCs from the South from that for those from the North. While there is variation across the first three periods, it is in-

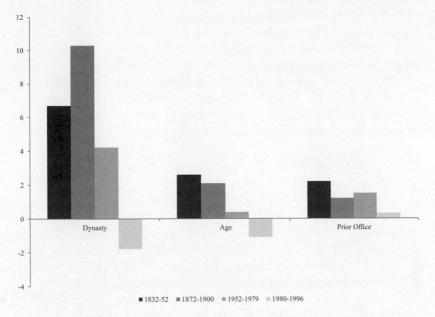

Figure 7.14 North-South comparisons of characteristics of politicians elected to the U.S. House

deed the case that the North and South were different from each other on all measures, in such a way that the evidence indicates politicians from the North were more "professional," while the South had less developed parties available for young careerists. The most recent era (post-1980) is sharply different, as the South "leads" the North for the first time on two of these indicators, while on the third, the two regions are essentially equal. That is, we can conclude that the evidence is consistent with the position that the South finally has a system that features two parties as fully professionalized as their northern counterparts.

CONCLUSION

This chapter has built upon the evidence in chapters 3–6 documenting that the South for most of its history had an underdeveloped party system to show that this state of affairs had an important consequence— less competitive elections. With time, elections in each period became more competitive, albeit only temporarily in the two nineteenth-century periods. Further, they became competitive, at least in part, through the systematic movement of ambitious politicians from lower to higher levels of political office. Moreover, we have seen that the maturation of the party system in elections, organization, and government is systematically associated with greater electoral competition. Finally, when elections finally became fully competitive in the South and in a sustained way, the parties were finally able to recruit politicians that were typical of politicians elsewhere in the sense that they were professionalized and, as we show next, positioned to represent the interests of voters.

8 COMPETITIVE PARTY SYSTEMS AND DEMOCRATIC RESPONSIVENESS

In chapters 3 to 6, we observed a substantial gap in the development of the party systems of the South and the North in the nineteenth and twentieth centuries. We have also seen (in chapter 7) that differences in the development of the party systems resulted in systematically less electoral competition in the South. Our theoretical claim in chapter 2 was that a competitive party system in equilibrium is a necessary condition for an effective democracy. We sought to show in chapter 7 that only in the last generation has the South caught up fully with the rest of the nation in terms of its party competition, such that, in the twenty-first century, the two major parties attract highly professionally oriented politicians, their pipeline for expressing and realizing that ambition is essentially full all around, and the two parties have settled into a sort of fully developed equilibrium individually and thus into a fully developed equilibrium as a two-party system in the North and in the South. Here, we examine whether this has indeed appeared to be reflected in the emergence, at least in the South, of an effective democracy and in particular whether elected officials are responsive to the policy preferences of their citizens.

More specifically, we examine regional differences in government responsiveness in two areas for each of the historical periods we have studied. First, we compare the relationship between public opinion and legislator roll call decisions in each region to determine if lawmakers in each region are equally responsive to citizens' policy preferences. In this we are able to make a complete and exhaustive testing, comparing between regions and over time. We then turn to compare regional measures of lawmaker responsiveness beyond roll call voting such as

per capita appropriations, legislative effectiveness, and constituent service activity, where and when we are able to do so.

RESPONSIVENESS

One critical way that we might judge whether democracy is effective
is to assess whether the outcomes of government decision making are
responsive to the policy preferences of citizens (e.g., Dahl 2000; Huber and Powell 1994; Przeworski, Stokes, and Manin 1999; Blais and
Bodet 2006; for a review see Powell 2004). We argued in chapter 2
that electoral competition is a necessary condition for democracies
to be effective. Thus, we would also expect that electoral competition
will enhance government responsiveness and its absence would lead
to government laxity.

One way that electoral competition induces responsiveness is by
enhancing the likelihood that voters will be afforded an opportunity to
support capable candidates. In the last chapter, we found that southern
lawmakers tended to possess characteristics that suggest they were of
lower "quality" as lawmakers compared to their more professionalized
northern peers. This is due in part to the failure of a fully articulated
two-party system to develop in the South until recently, and thus the
less developed party tended to attract less well qualified individuals. In
the twentieth century, for example, because the southern Democrats
had little in the way of organized opposition until around the 1980s,
they, too, allowed organization to wane (in the absence of reason to
invest heavily for competitive purposes), and they too attracted somewhat less well qualified figures. An inference from these findings in the
last chapter is that southern elected officials have historically been less
equipped to respond to the preferences of their constituents.

A second way that competition induces responsiveness is more
direct. Even given our findings in the last chapter, southern elected
officials still might have been perfectly capable individuals. Perhaps,
however, they simply did not face the necessary degree of electoral
pressure to induce their attention to constituents' needs. That is the
focus of this chapter.

Next, we examine in each region and for each period whether, when
citizens voted more liberally, their legislators also voted more liberally.
We examine, that is, what legislative scholars have termed "responsiveness" (e.g., Achen 1978; Erikson 1978; Ansolabehere, Snyder, and
Stewart 2001). If the estimated effect of district or state liberalism on
legislator roll call liberalism is greater in one region than in the other,
we will conclude that the legislators in that region are more responsive
to variation in regional public opinion.

We measure roll call liberalism using a legislator's first-dimension DW-NOMINATE coordinate in a given Congress (e.g., Ansolabehere, Snyder, and Stewart 2001; Clinton, Jackman, and Rivers 2004; Griffin 2006). These scores are reflected from their original and usual direction such that higher scores indicate more liberal voting behavior. We map this measure onto the liberalism of the legislator's district as measured prior to the legislator's roll call votes. So, an estimated positive relationship between the two will reveal that legislators who represent more liberal districts vote more liberally than do legislators who represent less liberal districts.

We measure congressional district and state liberalism using the congressional district (or in the case of senators, the state's) two-party presidential election vote share for the Democratic Party (e.g., Griffin 2006, among others). A few details are worth noting. First, for all our analyses where we pool data across years, we normalize the presidential vote measure by subtracting the national proportion of the vote received by the Democratic presidential candidate in that year. Doing so makes these data more comparable across years—districts and states that consistently support the Democratic presidential candidate at rates stronger than the national average will take on positive values and districts/states that are consistently more Republican than the national average in their presidential voting will take on negative values. Next, in the post–World War II period where data are more plentiful, we do not impute district/state ideology for Congresses that follow midterm elections, so our analyses focus only on those Congresses that follow presidential elections. In the Whig and post-Reconstruction periods, where data are sparser, our analyses impute presidential vote share (using the immediately preceding presidential election) for Congresses commencing after a midterm election. Finally, in a few instances the presidential vote measure precedes a round of redistricting while a legislator's roll call voting follows that round. We omit these cases from the analysis.[1]

We are interested in the total effect as well as specifically the direct effect of citizen preferences on MC roll call voting. Constituents' preferences affect whether a Democrat or a Republican is elected, and members' party affiliations independently affect their roll call decisions, so citizens' preferences indirectly affect roll call voting. At the same time, elected officials may be directly attentive to their constituents' preferences when making roll call decisions. To make both of these comparisons, we will examine the effect of constituent opinion on roll call voting both with and without factoring in legislator partisanship, which surely mediates the two (Lee, Moretti, and Butler 2004).

Jacksonian Period

We begin with the Jacksonian era. In some of our models, we control for legislators' party affiliations (Democrats and Jacksonians coded 1, Whigs and Anti-Jacksonians coded 0). Our data span the Twenty-Third to the Thirty-Third Congresses (1833–53). According to Poole and Rosenthal (1997, 66–67), the Whigs were the more "conservative" of the two parties on the first dimension, supportive of developing the nation's manufacturing sector via a high tariff, a growth-oriented monetary policy, and internal improvements to roads and canals. Thus, if MCs and senators are responsive to the regional variation in opinion across states, the district/state liberalism measure will be positively related to roll call liberalism. The results for the U.S. House and Senate are presented in tables 8.1 and 8.2, respectively.

Outside the South, House members in both chambers were responsive to the variation in opinion across states (tables 8.1 and 8.2, column 1). More liberal states were represented by representatives who voted more liberally on the economic dimension. We interpret the substantive magnitude of the Senate parameter estimate below. The same cannot be said for the South. Southern legislators were much less responsive than were northern legislators (in the House), or totally unresponsive altogether (in the Senate) (column 2).

The results in columns 3 and 4 of both tables first confirm that Democratic members were much more likely to vote liberally, as we have supposed, and that this was true in both regions. These results also indicate that the effect of House district liberalism in the North was in part direct, and in part indirect, while in the South the original positive effect observed in the House was entirely due to party affiliation. Once that was controlled, the southern House member was unresponsive to his district. In the Senate, meanwhile, the effect of roll call liberalism in the North was entirely indirect—more liberal states tended to elect Democrats who voted liberally. In the South, state liberalism is actually negatively related to senator roll call liberalism once we account for senators' party affiliations. Senator partisanship had similar effects on roll call behavior in each region, but in the South, state ideology was a much weaker predictor of senator partisanship, if it was a systematic predictor at all.

To illustrate the magnitude and importance of the regional difference in responsiveness, figure 8.1 reports regression lines for the relationship between state liberalism and senator roll call liberalism for U.S. senators serving between 1832 and 1852.[2] As the figure shows, in the North, senators clearly tended to vote more liberally when they

Table 8.1 House member responsiveness by region, 1832–52

	North	South	North	South
District liberalism	1.554**	0.353**	0.212**	−0.023
	[0.073]	[0.054]	[0.048]	[0.035]
Democrat			0.520**	0.409**
			[0.009]	[0.012]
Constant	−0.771**	0.099**	−0.398**	0.058**
	[0.037]	[0.031]	[0.022]	[0.019]
R^2	0.23	0.06	0.74	0.66
N	1,548	670	1,548	670

* $p < .05$; ** $p < .01$; standard errors in brackets.
Note: Dropping districts in which less than 50% of the population is contained in whole counties (method used by Ansolabehere, Snyder, and Stewart 2001) Dropping all districts with partial counties.

Table 8.2 Senator responsiveness by region, 1832–52

	North	South	North	South
State liberalism	1.295**	0.082	0.025	−0.247**
	[0.164]	[0.104]	[0.103]	[0.058]
Democrat			0.725**	0.520**
			[0.025]	[0.024]
Constant	−0.027	0.341**	−0.356**	0.063**
	[0.020]	[0.028]	[0.016]	[0.019]
R^2	0.14	0.00	0.72	0.71
N	399	199	399	199

* $p < .05$; ** $p < .01$; standard errors in brackets.

represented states that were more supportive of the Democrats' presidential candidates. For instance, we would expect a northern state where the Democratic presidential candidate's support was one standard deviation less than the mean to be represented by a senator with a roll call score of −.15 (on a −1 to +1 scale), while a state where the Democratic presidential candidate's support was one standard deviation above the mean to be represented by a senator with a roll call score of .28. In contrast, a southern senator representing the second state would vote no more liberally than the first. In sum, outside the South, as states became more liberal, their senators voted more liberally—that is, senators as a group were responsive to the variation in citizen ideology across states (and, of course, perhaps vice versa). In the South, senators were not similarly responsive, or indeed were not responsive to public opinion at all.

Thus far, we have examined lawmaker responsiveness on Poole and

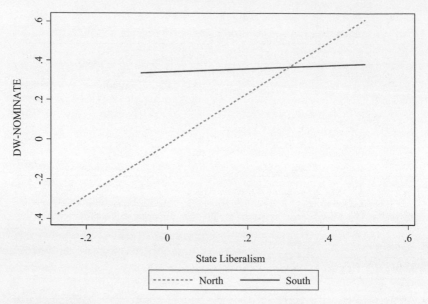

Figure 8.1 Effect of state liberalism on senator liberalism, 1832–52, by region

Rosenthal's first dimension of roll call voting, which they identify as reflecting social welfare and economic issues. Perhaps southern representatives' voting on noneconomic issues was more responsive to state preferences than was their northern counterparts' voting on these issues, in the same way that northerners' voting was more responsive to district/state liberalism on economic issues. This might be especially true on votes related to slavery. To examine this, following Poole and Rosenthal's guidance that the second dimension of roll call voting was dominated by slavery votes in the Thirtieth and Thirty-First Senates (1997), we regressed representatives' second-dimension roll call liberalism score in these Congresses on district liberalism, measured as above. Based on the manner in which we measure ideology, using presidential voting behavior in the district, we contend that this measure reflects citizens' first- and second-dimension preferences, perhaps weighted based on the importance of each dimension to the state's residents.

In the North, MCs were responsive directly and indirectly to citizens' preferences (see table 8.3). Democrats were more likely to uphold slavery, and independent of this, members representing districts that voted Democratic were also more likely to uphold slavery. In the South, district liberalism's effect on roll call voting was at least as large as in the North, and perhaps larger. However, the effect was totally indirect, at least statistically. That is, House members from the South did not vote more liberally when their constituents did, at least not significantly so, once we account for party.

In contrast, there is no evidence that southern senators were more responsive than northern senators to state preferences when voting on slavery (table 8.4). What is different is the mechanism. In the North, Democratic senators were much more likely to uphold slavery than were northern Whigs, and states that were more supportive of Democratic presidential candidates were generally more likely to elect Democratic senators.[3] Responsiveness was, in other words, entirely indirect. In the South, senator responsiveness to public sentiment was much more direct. Democratic senators were more likely than Whigs to uphold slavery, but the magnitude of this tendency was only half what it was in the North. This left substantial room for southern state liberalism to directly affect senator voting on slavery.

Table 8.3 House member responsiveness by region on slavery votes, Thirtieth and Thirty-First Congresses

	North	South	North	South
District liberalism	1.487**	1.896**	0.665*	0.249
	[0.265]	[0.304]	[0.260]	[0.265]
Democrat			0.003**	0.008**
			[0.000]	[0.001]
Constant	−0.527**	−1.438**	−0.367**	−1.208**
	[0.130]	[0.157]	[0.119]	[0.114]
R^2	0.10	0.25	0.27	0.62
N	293	120	293	120

* $p < .05$; ** $p < .01$; standard errors in brackets.

Table 8.4 Senator responsiveness by region on slavery votes, Thirtieth and Thirty-First Senates

	North	South	North	South
State liberalism	3.984**	3.154**	0.515	1.766*
	[0.753]	[0.709]	[0.602]	[0.703]
Democrat			0.875**	0.381**
			[0.088]	[0.100]
Constant	0.118	−0.675**	−0.212**	−0.840**
	[0.060]	[0.069]	[0.051]	[0.073]
R^2	0.28	0.37	0.70	0.56
N	74	36	74	36

* $p < .05$; ** $p < .01$; standard errors in brackets.

Post-Reconstruction

As a group, southern elected officials in the post-Reconstruction period again were less responsive than were northern lawmakers to the variation in opinion that existed across their region, even among voting citizens (i.e., white males).

When we compare the overall effect of citizen ideology on roll call liberalism in the House, we find that northern representatives were nearly six times as responsive as southern representatives in the post-Reconstruction period (table 8.5, columns 1 and 2). When we control for representatives' party affiliations, the estimated effect of district liberalism on legislator roll call liberalism drops dramatically in both regions (table 8.5, columns 3–4), indicating that the effect of citizens' preferences is mostly indirect, operating via their connection to legislators' party affiliations. We also note the difference in the substantive and statistical significance of the estimates—outside the South district liberalism continues to exert a direct effect whereas in the South there is no systematic, direct effect after accounting for party. The northern advantage in responsiveness during this period extends to both parties (columns 5–8).[4] Among Democrats in particular, northern MCs were responsive to variation in district ideology; however, among northern Republican MCs, there was a smaller but still statistically significant effect of district ideology on MC roll call liberalism.

In the comparable table for U.S. senators (table 8.6), northern legislators were more than twice as responsive as southern legislators overall. When we control for senators' party affiliations, the estimated effect of state liberalism on their legislators' roll call liberalism drops to zero outside the South (column 3), indicating that the effect of citizens' preferences is entirely indirect via their connection to senators' party affiliations. In the South, accounting for party reveals that within parties citizens' preferences were actually *negatively* related to their legislators' voting behavior. This is driven home by the results in the table's last two columns. In sum, in the post-Reconstruction period northern representatives were much more responsive than southern representatives to differences in the ideology of their constituents in district and in state.[5]

We illustrate the substantive difference between the regions in figure 8.2 for the U.S. House data. The figure fits trend lines to scatter plots of the association between district support for the Democratic presidential nominee (normalized against the mean) and the roll call behavior of the district's House representative. In the North, more liberal districts tended to be represented by more liberal legislators.[6] Northern

Table 8.5 House representatives' responsiveness by region and party, 1876–1902

	(1) North	(2) South	(3) North	(4) South	(5) North GOP	(6) South GOP	(7) North Dem	(8) South Dem
District liberalism	1.973** [0.062]	0.358** [0.045]	0.203** [0.023]	0.015 [0.018]	0.100** [0.026]	-0.023 [0.083]	0.563** [0.052]	0.017 [0.018]
Democrat			0.775** [0.005]	0.865** [0.011]				
Constant	-0.100** [0.007]	0.370** [0.010]	-0.431** [0.003]	-0.370** [0.010]	-0.439** [0.003]	-0.371** [0.011]	0.331** [0.004]	0.495** [0.004]
R^2	0.28	0.06	0.92	0.86	0.01	0.00	0.12	0.00
N	2,581	1,034	2,581	1,034	1,727	103	854	931

$* p < .05$; $** p < .01$; standard errors in brackets. District liberalism interpolated for midterm years using most recent presidential vote. Congress following 1882 elections omitted due to redistricting.

Table 8.6 Senator responsiveness by region and MC party affiliation, 1876–1902

	North	South	North	South	North	South
	All	All	All	All	Democrats	Democrats
State liberalism	1.354**	0.560**	−0.000	−0.286**	0.312**	−0.248**
	[0.118]	[0.118]	[0.042]	[0.064]	[0.115]	[0.068]
Democrat			0.835**	0.819**		
			[0.010]	[0.026]		
Constant	−0.675**	0.109	−0.322**	−0.074*	0.353**	0.720**
	[0.054]	[0.076]	[0.018]	[0.038]	[0.060]	[0.045]
N	782	310	782	310	234	271
R^2	0.14	0.07	0.91	0.78	0.03	0.05

* $p < .05$; ** $p < .01$; standard errors in brackets. Too few Republican and Populist senators to analyze separately.

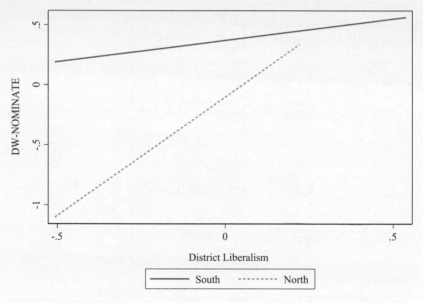

Figure 8.2 Effect of district ideology on U.S. representative roll call liberalism by region, 1876–1902

lawmakers were strongly responsive. In contrast, in the South, legis-lators representing more liberal districts voted only modestly more liberally than legislators representing more conservative districts.

If slavery was the dominant second-dimension issue in the Jackso-nian period, the dominant second-dimension issue in the 1890s was currency, or whether the nation would stay on the gold standard or move to bimetallism (Poole and Rosenthal 1997). As we note above,

Table 8.7 U.S. currency votes in Fifty-Second and Fifty-Third Houses (1891–95)

	North	South	North	South
District liberalism	0.609*	0.240	−0.143	0.232
	[0.245]	[0.171]	[0.269]	[0.177]
Democrat			0.315**	0.028
			[0.054]	[0.154]
Constant	0.127**	−0.108**	−0.077	−0.133
	[0.025]	[0.039]	[0.043]	[0.146]
R^2	0.02	0.01	0.09	0.01
N	407	155	407	155

* $p < .05$; ** $p < .01$; standard errors in brackets. Twenty-nine votes in Fifty-Second House; forty-one votes in Fifty-Third House (Poole and Rosenthal 1997).

farmers contended that tying the currency to the gold standard constrained the extent to which their debt would be managed by inflation. We test whether the regional gap in responsiveness we have just observed on the primary, economic dimension extends to the other primary sphere of conflict. As our source of data, we focus on the DW-NOMINATE second dimension of roll call votes from 1891 to 1895. Upon doing so, we find that the regional difference in responsiveness we observed with respect to the primary dimension of disagreement in this period is mirrored in currency votes (table 8.7). Northern MCs who represented strongly Democratic districts were much more likely to oppose the gold standard and kindred policies in these Congresses. In contrast, across the South no such relationship existed. Finally, the relationship in the North was indirect—Democratic districts elected Democrats who were more likely to oppose the gold standard (table 8.7, column 3).

These differences in responsiveness are consonant with the observations of historians of the period who conceptualize representation as proximity of interest between citizens and officials rather than responsiveness of officials to citizens' interests (Achen 1978). For instance, Woodward (1971) contended that officials who represented and were elected by farmers regularly did not represent their interests:

> Among the seventeen Democratic Congressmen elected by Mississippi between 1876 and 1890, a careful investigation was able to find only seven who sympathized with, worked for, and were approved by the farmers. (18)

And (Woodward 1971) goes on to say,

One heated contest after another arose to divide the white man's party. In each conflict—whether with bondholders over the state debt, with the bankers over a usury law, with the merchants over protection of fertilizer consumers, or with railroads over rates—the popular side of the issue was opposed by the Redeemers with striking consistency. (19)

And then there was the matter of sovereignty. As Woodward observed, in one southern state after another the ability of citizens to govern themselves evaporated at the local level. In North Carolina, state law provided that "the legislature should name the justices of peace, who in turn were to elect the commissioners of their respective counties, thus making the principal county officer appointive" (Woodward 1971).

> In . . . North Carolina, almost the first step taken by the legislature after the downfall of Republican power was the passing of a county-government act that, according to one historian, "violated every principle of local self-government." The law provided that the legislature should name the justices of peace, who in turn were to elect the commissioners of their respective counties, thus making the principal county officer appointive. By this means the "black" counties of the east were assured white government, but by the same device western "white" counties lost control of their local affairs to a highly centralized party machine. Thirty members of the legislature of 1876 signed a "solemn protest" against the act upon its passage. Twenty years later they were echoed by a Populist outburst that pronounced the system "as mean a piece of political machinery as ever was devised," for it put the financial affairs of every county into the hands of an irresponsible oligarchy.[7] (54)

In Louisiana (Woodward 1971),

> In the hands of the governor, instead of the legislature, was placed "an inordinate appointive power." He appointed the police jury of every parish, which levied local taxes and enacted local laws, as well as all rural school boards, all executive boards and boards of trustees of state institutions, numerous judges, and all registrars, who passed upon the eligibility of voters. (54–55)

"The corresponding device in Florida was even simpler. In the hands of the governor, instead of the legislature, was placed 'an inordinate appointive power'" (Woodward 1971).

> The constitution placed in the hands of the governor the power to appoint (with confirmation by the senate) in each county the tax collector and assessor, treasurer, surveyor, superintendent of schools, county

commissioners, sheriff, clerk of court, county judge, and justices of the peace—thus leaving to the uninhibited franchise of free Floridians the choice of constables. . . . Clearly the restoration of "home rule" in Florida did not bring sovereignty very close to home. (54–55).[8]

And, as a last illustration:

> Describing the situation in the Upper South, William L. Royall stated that "the elections in Virginia became a farce. We got rid of negro government but we got in place of it a government resting upon fraud and chicanery, and it very soon became a serious question which was worse, a negro government or a white government resting upon stuffed ballot boxes." (58)[9]

The Modern Period

In keeping with the periodization of the modern era above, we first present responsiveness analyses for the period 1952–80. Our purpose in analyzing just the first portion of the modern era is to compare lawmaker responsiveness prior to the full emergence of a two-party system and electoral competition across the South to the results of an analysis upon its emergence (1980–2012). Again, we choose 1980 as our break point based on Black and Black's claim that "Reagan's presidency was the turning point in the evolution of a competitive, two-party electorate in the South" (2002, 25).

We begin with the House of Representatives (table 8.8). Looking first at the total (direct and indirect) effect of district preferences on MC roll call voting prior to 1980 (columns 1 and 2), the ratio of responsiveness outside the South to inside the South is a little less than 4.0 (2.12/.55). When we control for MC party to examine the direct effect of citizens' preferences (columns 3 and 4), the responsiveness gap remains—northern MCs were still nearly three times as responsive as southern MCs. Outside the South, the direct effect of citizens' preferences exceeds the estimated size of the total effect within the South. Last, the estimated indirect effect of MC party affiliation is again somewhat larger in the North than in the South.

Next, responsiveness might differ by party. This might account for the results thus far if Republicans are more responsive than Democrats, since a much larger proportion of northern than southern MCs during this period were Republicans. To investigate this possibility, we estimated the effect of citizens' preferences on MC roll call liberalism by party and region (columns 5–8). The MCs of both parties were more responsive outside than inside the South. Northern Democrats were nearly three times as responsive as southern Democrats (columns

Table 8.8 House representatives' responsiveness by region and party, 1952–80

	(1) North	(2) South	(3) North	(4) South	(5) North Dem	(6) South Dem	(7) North GOP	(8) South GOP
District liberalism	2.120** [0.051]	0.552** [0.054]	0.773** [0.033]	0.262** [0.046]	0.703** [0.034]	0.246** [0.052]	0.973** [0.070]	0.388** [0.090]
Democrat			0.546** [0.007]	0.342** [0.017]				
Constant	−0.011 [0.006]	−0.021** [0.008]	−0.253** [0.004]	−0.298** [0.015]	0.299** [0.005]	0.045** [0.008]	−0.245** [0.005]	−0.289** [0.012]
R^2	0.43	0.12	0.83	0.42	0.27	0.04	0.15	0.13
N	2,301	752	2,299	752	1,157	628	1,142	124

* $p < .05$; ** $p < .01$; standard errors in brackets.

5 and 6). Because there were relatively few Republican MCs in the South during this period, we must be more cautious about our conclusions. When we compare the estimated effect of citizens' preferences on Republicans' roll call liberalism in each region (columns 7 and 8), we find that northern Republicans were more than twice as responsive as southern Republicans. The substantive effect of these findings is illustrated in figure 8.3. Prior to 1980, and within the South, districts that were somewhat more liberal-leaning were represented by only slightly more liberal members of the House. In the North, responsiveness to the variation in public sentiment across districts was much more vibrant. The figure also suggests that this phenomenon was not owing to restricted variation in southern district liberalism. Appendix B to this chapter provides a more careful consideration (and dismissal) of this alternative interpretation.

The story in the Senate prior to 1980 is much the same (table 8.9). The total effect of state liberalism on senator roll call liberalism is much greater in the North than in the South; indeed, there is no systematic relationship between these phenomena in the South at all (columns 1 and 2). The magnitude of the effect in the North is about the same as we observed among northern House members in table 8.8. After we account for senators' party affiliations, there remains a direct effect

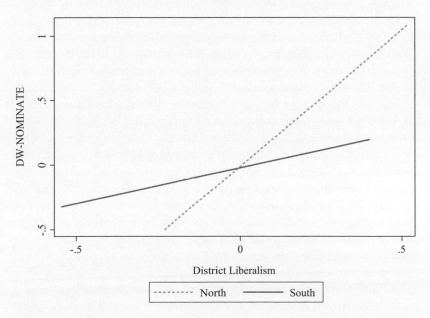

Figure 8.3 Effect of district liberalism on U.S. representative liberalism by region, 1952–80

Table 8.9 Senator responsiveness by region, 1952–80

	North	South	North	South
State liberalism	2.179**	0.089	0.937**	−0.037
	[0.161]	[0.106]	[0.095]	[0.082]
Democrat			0.585**	0.495**
			[0.012]	[0.034]
Constant	0.076**	−0.009	−0.223**	−0.438**
	[0.010]	[0.015]	[0.009]	[0.032]
R^2	0.14	0.00	0.72	0.41
N	1,096	313	1,096	313

* $p < .05$; ** $p < .01$; standard errors in brackets.

of state preferences on senator roll call voting in the North, although it is about half the size of the total effect. After controlling for party in the South, we see that senator partisanship affected roll call voting similarly in both regions, and there remains no relationship between citizens' preferences and senator roll call voting. So, southern Democrats tended to vote more liberally just as they did in the North, but the more liberal (i.e., moderate) of the southern states did not reliably elect Democratic senators. Even when southern senators all hailed from one party, the variation in state ideology reflected in presidential voting did not systematically affect senator roll call liberalism.

What, then, of the most current period, 1980–2010? Looking first at the total effect of citizens' preferences on legislator roll call liberalism (table 8.10, columns 1 and 2), responsiveness inside the South over the last three decades has caught up to, and nudged in front of, responsiveness among northern MCs. When we account for MC party to examine the direct effect of citizens' preferences (columns 3 and 4), the degree to which responsiveness in the South surpasses responsiveness in the North is even clearer. In both regions, the direct effect of citizens' preferences is relatively small compared to the total effect, indicating that a good deal of the responsiveness mechanism works indirectly through members' party affiliations. Indeed, the estimated effect of MC party affiliation on legislator roll call liberalism in both regions is relatively large compared to the estimated effects in table 8.8. Among Democrats, southern MCs appear quite a bit more responsive than northern MCs (columns 5 and 6). Finally, among Republicans (columns 7 and 8), we find that northern Republicans exhibit somewhat higher levels of responsiveness than southern Republicans.

Overall, however, legislators today appear to be just as responsive to the public in the North and in the South when they cast roll call votes. This is illustrated most starkly in figure 8.4, which again plots the

Table 8.10 House representatives' responsiveness by region and party, 1980–2010

	(1) North	(2) South	(3) North	(4) South	(5) North Dem	(6) South Dem	(7) North GOP	(8) South GOP
District liberalism	2.091**	2.223**	0.766**	0.937**	0.688**	0.995**	1.049**	0.804**
	[0.046]	[0.078]	[0.026]	[0.048]	[0.025]	[0.060]	[0.065]	[0.083]
Democrat			0.671**	0.575**				
			[0.007]	[0.012]				
Constant	−0.072**	−0.100**	−0.376**	−0.406**	0.304**	0.166**	−0.367**	−0.415**
	[0.007]	[0.010]	[0.005]	[0.008]	[0.004]	[0.008]	[0.006]	[0.009]
R^2	0.45	0.48	0.87	0.86	0.36	0.37	0.19	0.19
N	2,534	880	2,529	879	1,402	465	1,127	414

* $p < .05$; ** $p < .01$; standard errors in brackets.

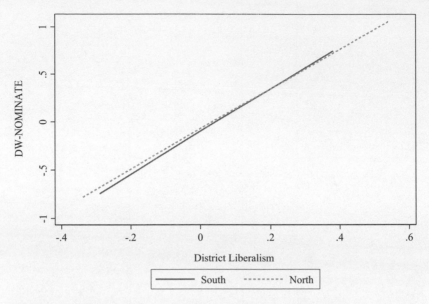

Figure 8.4 Effect of district liberalism on U.S. representative liberalism by region, 1980–2010

regression line for both regions. At long last, the regression lines for the two regions are parallel; indeed, they are nearly identical as they almost intersect the horizontal axis at the same point as well.[10]

In this modern period we are fortunate to also be able to measure citizen opinion using public opinion surveys rather than voting behavior. To examine the robustness of our finding that representation among southern MCs rivaled that of northern MCs by century's end, we modeled House roll call voting (CQ Key Votes 2000–2012)[11] using measures of public opinion in the same policy domain (National Annenberg Election Study, Cooperative Congressional Election Study). For instance, we modeled whether a legislator cast a conservative roll call vote on the Child Health Insurance Program as a function of district opinion on government providing health insurance to citizens. In doing so, we pooled across multiple issues such that our model included approximately 8,400 observations. When we estimate this model among southern and northern states, we find that the estimated effect of opinion in the South (.77) is statistically indistinguishable from its estimated effect in the North (.83). This is as we would expect for this period and given our findings reported above.

When we model senator voting after 1980, we find that there has been substantial regional convergence. Whereas prior to 1980 southern senators' roll call voting was not at all responsive to state liberalism, af-

Table 8.11 Senator responsiveness by region, 1980–2010

	North	South	North	South
State Liberalism	2.185**	1.471**	0.985**	0.245*
	[0.104]	[0.291]	[0.047]	[0.113]
Democrat			0.629**	0.661**
			[0.008]	[0.014]
Constant	0.002	−0.127**	−0.306**	−0.436**
	[0.009]	[0.019]	[0.006]	[0.010]
R^2	0.26	0.07	0.87	0.87
N	1,261	356	1,261	356

* $p < .05$; ** $p < .01$; standard errors in brackets.

ter 1980 responsiveness is considerable, and about two-thirds as strong as among northern senators. In the North, responsiveness prior to and after 1980 was virtually the same (compare tables 8.9 and 8.11, column 1). Taken together, these findings point to substantial movement toward similarity of responsiveness across regions. When senators' party affiliations are incorporated into the model it is observed that almost all of the responsiveness in the South is indirect, whereas about half of the responsiveness in the North is indirect. That indirect action through party, however, is about the same in the two regions.

In earlier periods we examined responsiveness on the second dimension of roll call voting (covering slavery issues and currency votes in the two nineteenth-century periods, respectively). An interpretation of those two dimensions is that they tapped the domains that were particularly at issue in the South. Slavery is obvious, but the threat of the Populist Party in the South was to unite working-class blacks and whites against the middle- and upper-class whites, and that would be done on economic issues such as bimetallism. Perhaps southern legislators were much more responsive than northern legislators in the contemporary period on civil rights roll calls, given the special salience of these votes for southerners, even though civil rights was changing in this period from essentially defining the second dimension (such as in the House data, below) to becoming fully aligned with the first dimension (over the period included in the Senate votes, below). To test this, we repeated our responsiveness analyses using legislators' civil rights roll call coordinates in selected Congresses. Specifically, Poole and Rosenthal (1997, 49) identify one Congress (the Eighty-Ninth, 1965–67) during this period in which House representatives' roll call voting exhibited a second dimension that they identify (based on roll call content) as civil rights/desegregation/busing. Poole and Rosenthal identify nine Senates during the modern period in which voting exhibited a second, at least partly civil rights, dimension—the Eighty-Sixth–

Table 8.12 House representatives' responsiveness on civil rights votes by region and party, Eighty-Ninth House

	North	South	North	South	North Democrats	South Democrats
District liberalism	−0.405	−0.077	1.063**	0.377**	0.713**	0.273
	[0.244]	[0.201]	[0.213]	[0.142]	[0.268]	[0.153]
Democrat			−0.599**	−0.686**		
			[0.040]	[0.061]		
Constant	0.340*	−0.692**	−0.232	−0.338**	−0.595**	−0.969**
	[0.158]	[0.107]	[0.128]	[0.079]	[0.182]	[0.083]
R^2	0.01	0.00	0.41	0.55	0.03	0.03
N	326	108	326	108	200	92

$* p < .05; ** p < .01$; standard errors in brackets.

Eighty-Eighth, Ninetieth–Ninety-Second, Ninety-Fourth, Ninety-Sixth, and Ninety-Seventh (Poole and Rosenthal 1997, 50–51).

The results of these analyses, reported in table 8.12 for the House, indicate that southern representatives were not more responsive than their northern peers on these votes in the Eighty-Ninth Congress. In general, district liberalism was not a good predictor of civil rights roll call voting in either region. The reason, it appears, is that while Democrats generally tended to vote more conservatively than Republicans on civil rights matters, among Democrats those representing districts that were more supportive of Johnson in 1964 tended to vote more liberally on civil rights matters. This was especially true in the North.

In the Senate, only northern senators were responsive to the variation in civil rights liberalism across their constituencies (table 8.13). As in the House, Democratic senators voted more conservatively on civil rights roll calls, but after accounting for this, districts that supported Democratic presidential candidates were represented by senators who voted more liberally on civil rights.

In sum, the lack of a mature party system and the less competitive elections associated with it for much of the South's history led its politicians to be less responsive to constituents' concerns. When the region's elections became more competitive after 1980, legislator responsiveness came to look very much like that in the remainder of the country.

BEYOND ROLL CALL VOTING

We can also evaluate the attentiveness of legislators to their constituents using a host of other measures beyond roll call voting. Legis-

Table 8.13 **Senator responsiveness on civil rights votes by region, selected Senates**

Region	North	South	North	South
State liberalism	1.069**	−0.224	2.145**	−0.088
	[0.255]	[0.248]	[0.168]	[0.148]
Democrat			−0.707**	−0.894**
			[0.022]	[0.048]
Constant	0.164**	−0.693**	0.529**	0.034
	[0.017]	[0.031]	[0.016]	[0.043]
R^2	0.02	0.00	0.59	0.65
N	710	197	710	197

* $p < .05$; ** $p < .01$; standard errors in brackets.

lators work to secure federal appropriations for their districts, they sponsor and cosponsor legislation, and they help their constituents in their interactions with the federal government, among other activities. All of these efforts have been the subject of studies concerned with congressional representation, whether it be appropriations (Stein and Bickers 1994; Griffin and Flavin 2011; Martin 2003), bill sponsorship (Frantzich 1979; Schiller 1995; Whitby 2002), constituent service (Johannes and McAdams 1981; Dropp and Peskowitz 2012), or all of these (Wawro 2001; Canon 1999; Volden and Wiseman 2014).

Committee Leadership

We begin with committee leadership, an institutional position that confers significant advantage in the lawmaking process (e.g., Shepsle and Weingast 1987). To assess whether the South's occupation of committee chairs was commensurate with the region's size, we compare the proportion of U.S. House committee chairs occupied by southerners in each Congress with the proportion of House seats occupied by southerners.

Upon doing so, in the Whig era we find that the share of House committee chairs occupied by southerners rivaled and even exceeded the region's share of the chamber from the 1832 to the 1844 elections (figure 8.5[a]). Thereafter, the South's representation among committee chairs tracked its composition of the chamber until the end of the Whig era.

In the period after Reconstruction, after a brief period in which southerners were somewhat underrepresented among committee chairs, for the remainder of the period the southern share of committee chairs and the region's share of the House chamber tracked quite closely (figure 8.5[b]). The conventional wisdom is that southern MCs, by virtue of their greater seniority, have been disproportionately

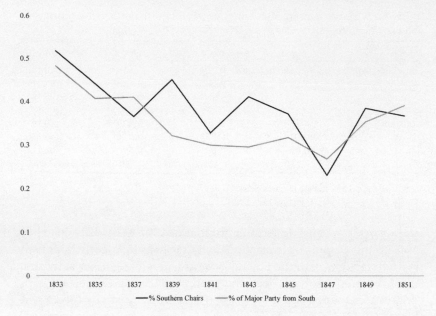

Figure 8.5(a) Southern committee chairs in the U.S. House, 1833–51

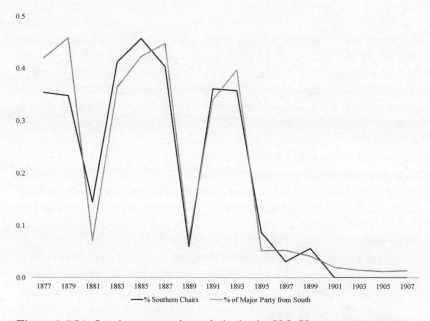

Figure 8.5(b) Southern committee chairs in the U.S. House, 1877–1907

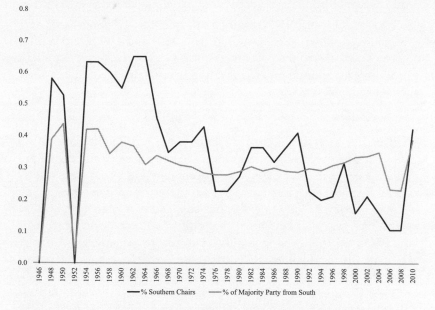

Figure 8.5(c) Southern committee chairs in the U.S. House, 1946–2012

likely to chair the committees of Congress, and used this perch historically to derail, among other things, civil rights reforms in the 1950s. Figure 8.5(c) presents the proportion of committee chairpersons who represented a southern district from 1946 to 2012 (the One Hundred Twelfth Congress), together with the proportion of the majority party hailing from the South. Overall, during this period southern representatives comprised between 25% and 30% of all MCs. Turning our attention to the committee chair data, the first thing to notice is its significant variability, especially in the late 1940s and early 1950s. The dramatic changes in southern chairs from Congress to Congress highlight the downside of one-party dominance in the South. When the Democrats held a majority and controlled chair assignments, southerners enjoyed a much greater representation among chairs than their numbers in Congress (and the majority party) merited. However, when the Democrats (briefly) lost the majority, southern fortunes were reversed. The second thing to notice from these data is that from the 1950s to the 1990s the share of chairs that were southern dropped from three in five to approximately one in four such that by 1992 southerners were underrepresented among chairs compared to both their contribution to the Democratic majority and to the House as a whole (at this point 30% of House members were southern).

Thereafter, the share of chairs that were southern continued to fall until 2010 when the GOP regained control (for a second time) and the southerners that were elected in the 1980s and 1990s had gained sufficient seniority in the party to assume a chairperson role. In 2010, the South's representation among committee chairs again matched its share of the majority party.

Appropriations

We have not located a source for federal appropriations data in the 1800s disaggregated to the state level. So, we proceed directly to the modern period to ask whether in the modern period southern lawmakers have trailed their northern counterparts in bringing money home to the district, and how this has changed over time. For an early perspective, we relied on federal expenditures data reported in Mushkin (1957). In 1952, the regional gap in federal expenditures, or the extent to which northern states received more federal dollars than did southern states, was more than $18.00 per capita ($461 to $442), or 104%.[12] Among the states receiving the lowest per capita federal dollars were South Carolina (ranked thirty-ninth of the forty-eight continental states), Virginia (forty-third), and North Carolina (forty-eighth).

To examine how the regional gap in federal appropriations has changed over time, we utilize data from the U.S. Census Bureau on federal expenditures by state per capita.[13] Figure 8.6 reports the ratio of northern to southern expenditures per capita in 1970, or when regional differences in party competition were starker, in 1981, when the transition to two-party competition in the South was beginning to gain steam, in 1991, and in 2005. In 1970 and in 1981 per capita federal expenditures were 5%–6% greater in northern than in southern states. In 1993 the northern advantage had dropped to 1%, and in 2005 southern states received 4% more federal expenditures on average than their northern counterparts. In 2010, according to the Consolidated Federal Funds Report this ratio remained .96. In sum, in the period that elections in the South were more competitive, southern legislators rivaled their northern colleagues in bringing federal dollars to their districts.

Next, because federal expenditures are affected by a number of factors beyond legislator effort to direct funds to their state or district, we examine a more fine-grained measure of such effort—congressional earmarks. According to the Office of Management and Budget, "Earmarks are funds provided by the Congress for projects, programs, or grants where the purported congressional direction (whether in

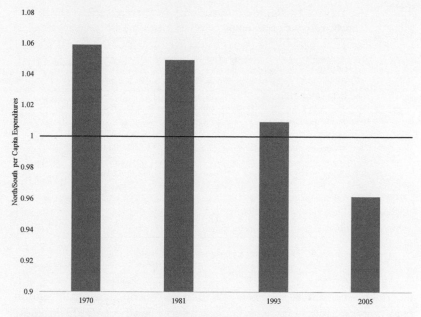

Figure 8.6 Ratio of northern to southern federal per capita expenditures, selected years

statutory text, report language, or other communication) circumvents otherwise applicable merit-based or competitive allocation processes, or specifies the location or recipient, or otherwise curtails the ability of the executive branch to manage its statutory and constitutional responsibilities pertaining to the funds allocation process."[14] We assume that constituents like earmarks, although we acknowledge that some are ambivalent about them.[15] Unfortunately, for our purposes, earmarks are a creature of the modern Congress, so we are unable to compare the regional allocation of earmarks prior to and after 1980. Instead, we simply compare contemporary earmarks by region. Given our observations thus far, we anticipate that we will not observe a regional difference.

Table 8.14 reports models of per capita state earmarks in fiscal years 2008 and 2010 as a function of a southern district indicator, state population (Lee and Oppenheimer 1999), and the proportion of each state's House and Senate delegation that was affiliated with the chamber's majority party in the One Hundred Tenth and One Hundred Eleventh Congresses, respectively. We report multiple fiscal years to account for change in party control of the White House in 2008 and greater Democratic control of the Senate after the 2008

Table 8.14 **Regional similarity of federal**
appropriations, fiscal years 2008 and 2010

	2008	2010
South	11.82	3.845
	(13.85)	(16.44)
Pop. (millions)	−3.031**	−3.030**
	(0.851)	(1.020)
% House major	17.24	29.95
	(19.08)	(19.50)
# Senate major	9.811	−1.981
	(7.002)	(8.185)
Constant	54.67**	54.64**
	(13.82)	(17.12)
N	48	48
R^2	0.24	0.21

* $p < .05$; ** $p < .01$; standard errors in parentheses.

elections. According to these models, there was no statistically significant regional difference in state earmarks in fiscal year 2008 or 2010.
Substantively, in 2008 southern earmarks were $55.84 per capita and
northern earmarks were $58.26 per capita; in 2010 the figures were
$51.80 and $50.94, respectively. We cannot say there was a regional
difference historically, but there certainly is not one today.

Legislative Effectiveness

Legislators engage in a number of bill-related activities beyond roll
call voting that affect the interests and concerns of their constituents.
Indeed, it is in these other domains such as bill introduction, floor
speeches, and the like that legislators can pursue policy agendas that
are not already structured by party leaders.

Our early data on legislative effectiveness come from Johannes and
McAdams (1981). Below, we report comparisons of North/South
mean lawmaker activity using data for the period 1975–81 (annual
bills sponsored); 1975–82 (annual floor speeches); and casework
(1982) (figure 8.7), or at the close of what we have termed the post–
Jim Crow era. For each of these activities we calculated the ratio of
the regional averages (North/South) minus one, so a positive value
reflects the degree to which northern legislators were more engaged
in these activities, and a negative value the extent to which southern
legislators were more engaged. According to these data, in the 1970s
and 1980s southern lawmakers were decidedly less likely than their
northern counterparts to propose legislation and to make speeches on

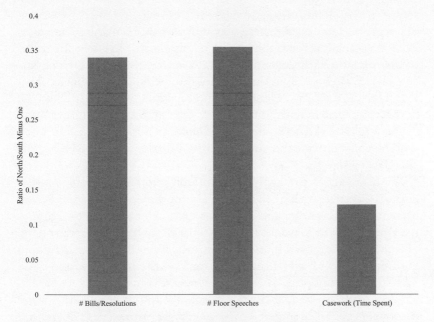

Figure 8.7 Regional comparisons of lawmaker effectiveness, 1975–83

the floor of the House chamber. By both of these measures, southern lawmakers fell behind their northern peers in representing the interests of their constituents, with the latter on average introducing 33% more bills and giving 35% more speeches per MC. This is a considerable disparity. In the third domain we examined, constituent casework, southern legislators devoted less time to this activity than did northern legislators, with the latter devoting approximately 12% more time to the activity. To summarize, in the 1970s southern MCs were less effective legislators in terms of proposing legislation, advocating on behalf of it (or other legislation) on the floor, and devoting time to serving constituent concerns.

These observations are corroborated in recent work by Volden and Wiseman (2014). Using data from 1973 to 2008, and excluding African American legislators from their definition of "Southern Democrats," they found that the "Legislative Effectiveness Scores"[16] of southern Democrats were 20% lower than other Democratic MCs when the Democrats were in the majority (prior to 1994) and 10% lower than other Democrats when Democrats were in the minority. So, southerners' effectiveness was not solely attributable to their tendency to affiliate with one of the parties, combined with which party was in the majority. Following the elections in 2000 and again in 2004, southern Democrats' legislative effectiveness equaled the effectiveness of northern Democrats. Where we differ from Volden and Wiseman is in the explanation for southerners' relative ineffectiveness for much of this period. Their account emphasizes that southern Democrats' votes were, after 1982, not needed by the Democratic majority for it to pursue its legislative agenda, and were similarly not needed by the new Republican majority after 1994. Our alternative interpretation is that a relative dearth of electoral competition in the South did not, until recently, provide the same incentive for southerners to be equally effective legislators.

We also extend the analyses in Volden and Wiseman to another domain—cosponsorship of lawmakers' proposed bills. In figure 8.8 we present data from Adler and Wilkinson (2012) for the Ninety-Third to the One Hundred Eleventh Congress (1972–2010) on cosponsorship of legislators' proposed bills by other lawmakers. When we compared the frequency with which northern and southern legislators' House bills were cosponsored, we observe regional convergence. At the beginning of the period, there is a northern advantage of 20% more cosponsors per bill, compared to southern bills introduced. By the end of this period, the northern advantage had disappeared altogether. It would be a mistake to attribute this trend entirely to the increase in southern Republican MCs together with the party gaining a majority in 1994. Although cosponsorships of southern bills enjoyed their heyday in 1995 and 1996, there are both years prior to 1994 when southerners held an advantage (1976, 1988, 1991, and 1993) as well as years after 1994 when northerners held an advantage (1998–2001 and 2007–10). Indeed, the trend line does not suggest regional parity until 2002. For our purposes the critical point is that bills introduced by southern MCs are now cosponsored at rates that rival their northern peers, where this was not generally the case in the 1970s.

For a more recent regional comparison of constituency service, we turned to the ANES, which queried its respondents from 1978 to 1994 on whether they had ever contacted their House representative to seek help concerning a problem. Because the volume of constituent requests is in part a reflection of how strongly incumbents solicit inquiries by offering up assistance in a visible manner (Yiannakis 1981), the proportion of constituents who report contacting their House incumbent reflects the member's commitment to constituency service. Figure 8.9 reports the proportion of ANES respondents in each region reporting that they had sought help from their House member. According to these data, southerners were often less likely than northerners to seek assistance from 1978 to 1990, and in just one year during

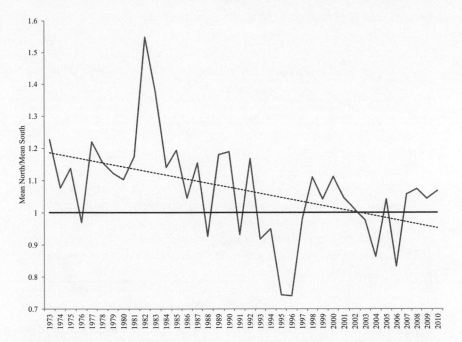

Figure 8.8 Mean cosponsorships per House bill introduced, regional ratio, 1973–2010

this interval were they more likely to do so. However, there is clearly an upward trend evident in southerners' contacting behavior, but not among northerners, and we can conclude that there was little regional difference by the middle of the 1990s.[17]

Finally, to supplement all of this objective evidence of regional differences in political representation we report constituents' subjective impressions of whether their representative is doing a good job. Unfortunately, these data from ANES are only available beginning in 1978 (they continue until 2012); in this era we would generally expect that evaluations of southern MCs should rival the ratings of northern MCs by their constituents. Comparing the regional means of incumbent thermometer ratings by year, we see that indeed southern MCs were just as well liked, and even slightly better liked, by their constituents during this period. Again, this is not terribly surprising given that we have already seen that in the period after 1980 southern representatives were just as responsive to constituent opinion as were northern representatives, southern representatives were as successful in securing federal monies, and southerners were just as effective legislatively.

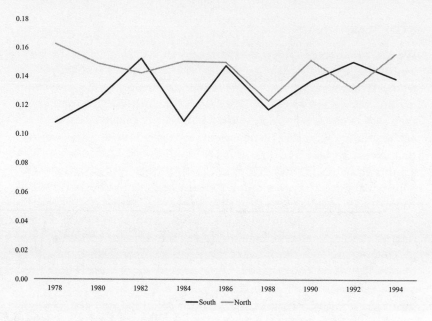

Figure 8.9 Contacting member of Congress for assistance by region, 1978–94

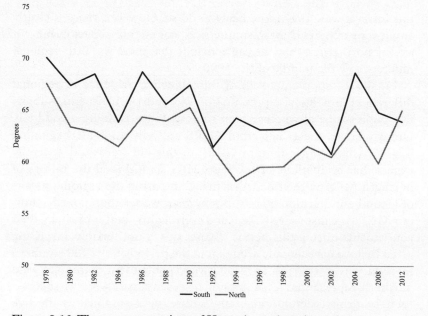

Figure 8.10 Thermometer ratings of House incumbent by region

CONCLUSION

We saw (in chapter 7) that southern lawmakers were, in the 1800s as well as in the middle of the 1900s, less experienced, more likely to hail from a family legacy, and younger than their northern colleagues, a situation that persisted until the last decades of the twentieth century. We then saw a similar pattern in this chapter—prior to about 1980 southern legislators were less responsive to the variation of public opinion that existed in their region than were northerners. Since about 1980, southern lawmakers have completely closed the responsiveness gap. Third, we compared other measures of responsiveness beyond roll call voting. Once again we find that while there were substantial differences in the degree to which southern MCs brought money home to their districts and successfully ushered their bills through Congress prior to 1980, in the last thirty years southern lawmakers have caught up to their northern counterparts on almost every responsiveness measure we compare. Of course, this is just as we would have anticipated, given the convergence in regional party development and electoral competitiveness observed over the last quarter century in chapters 6 and 7.

Has the movement of the southern party system toward equilibrium and the sustained competitiveness of elections since 1980 also yielded more effective democratic governance in the South? That is the question to which we now turn.

APPENDIX A: TECHNICAL ISSUES WITH RESPECT TO RESPONSIVENESS DATA FOR THE U.S. HOUSE

1. For the 1832–52 responsiveness analyses in chapter 8, we aggregated county-level presidential vote data into congressional districts. Two decision rules are typically used when aggregating election data at the level of congressional districts that contain partial counties. In some cases, districts in which less than 50% of the population was contained in whole counties were dropped. This is consistent with the "county aggregation method" used by Ansolabehere, Snyder, and Stewart (2001): "All districts that were composed completely of whole counties were, of course, included. Furthermore, we included cases where the percentage of the district's population that was contained in whole counties was at least 50 percent" (155). The article by Ansolabehere et al. does not explain how they dealt with the partial counties in districts where the percentage of the population contained in whole counties was at least 50%. In this analysis, when at least 50% of the district population was contained in whole counties, only the whole

counties in these districts were used in calculating the district's presidential vote totals. In addition to this method used by Ansolabehere et al., the models were also run after dropping all districts that contained partial counties. Another possibility for future analyses is to use all partial counties through some type of apportionment approach.

2. To construct congressional district-level measures of presidential support for the 1832–52 period in chapter 8, county-level presidential vote data were obtained from the Interuniversity Consortium for Political and Social Research (ICPSR) Study 0001, United States Historical Election Returns, 1824–1968. Information regarding the congressional district number for each county was also available in this ICPSR data set in most cases. However, because the district information was not included in these data for all observations, all information in the ICPSR data set regarding the district number for each county was verified with congressional district maps (Parsons, Beach, and Hermann 1978; Parsons, Beach, and Dubin 1986). Missing or inconsistent district information in the ICPSR data set was filled in using these congressional district maps. These district maps were also used to determine which districts contained partial counties and what proportion of the district population was contained in whole or partial counties.

3. When dividing states into North and South for these models, the southern states included all states that were members of the Confederacy (Alabama, Arkansas, Florida, Georgia, Louisiana, Mississippi, North Carolina, Tennessee, Texas, Virginia), except for South Carolina. County-level presidential vote data for South Carolina was not available in ICPSR 0001 until 1868.

4. When controlling for party affiliation in these models, Democrats and Jacksonians were coded 1 and Whigs and anti-Jacksonians were coded 0. For all House models, members that were not affiliated with these parties were dropped from the analyses.

APPENDIX B: CHECKS ON SENATE RESPONSIVENESS BY REGION IN THE CONTEMPORARY PERIOD

To probe this comparison further, we take advantage of an alternative measure of state-level constituent preferences. Wright, Erikson, and McIver (1993) generated a measure of citizen ideology using CBS/*New York Times* surveys aggregated to the state level for the period 1978–93. We used these data to model senators' DW-NOMINATE coordinates (see table 8.A-1). The results of these models lend support to the view that the responsiveness of southern senators is today much more on par with that of northern senators. After accounting for senators' party

Table 8.A-1 Senator responsiveness by region using a survey measure of state ideology, 1978–93

	North	South	North	South
State liberalism	0.964**	0.342	0.481**	0.391**
	[0.115]	[0.359]	[0.059]	[0.145]
Democrat MC			0.601**	0.621**
			[0.015]	[0.021]
Constant	2.102**	0.714	0.775**	0.442
	[0.244]	[0.792]	[0.128]	[0.320]
R^2	0.11	0.01	0.77	0.84
N	597	176	597	176

* $p < .05$; ** $p < .01$; standard errors in brackets.

affiliations, which improves the precision of the estimate of state liberalism's effect, there is only a modest regional difference in senator responsiveness. Note also that since these data are not available after 1993, the regional difference in responsiveness today may be even smaller.

9 COMPETITIVE PARTY SYSTEMS AND DEMOCRATIC EFFECTIVENESS

We have developed two principal findings to this point. The first concerns the development of a multiparty (i.e., two-party) system in the South. Since the Jacksonian era, the South has generally been a one- or no-party system, similar to the period that Key (1949) studied in depth. There were three times, however, in which the South was open to the development of a two-party system, and we considered them and contrasted them with the one-party eras in supporting this finding empirically. The second finding concerns the consequences of having a two-party system in the southern states, and that is that the government is expected to become more democratic and more responsive to the public. We will extend that analysis even further in this chapter to provide at least a first look at whether the coming of a more genuine democratic politics in the South has, indeed, made the public's lives better off and fortunes and futures stronger. Key (1949) had argued that democracy failed in a one- or no-party system. The inference therefore would be that in a two-party or more general multiparty system, democracy should succeed and the therefore the public should also flourish—at least relative to the public not living in an effective democracy.

TWO GENUINE, "IN-EQUILIBRIUM" PARTIES COME TO THE SOUTH AND, WITH THEM, A GENUINE TWO-PARTY SYSTEM

In the Jacksonian era itself, the South started behind the North in these terms, but had a reasonably extended period in which the second party, in this case the Whigs, was able to develop. Virtually at the very moment that the Whigs collapsed, the South was just nearing the North's level of development of that party system, and thus the 1840s stand as the most similar period to the current one in these terms, but with the South modestly behind the North. That is, a two-party system was reasonably well developed for the first time in history, it was so throughout virtually the entire nation, and the South's parties and party system were coming to approximate those of the North. Even though both major parties focused on forging and maintaining inter-sectional alliances, as we saw in figure 3.2 above, regional divisions within each party were quite as similar in extent as were the differences between the two parties (at least in terms of roll call voting and thus in terms of policies actually reaching the floor of Congress). And thus, in terms of party reputation on policy, the Democrat-Whig party system was considerably less strong than later ones. Thus, we cannot be confident that the consequences of a two-party system in terms of democratic effectiveness would be clear yet in the South.

The second time was even briefer, justifying why Goodwyn called it the "Populist Moment" (1978). While Reconstruction saw a dominant (if not quite one-party) party system of Republicans, "Redemption" saw the return of the Democrats to majority status and, then, briefly the rise of a Populist threat to become a serious second party. Defeating it rapidly and soundly allowed Key's one-party South to develop and prevented a genuine system of Democrat and Populist Parties to solidify.

The third moment is the contemporary one. While the Civil Rights and Voting Rights Acts of the mid-1960s mark the end of the legal portions of Jim Crow, resistance to integration continued, and as a parallel consequence, the development of the Republican Party in the South was slowed. As we have seen, it was not really until Reagan's success in the 1980s that the GOP's southern strategy was able to succeed. That is, Reagan, like Goldwater and Nixon before him, felt the need to develop an explicit southern strategy for voting even for president, let alone for state-level party building. So, it was not until the 1980s that the party began to succeed in organizational development and not until the mid-1990s that it paid off in a competitive Republican Party in most southern states. We can therefore turn to look at southern parties and the southern party system in the period before 1980 and afterward to assess the contrast between a South without and then with two fully developed parties and therefore, by today, with a fully developed, in-equilibrium, two-party system.

One of Key's legacies was that it is helpful to study a political party as consisting of three parts: a party in government, a party in elections, and a party as an organization. These of course are simply subcomponents of a complete political party, and we can't meaningfully ask the question of whether one part "causes" changes in other parts, and not the reverse. They are simply the related components of a political party. Unlike this case of thinking about the pieces of a single political party, we can speak meaningfully about how two or more parties interact in a fully developed party system. In particular, as Key himself argued, in the absence of a second (or third, or more) reasonably fully articulated political party, the "first" party will decline in organizational vigor, to the point that he concluded that the absence of an alternative meant that the southern Democratic Party might be a full party in the nation (where it was embedded in a fully developed party system in the North) but it could not even rise to the status of a complete party in the South, and so southern politics in the states was a politics in a no-party system.

Key's description of southern politics continued to apply into the 1950s and onward, to a time roughly approximated by the 1980 election of Reagan, a Republican Senate majority, and a strong minority base in the House. That election, at least, provides us with a convenient point at which to divide time into that with a no-party and that with a two-party South. Let us begin consideration of the southern parties with their organization. As we documented in chapter 6, the best studies of state party organizations led us to the observation that the southern parties were indeed considerably less well developed in the South than the North in the 1960s (figure 6.11). They strengthened considerably in the 1970s and 1980s, nearly (but not completely) closing the regional gap. By the next survey in 1999, southern parties had strengthened (and northern parties weakened) such that the southern parties were the more strongly organized, and by the 2012 survey, both regions had strongly organized parties.

As we showed in chapter 7, beginning no later than the 1980s, the organizational strength of the southern Republicans had, indeed, emerged sufficiently clearly that ambitious young politicos were entering the ranks of the GOP and beginning to climb Schlesinger's opportunity structure in that party as well as their more liberal counterparts doing likewise on the Democratic side. While regional differences in turnout are both reflections of the ability of the parties' organizations to mobilize supporters and of the strength of partisan identification of the public in the electorate, it is worth noting that the heretofore huge gap between the regions disappeared completely in and after the 1980s, suggesting another dimension by which the southern party organizations had muscle to flex (see figure 6.15).

In the electorate, we saw that there was another huge gap between levels of identification in the South with the Democrat as compared to the Republican Party. There was a convergence in southern partisan identifications that achieved a close parity between the two parties at about 1980, and advantaged the Republicans thereafter, until coming back to parity in 2012. A fully developed party need not hold the loyalties of 50% of every region, of course, but it is clear that by 1980, southerners had the opportunity to choose and were choosing between identifying with Republicans and with Democrats, quite unlike in, say, 1960 (figure 6.16). This was followed by regional differences in party loyalty in presidential voting (i.e., voting for the nominee of the party one identifies with) around 1976 and in congressional voting in the mid- to late 1990s (figures 6.20 and 6.21). Another feature of the new-found importance of party identification in a two-party South is that the regional difference in perceptions of party differences fell under 2% in 1980 and by 2012 became slightly negative (i.e., the southern respondent is now more likely to report seeing differences than the northern respondent; see figure 6.17). Presumably this is because ideological sorting was completed such that the southern Democrat (the case of special interest is in the "out-of-equilibrium" one-party South) was if anything more ideologically consistent in their voting starting in 1978 or 1980, and full convergence to eliminate regional differences was achieved early in the twenty-first century (see figure 6.21). Both parties appeared to have policy reputations that were perceived and acted upon, that is, as meaningful to voters, in the South as in the North after 1980.

We have only modest data on parties in government in the states, although considerably more that can be applied to assessing the southern parties in the nation. In figure 6.9 we observed that, if anything, state legislatures were, on average, more polarized than the national one. More to the point here is that there is a consistent but reasonably modest difference in the estimated extent of polarization in the southern states compared to the northern ones, with the important story being that this regional difference was small and with both regions being more polarized than in the nation. And, of course, we have observed the rise of Republican success in securing strong nominees for state legislature, and in electing them (see figure 7.5). This suggests that the South is now a two-party region in the government, as it appears to be in its organization and in elections.

In postwar America, the South was a one-party system in the Congress, and in many ways they were the third party in the Congress. Figure 6.1 shows that the two possible (and not necessarily disjoint) roll call voting coalitions, that of party unity and that of the conservative coalition, were common throughout the 1950s, 1960s, and 1970s. Indeed, the latter was nearly as frequently formed as the party unity coalition in many years in this period. That lasted until the early 1980s, when the conservative coalition declined in frequency of appearance, and indeed became so rare that even the counting of conservative co-alition votes ended by the end of the century. The South (i.e., the southern Democrats in Congress) went from being the oft-decisive balancer between liberal northern Democrats and Republicans to be-coming simply a part of the Democratic Party by the end of the twen-tieth century.

We can see why by looking at regional and partisan DW-NOMINATE scores (see figures 6.3–6.7). On the Republican side, after 1980, there was very little differentiation between northern and southern wings, and both began to climb dramatically in a conservative direction to-gether and in near lockstep. On the Democratic side, the northern Democrats hardly changed at all, as they were reasonably liberal (about as much to the left as their Republican peers—almost exclusively from the North in those days—were to the right) at the beginning of this period as at the end (unlike their now two-regional GOP peers who are now apparently considerably more conservative than Democrats are liberal). The Democratic polarization is due first to the declining proportions of southern Democrats and then to the slowly but consis-tently increasing liberalization of the southern Democrat in the House. By 2012, for the first time, the southern Democrat is essentially just as liberal as the northern Democrat. In short, the regional delegation to the House (and in most respects to the Senate) from the South was once a solidly Democratic group that acted as if it were a united bloc—Key's one party in the nation. It was (as Aldrich 2015 shows) almost entirely due to the actions of this one-party South, acting es-sentially as if it were a third party embedded in a two-party system in the North that explains the depolarization of the American parties in the post-1936 period, ending with the repolarization as the southern system began to be a two-party system. And, perhaps even more im-portantly, those two southern parties now are nearly identical to their northern counterparts in their actions and choices. It is a two-party system of the South in the nation, but it is the same two-party system as in the North. The South has merged with the North in its national partisan politics.

The Consequences of a Two-Party System

Our second principal finding is to observe one of the consequences that flows from the failure of a fully developed (or "in-equilibrium") two-party system. That consequence is the resulting failure to have a fully developed democratic politics. And since the South generally was extremely far from having a fully developed two-party system until 1980 or after, we found that, indeed, central characteristics associated with a well-functioning democracy were missing in the South relative to the North. Perhaps the clearest and most systematic illustration of that point is our finding in chapter 8 that southern members of both the U.S. House and Senate were far less responsive, and often fully unresponsive, to their citizens' preferences. At the very least, when (invariably northern) Democratic presidential candidates did better in the North, northern MCs voted more in support of Democratic/liberal policies. In the South, MCs voted without much variation over time, no matter for whom the citizens had voted. Almost immediately upon the emergence of a fully developed two-party system in the South, however, southern elite responsiveness looked just like that found in the North. Democracy appeared to work generally in that, for the first time, southern political elites paid attention to the choices of their constituents. And, while that is perhaps the most systematic set of observations, our other empirical investigations support that claim as well.

In this chapter we turn to one more set of observations, and one more general finding—more tentative and less fully developed, but apparently regular and strongly suggestive. That finding is the fuller test of the second side of Key's argument. Key argued that, in the absence of a fully developed (or in-equilibrium) multiparty system, democracy fails. And that, of course, is what he showed was true of the South under Jim Crow. He provided, that is, one careful empirical case study to support the claim that a fully developed multiparty system was necessary for effective democracy. While he referred to the North in these terms, he did not truly assess with any similar care the flip side of the inference. Is a fully developed multiparty system sufficient to ensure an effective democracy? While responsiveness and accountability as studied so far seem to suggest that may be empirically true in the United States, we extend that empirical case more broadly here, by way of making the simple claim that a competitive multiparty system makes democracy work (see also Rosenblum 2010). By way of conclusion, that is, we examine the effect of historically disparate party competition across regions on a variety of outcomes largely external to, but arguably influenced by, what happens in government, as well as whether and how these outcomes have converged across regions over time as electoral competition has come to the South. That is, we ask whether democracy's effectiveness correlates with partisan competition and a more responsive political leadership.

The democratic outcomes we will discuss fall into three categories—the extent to which democratic attitudes are embraced among the population, the degree to which citizens exercise their opportunity to participate in political activities, and the social conditions under which citizens live. We will show that as a result of the coming of regularized party competition in the South that works just like national democracy works, life in the South has improved alongside this political modernization.

While positive evidence would support the claim that competitive parties improve democratic performance for its citizens, we are not making a precise causal claim. Many things go together to explain such features of the contemporary South as economic growth, improved health among its citizens, and so on. What we do argue is that political development is one part of the complex of political, economic, and social developments that have led the South to more closely approximate the North and to be making the life chances of its citizens better and richer. A fully developed, competitive multiparty system is part of the penumbra of forces that help us understand how patterns of living have changed in the South—for the better. But it is a complex set of conditions that explain the outcomes we measure. Besley et al. (2010), for example, study the intertwining of economic development and political competition with the passage of the civil and voting rights legislation in the mid-1960s. They have a convincing claim that federal intervention in these ways can be considered exogenous from microlevel forces inside the South, especially in terms of the statistical model they estimate, and the inferences they can draw from it. Yet, in a larger sense, it is probably not really exogenous. Wright (2013) has subsequently shown, for example, that southern businessmen, often members of white citizens' councils themselves, were happy to have an end to segregation so that they could expand their businesses, and thus objected less strenuously (if at all) to the coming of the Civil Rights Act than they might have if politics would have truly been exogenous from the success of their business. Indeed, they might well, as Wright suggests, have been hoping for just such an opportunity to end the economic system they felt social pressure to support.

Many of our comparisons have sufficient data to support a more detailed investigation than the data from the earlier years of our study support. Rather, our study of the contemporary period is aided by richer data especially in the post–World War II period. We can also study a bit more than a simple North-South dichotomy. For example, we add a few comparisons of the border states to go along with the simpler North-South comparisons.[1] The border states shared a good deal more with the southern states than did the North share with the

South. These states, for example, had large black populations and retained slavery up to the Civil War.[2] Their connection to the South was
geographic, social, political, and economic. In Kentucky and Missouri,
there were pro-Confederate (and pro-Union) governments. Like every
slave state except South Carolina, the border states contributed some
white troops to the Union as well as the Confederate side. After 1880
most of the border states adopted the Jim Crow system. What sets the
border states apart, of course, is that they never declared secession.
Staying in the Union (whether their people and leadership wanted to
or not) yielded great consequences, including being on the victorious
side of the Civil War and thus also including the absence of Reconstruction and subsequent local reactions against Reconstruction.

We also are able to make more comparisons between the two races.
Given the radically different racial makeup of the North and South,
we want to be certain that the differences we observe are not simply
attributable to racial differences between the regions. Second, the
costs associated with the lack of southern party competition fell disproportionately on the black population, and we will be able to make
at least some observations of the effect of party competition on Key's
"have-nots." Finally, we are also genuinely interested in comparing
whites across regions if only to determine whether the dearth of party
competition in the South was injurious not just to blacks but in some
ways as well to the very whites who established the institutions that
halted the progress of political competition.

DEMOCRATIC ATTITUDES

We begin by looking at differences in the attitudes of citizens toward
democracy. If the South had, at best, a stunted brand of democracy,
if democracy at all, then we should observe sharp differences, at least
between those living in the North and in the South. And, if a stronger, more effective democracy does emerge, we would expect that the
public would see the benefits that flow from that change. We are particularly interested in three measurable aspects of citizens' beliefs about
democracy: freedom of speech; support for equality; and beliefs that
the government is responsive to the actions of its citizens. These three
items tap different dimensions of democracy, and each was notably
absent or at least weaker and under greater threat in the South than
in the North, especially during Jim Crow. In 1963, for example, the
state legislature banned speeches by communists on the University
of North Carolina, Chapel Hill, campus, leading to a dramatic confrontation between the state and students there. And that was just one

of the more notable instances of restricted speech. Everywhere there were such threats in the McCarthy era (early 1950s), but nowhere were they greater than in the South. Freedom of expression is often cited as a prerequisite of democracy (Dahl 1971, 1998), or at least as a "procedural minimum" of democracy (Collier and Levitsky 1997, 433). Support for freedom of expression may also tend to coincide with support for democracy.[3] Freedom of expression permits citizens to convey their policy preferences to government, and to criticize government decisions with which they disagree. Curtailing freedom of expression also gives some citizens an advantage in their efforts to influence policy. So, we will compare the support for controversial free speech in each region.

The system of Jim Crow, to take a second example, was one of segregation, of separation of the races, and as the Warren Court proclaimed as the centerpiece of the *Brown v. Board* decision (1954), "separate is inherently unequal." While nowhere is there full equality, the Jim Crow South was especially and perniciously unequal. Equality, too, "is central to any conception of democracy" (Verba and Orren 1985, 8). Democracy may depend on a certain amount of actual equality. The amount of equality that exists, though, will depend in at least some part on how much citizens value it. So, we will compare attitudinal support for equality in each region as well.

Finally, we need only note our findings in the last chapter to see that, at least in terms of how political elites in Congress voted, southern voters were indeed inefficacious in affecting the actions of their MCs. As Key famously contended, "Unless mass views have some place in the shaping of policy, all the talk about democracy is nonsense" (1961, 7). As a result, we are able to ask if citizens perceive that elected officials are attentive to their preferences and concerns. This is simultaneously an attitude that reflects the quality of democracy, or how effective the democratic process is working, and supports democracy, because citizens who feel the government is "efficacious" or, that is, that it heeds the populace, are themselves more likely to engage in politics (Abramson and Aldrich 1981). So, our final attitudinal comparison will be the reported level of external political efficacy in each region over time.

Freedom of Speech

Using data from the General Social Survey over the period 1973 to 2000 (when this question was discontinued), figure 9.1 shows how a regional difference in support for free speech waned over the same years as the Republican Party grew to be competitive in the South.

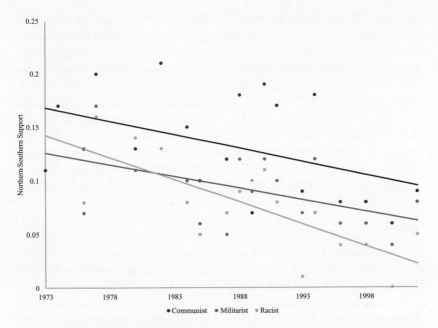

Figure 9.1 Support for free speech protections among southern and northern whites, 1973–2000

This figure reports the difference in the percentage of northern and southern white residents who supported allowing an "admitted Communist," a person who "advocates doing away with elections and letting the military run the country," or someone who "thinks that blacks are genetically inferior" to make a speech in their community. Positive values in the figure indicate weaker support for free speech protections inside the South than outside the South. For all three series, northern whites were initially much more often supportive of free speech protections than southern whites. For instance, in the 1970s southern whites were between 13 and 23 percentage points less likely than northern whites to support the idea that a Communist should be allowed to speak in their community. Somewhat smaller regional differences existed for the free speech rights of militarists and racists. By the year 2000, though, southerners were just as likely as northerners to back free speech protections for militarists and racists, while southerners were nearly as likely to support the free speech rights of Communists.

Note that this regional convergence was due primarily to more rapid growth in support for free speech in the South. For instance, while only 51% of southern whites supported allowing a Communist to speak in their community in 1973, 67% supported allowing such speech in 2000, more than double the increase outside the South (where support grew from 64% to 71%). The increase in southern support for the free speech rights of militarists over this period was of nearly identical size (17 percentage points), compared to just 9 points for northern whites. The increase in southerners' support for the free speech rights of racists was only 8 percentage points. However, absolute support for the free speech rights of racists outside the South was virtually unchanged over this period. In sum, southern support for free speech protections has increased considerably in the last quarter of the twentieth century, making the South indistinguishable from the remainder of the country by the century's end.

Equality

To gain an early perspective on attitudes about equality, we turned to a 1948 survey by the Gallup Organization. That survey contained an item that asked the following, "One of Truman's proposals concerns employment practices. How far do you yourself think the Federal Government should go in requiring employers to hire people without regard to their race, religion, color, or nationality?" Among southern whites, 83% replied that the federal government should not be involved in this at all. Outside the South, only a narrow majority of whites (51%) held this view.

How have regional attitudes about equality evolved? One measure of attitudes about equality that we have access to over time is ANES responses to the item "Do you strongly agree, agree somewhat, neither agree nor disagree, disagree somewhat, or strongly disagree that the country would be better off if we worried less about how equal people are?" These response options are coded 1–5, respectively, so, for example, a mean response of 2.0 indicates that a region generally supports the value of equality (or disagrees that we should worry less about it). Note that this question wording makes no mention of racial equality specifically. Figure 9.2(a) reports the mean response to this item among southern and northern state whites from 1984, when the item was first introduced by the ANES, to 2012. Because we have seen that by many measures the South had come to look much like the North by 1980 or so, the duration of this time series is not ideal. However, to the extent that we do observe regional differences at the opening of this period, we might infer that the differences were even more dramatic in the decades preceding.

According to the figure, southerners generally have become more supportive of equality over time, with the mean increasing from

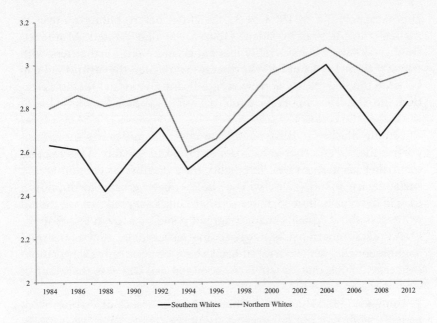

Figure 9.2(a) "The Country Would Be Better Off If We Worried Less about How Equal People Are," among whites, 1984–2012

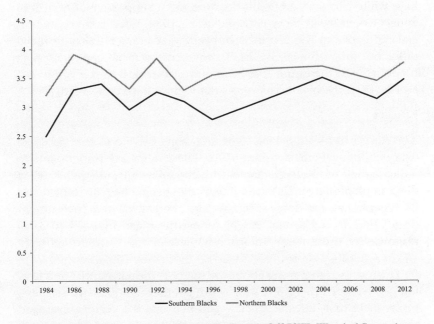

Figure 9.2(b) "The Country Would Be Better Off If We Worried Less about How Equal People Are," among blacks, 1984–2012

approximately 2.6 in 1984 to 3.0 in 2004, before falling quite dramatically in the year President Obama was first elected. Moreover, southerners were considerably less concerned than northerners with equality from 1984 until 1992, whereas since then the attitudinal gap between the regions has narrowed significantly. Prior to Obama's election, the South's support for equality rivaled support for this value in the rest of the country.

Among blacks, in 1984 northerners were significantly more supportive than southerners of efforts to promote equality. This is quite surprising insofar as racial inequality on a number of economic and social measures has (as we will see below) been greater in the South than in the North. Indeed, more southern blacks agreed that we should worry less about equality than disagreed (yielding a mean less than 3). Over time, southern blacks have become substantially more concerned about inequality while northern blacks have become only slightly more concerned, such that by 2008 the regional gap was less than half of what it was in 1984.

Comparing racial groups within regions, in the South whites were actually slightly more concerned about inequality than were blacks in 1984. Beginning in 1986 and continuing until 2008, with special distinction in 1988, blacks have been more supportive of equality than have whites. In the North, blacks were more supportive of efforts to enhance equality in every year, including 1984. What is more, the racial difference in the North is in every year greater than the racial difference in the South. By 2008, however, the racial gap in support for equality in the South (.46) was almost identical to the gap in the North (.53). By this measure, too, the regions have converged.

Efficacy

The ANES has been asking its respondents two items that relate to external political efficacy since 1952. These items ask respondents to indicate their level of agreement with the following statements: 1) "I don't think public officials care much what people like me think"; and 2) "People like me don't have any say about what the government does." Figures 9.3(a) and 9.3(b) report the mean indexed (0–100) response for these items among northerners and southerners from 1952 to 2012.

The most striking thing about the figure is the substantial and lasting gap between the efficacy of white southerners and northerners. From 1952 to 1980, the efficacy gap between the regions averaged almost 10 points. By comparison, from 1980 to 2012 the average gap in the external efficacy of the regions was about 1 point, and the two

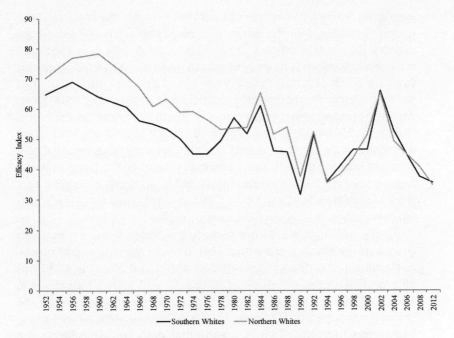

Figure 9.3(a) External efficacy index among whites by region, 1952–2012

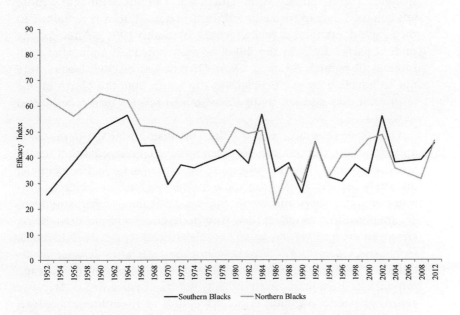

Figure 9.3(b) External efficacy index among blacks by region, 1952–2012

have been virtually identical since 1988. On this measure of democratic attitudes, too, the South has caught up with the rest of the country. As political efficacy in the North has declined, in the South it has been somewhat more resilient. In addition, as we will continue to see, in terms of attitudes and behaviors of the mass public, much of the South's transformation in this sphere had occurred by 1980 or so. Among blacks, external efficacy was dramatically higher in the North than in the South as this period opened (38 points), among the biggest differences we observe in any of our comparisons. This regional efficacy gap continued, with some variability, until 1984. Since then the regions have tracked relatively closely, although northern blacks were somewhat more efficacious in the Clinton years, while southern blacks felt more efficacious when Obama was elected.

Finally, although we do not include a separate figure we note the change in the efficacy gap within regions between whites and blacks. In the South, the efficacy gap between whites and blacks in 1952 was 39 points. With the exception of Johnson's and Carter's elections in 1964 and 1976, this gap remained more than 8 points until 1984 (when it was 4 points). Thereafter the gap fluctuated between 3.6 and 14.8 points until 2008, when, for the first time, southern blacks felt more efficacious than southern whites (albeit by a mere 1.6 points). The pattern outside the South was by no means identical. In 1952 the racial gap in efficacy in the North was 7 points, with whites more efficacious. The gap rose and fell until under Clinton it remained in the single digits (and actually favored blacks in 1996). After spiking under George Bush in the 2000s it even remained somewhat high in 2008 (9 points). So, in the year Obama was elected, blacks were not only feeling more efficacious in the South than the North in real terms, but they also felt more efficacious in relative terms, compared to whites.

One concern about reaching the conclusion that the democratic attitudes of southerners and northerners have converged is that southerners may simply have become more likely to dissemble. For example, one study has shown that the apparent convergence in the racial attitudes of southerners and northerners is misleading; when southerners are permitted to reflect their true preferences without them being known to the interviewer, a gap in racial attitudes persists (Kuklinski, Cobb, and Gilens 1997). This behavior may extend to democratic attitudes as well; that is, southerners may have "learned" the democratic response to these items, even if this is not their true attitude. Because actual behavior presumably is less susceptible to this influence, we turn to this topic next.

DEMOCRATIC BEHAVIOR

A second way we assess the quality of democracy is to compare the involvement of citizens in political decision making (Dahl 1998; Verba and Nie 1972; Altman and Pérez-Liñán 2002). According to Seymour Martin Lipset, "democracy in a complex society may be defined as a political system which supplies regular constitutional opportunities for changing the governing officials, *and a social mechanism which permits the largest possible part of the population to influence major decisions by choosing contenders for office*" (1959, 27; emphasis added). Moreover, we might care if this "social mechanism" not only permits political participation but also actively encourages or facilitates it such that a large portion of the population actually does participate in elections.

Electoral Participation

According to Lijphart (1999, 284), "voter turnout is an excellent indicator of democratic quality" (see also Moon et al. 2006). Figures 9.4(a) and 9.4(b) reflect the regional difference in reported turnout in presidential-year (1952–2012) elections by region, building on what we reported in chapter 6. Comparing the North and South, in every election from 1952 to 1972 reported turnout outside the South exceeded reported turnout in the South by at least 10 percentage points. In 1976, when a southerner led the Democratic ticket, the gap shrunk, and then, when Carter ran for reelection in 1980, the turnout gap was eliminated entirely. Under Reagan the regional turnout gap reemerged, but from 1988 to 2012 the regional gap fell from 17 points to just 3 points.

Among blacks, more than six in ten northerners reported voting in 1952, compared to just one in ten southerners. The regional gap persisted, save for the McGovern race, until 1980. In 1988 a regional gap reemerged, but it has since narrowed dramatically, leaving almost no regional gap among blacks in 2012.

Comparing racial groups within regions, in the South there was a 50 point reported turnout gap in 1952 with whites reporting higher turnout. As late as 1964 this gap was 26 points, but since 1968 it has always been less than 10 points, except 1996 when it was 12.8. In 2008, reported black turnout exceeded white turnout by 2 points, an event that had only happened previously in 1968 (0.5 points). In the North, reported white turnout exceeded reported black turnout by 19 points in 1952. This considerable gap persisted until 1964, when reported black turnout exceeded white turnout by 2 points. Since then, white turnout has usually exceeded black turnout in the North, but

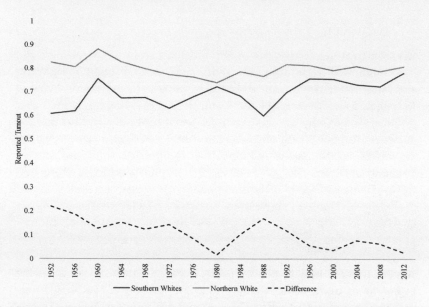

Figure 9.4(a) Regional differences in reported turnout among whites, 1952–2012

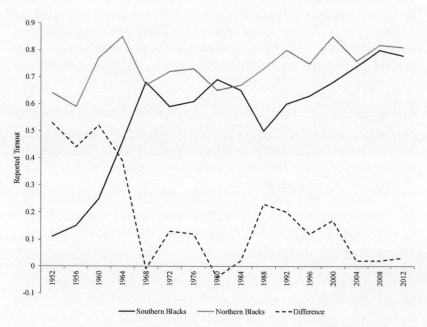

Figure 9.4(b) Regional differences in reported turnout among blacks, 1952–2012

seldom by more than 10 points (in 1984 it was 11.6). In both 2000 and 2008, black reported turnout exceeded white turnout, by 5.8 and 2.9 points, respectively.

A final look at figures 9.4(a) and 9.4(b) reveals that turnout in the South also has increased in real, as opposed to relative, terms. In presidential years reported turnout *within* the South among whites increased over this sixty-year period from about 60% to 77%. Meanwhile, reported turnout outside the South remained essentially unchanged.[4] Among blacks, reported turnout increased in both regions over this period, but much more dramatically in the South, especially in the 1960s and again in the 1990s.

Reported turnout regularly exceeds actual turnout, and if this tendency grew more in the South than the North, it might account for, or at least contribute to, the trends observed in figures 9.4(a) and 9.4(b). To address this concern, in figure 9.5 we report the actual regional difference in turnout of the voting-age population from 1952 to 2012. We are unable to limit this comparison to whites because most states do not keep a record of an individual's race in their voter file. According to these data, turnout was more than 30 percentage points higher in the North than in the South in 1960, and 23 percentage points higher

Figure 9.5 Regional difference in actual turnout of voting age population, 1952–2012

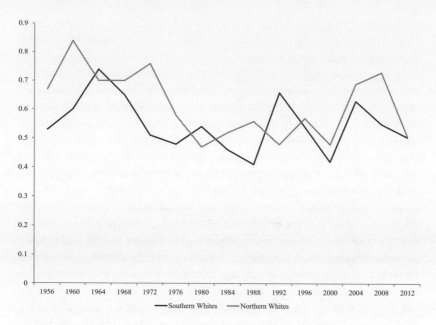

Figure 9.6 Reported campaign activity in presidential elections among whites, 1956–2012

in border states than in the South. These differences have declined, such that in 2012 the North-South and border-South turnout gaps were about 2.5 points.

We now turn to consider other forms of political participation. Figure 9.6 reports the mean level of nonvoting presidential election campaign activity among whites in each region. Using the ANES data, their measures of campaign activities include trying to influence others' votes, attending political meetings, working for a party or candidate, displaying a candidate button or sticker, and donating money to a party or candidate. Comparing the regions, we observe that from 1956 to 1980 northern whites participated at higher rates than southern whites in every election except Johnson's victory over Goldwater in 1964. In 1980, southern campaign activity exceeded northern activity, owing to an ongoing decline in northern activity while southern campaign activity remained fairly steady. Thereafter, neither region consistently was more active, with a southern advantage in 1992 and a northern advantage in 1988 and 2008 and complete regional convergence in 2012. Unfortunately, there are too few yearly observations to meaningfully make comparisons of campaign activity among blacks.

Were these changes in southern attitudes and behaviors a result of the heightened competitiveness the region experienced in the same era, as we argued in chapter 2? The evidence thus far is certainly suggestive, but requires more rigorous examination. We thus modeled three of the outcomes described above—external efficacy, support for equality, and reported election turnout—using ANES data mapped onto presidential and congressional election competitiveness data. The unit of analysis is the state/year in the continental United States from 1956 to 2012. We also control for educational attainment, household income, and year. The results for the model of external efficacy, reported in table 9.1, column 1, show that where the presidential election was more competitive citizens reported feeling that the government cared more about what they think and that people like them had greater a say in what the government does. Respondents reported greater support for doing more to promote equality when and where congressional elections were more competitive (column 2).[5] Finally, where presidential

Table 9.1 Effect of electoral competitiveness on democratic attitudes and behavior

	External efficacy	Support for equality	Voter turnout[1]
Presidential competitiveness	0.125*	−0.057	11.891*
	[0.049]	[0.291]	[5.321]
Congressional competitiveness	−0.002	0.191*	3.429
	[0.018]	[0.092]	[2.339]
Educational attainment	0.093**	0.382**	2.267
	[0.022]	[0.089]	[3.296]
Household income	0.091**	0.031	10.201**
	[0.017]	[0.075]	[2.500]
Year	−0.007**	0.004	0.007
	[0.001]	[0.004]	[0.072]
Northern state	0.029*	0.046	6.671**
	[0.013]	[0.059]	[1.401]
Constant	14.663**	−6.001	23.230
	[1.091]	[7.399]	[140.770]
R^2	0.47	0.17	0.42
N	486	219	240

* $p < .05$; ** $p < .01$. Models include controls for educational attainment, household income, and year.
[1]Only includes state/years with at least forty respondents.

elections were more competitive, citizens were more likely to report that they voted. These findings are consistent with prior studies showing that in competitive electoral environments, parties are incentivized to mobilize voters (Powell 1986; Jackman 1987; but see Ferejohn and Fiorina 1975; Ansolabehere and Iyengar 1994). In sum, the evidence certainly suggests that electoral competitiveness does improve democratic attitudes and behaviors.

CONDITIONS

Do the efforts of the parties to compete over valence issues in democratic elections redound to the benefit of the public? If our claim in chapter 2 is correct, we should expect to observe that after sustained party competition arrived in the South, and competitive elections followed, there should be observable gains made in the region on valence issues. Specifically, another way to compare the fruits of partisan competition is to compare whether citizens are, for example, more economically secure, healthy, educated, and safe from crime than they were without democratic competition (Dahl 1998; Lijphart 1999).[6] A healthy party system may promote government performance by building a bridge between the executive and the legislature (Levitsky and Cameron 2003), or competitive parties simply may improve government performance by increasing the likelihood of removal from office in the event of poor performance. Regardless, we are most interested in whether electoral competition yields improved democratic performance in this way.

In making these comparisons, we anticipate observing two patterns if our argument in chapter 2 is correct. First, we expect to observe more rapid convergence of border than southern states with the northern states, because electoral competition came to these states earlier than to the South. Second, we expect to observe eventual convergence of southern and border states as southern states reached a level of competition that rivaled that in the border states.

Our first regional comparison is of the rate of illiteracy. Figure 9.7(a) reports the illiteracy rate among whites by region from 1850 to 1930, when the U.S. Census stopped measuring this. Recall that this period includes the final breath of the Whig period, the Civil War, Reconstruction, and the portion of the Jim Crow era leading up to the New Deal. For the entirety of this period, as we have documented, electoral competition in the South was weaker than competition in the North. Thus, in this era we would not expect to observe convergence in conditions across regions. Indeed, while there is substantial evidence of

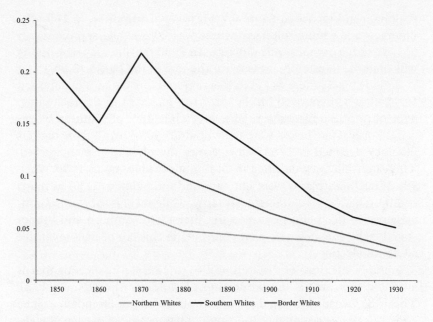

Figure 9.7(a) Illiteracy among whites by region, 1850–1930

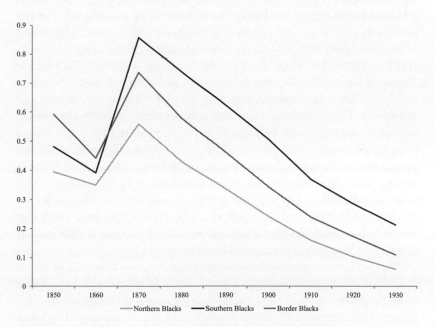

Figure 9.7(b) Illiteracy among blacks by region, 1850–1930

regional convergence in figure 9.7(a), it is not complete. In 1850 the illiteracy rate among southern whites was 20%, while approximately 8% of northern whites were illiterate. In 1930 the illiteracy rate among whites in the South (5%) was twice the rate in the North (2.6%).

Among blacks there was even less regional convergence in illiteracy. In 1850, when enslaved blacks were not included in the reckoning, 40% of northern blacks were illiterate, while 48% of southern blacks were. Border state blacks were the worst off (60%). In all three regions illiteracy declined in 1860 before rising sharply after Emancipation. Thereafter illiteracy declined in all regions leading up to 1930, when 7% of northern blacks were illiterate and three times (21%) as many southern blacks were illiterate. Notably, while there is substantial convergence in this period between the literacy of southern and border state blacks, it is nowhere near complete in this era of uncompetitive southern elections.

Another measure of a state's ability to educate its citizens that is available over time is the proportion of children who attend school. The U.S. Census has regularly asked about school attendance since 1850. We report regional proportions of whites under the age of eighteen attending school from 1850 to 2010 in figure 9.8(a), and a parallel figure for blacks (figure 9.8[b]). The figure for whites indicates that in the latter half of the nineteenth century school attendance of southern white children lagged far behind northern white attendance. For instance, in 1870 less than one in five southern white children attended school while more than two in five northern children did so. It was really not until 1980 that the two regions fully converged. School attendance among border state whites was similar to that in the South in 1850, and converged sooner and more quickly with the North than did the South. There was also a considerable regional difference in blacks' school attendance from 1850 to 1950, with around 15% more blacks attending school in the North in any given year. The rate of school attendance among border state blacks in 1850 was identical to the rate among southern blacks (2%). However, the rate in the border states more rapidly converged with the northern states as a whole, such that from 1900 onward the two tracked quite closely. The year 1980 was the first that southern blacks' school attendance equalled (and indeed surpassed) that of northern (and border state) blacks.

We also possess census data on total family size from 1850 to 2010. It is well established in prior studies that family size is associated with "increased illness, less satisfactory growth and intellectual development, increased illness in parents, and economic and emotional stresses" (Wray 1971; see also Downey [1995] for a review of stud-

Figure 9.8(a) School attendance of whites < 18 years old by region, 1850–2010

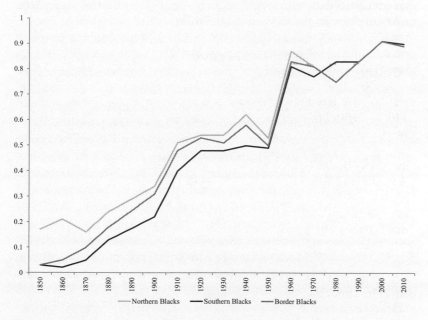

Figure 9.8(b) School attendance of blacks < 18 years old by region, 1850–2010

ies concerning family size and educational performance). Comparing family size among whites and across regions (see figure 9.9[a]), border and especially southern white families were larger than northern white families from 1850 to 1970. Thereafter family size in the three regions was virtually identical on average. Among blacks, in 1850 family size was similar (about 4.75) in the South, the North, and the border states. Southern blacks' family size then grew to 5.75 by 1900, and this increase coupled with falling family sizes among northern blacks opened up a considerable regional gap in black family size that continued until 2000. Today, black families in the South and North are similarly sized on average. In the border states, black family size began to look like black family size in the rest of the North somewhat earlier, around 1980.

Next, we compared the household incomes of whites in each region using census data, which is available from 1950 to 2010. To enhance comparability of the data over time, all of the figures are presented in 2010 dollars. According to these data, the incomes of northern whites substantially exceeded those of southern whites in 1950, the regions converged in 1980 due to a decline in northern whites' real incomes from 1960 to 1980, but then regional incomes became unequal again from 1990 through 2010. However, southern whites' incomes as a percentage of northern whites' incomes in 2010 were much larger in that year than they were sixty years earlier.

Among blacks, there is not much evidence of regional convergence in household incomes between North and South. There is some indication that border state blacks' incomes converged with northern blacks' incomes, although some difference between them reemerged in 2010.

Figure 9.11(a) reports the life expectancy of white males from 1940 to 2000, the latest date for which state figures are available. From 1940 to 1960, life expectancy in the northern, border, and southern states was similar,[7] though northerners were expected to live more than a year longer than southerners. "Most of the difference between North and South [was] attributable to higher mortality in childhood" (Ferleger and Steckel 2000, 173). In 1970 this regional difference actually grew, with life expectancy 2.25 years longer in the North than the South and one year longer in the border states than in the South. From 1970 to 2000 the North-South gap closed somewhat, to 1.5 years, while the gap between the South and border states is no more.

Among nonwhite males, there is little evidence of regional convergence. In 1960, the first data for which northern black life expectancy data are available from the CDC, life expectancy among northern

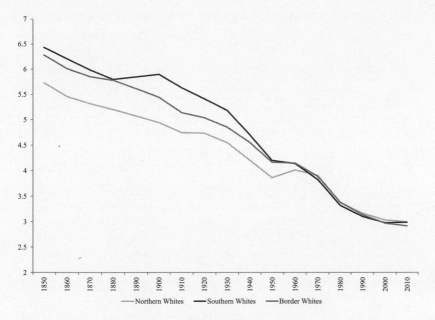

Figure 9.9(a) Mean family size among whites by region, 1850–2010

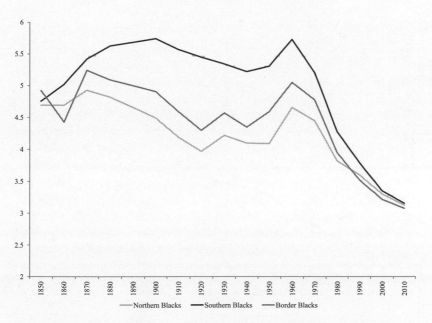

Figure 9.9(b) Mean family size among blacks by region, 1850–2010

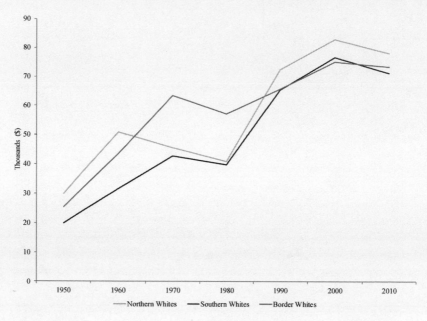

Figure 9.10(a) Household income among whites by region, 1950–2010

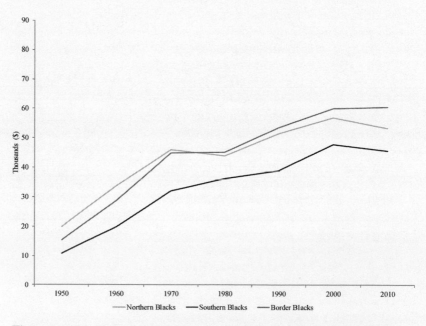

Figure 9.10(b) Household income among blacks by region, 1950–2010

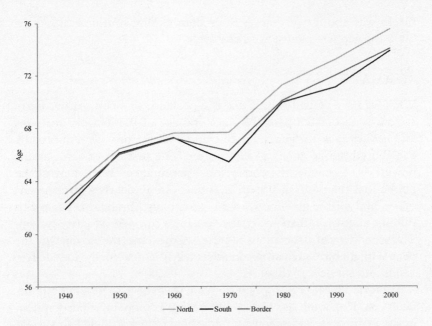

Figure 9.11(a) Life expectancy at birth among white males by region, 1940–2000

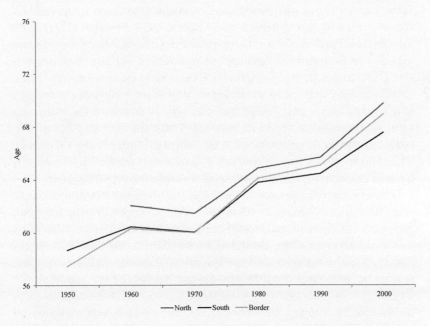

Figure 9.11(b) Life expectancy at birth among nonwhite males by region, 1950–2000

blacks was about two years greater than among southern blacks. In 2000 the gap was almost the same size.

SUMMARY

What we have argued here is that the presence of a competitive party system is associated with the development of democratic attitudes and behaviors in the general public and with the provision of broadly distributed public goods to that public. The first set of associations reflects, we presume, the comfortable acceptance on the part of the public that the political system is, indeed, more nearly a government of, by, and for the great body of the people (as Abraham Lincoln and Publius might say) than any system lacking a competitive party system. The second set of associations reflects, we presume, the reason why the people might have such an acceptance: the system actually does deliver goods and services to them.

We tested these presumptions in what we believe to be a fair but difficult test. The South had flirted with having a competitive party system in the eighteenth and nineteenth centuries, but had failed to sustain such a competitive system even then. The Federalist and Democratic-Republican party system was short-lived everywhere. The Democratic-Whig party system was established, according to most historical accounts, in 1840 and collapsed in or about 1854 (Aldrich 2011). The Republican Party did not emerge in the South, and the Confederacy chose to be nonpartisan. And it was the threat of the rise of an opposition party to the newly "redeemed" Democratic Party in the late nineteenth century that led to the undermining of the ability of democracy and a competitive party system to emerge for much of the twentieth century, throughout the Jim Crow era. Thus, the potential for a two-party system was barely realized at all—until the current era. Of course, while the southern system was not a democracy until then, it was embedded in a national democracy with a competitive party system.

The evidence we summarize in table 9.2 suggests that this account is in fact the case. There, we report the result of regressing the biennial, regional difference of each social condition's measure on a linear time trend to ascertain if the declining North-South regional differences observed in the figures above are statistically significant. The reported parameter estimates indicate the annual decline in the regional difference for the relevant measure. In addition, in table 9.2 we report the estimated regional difference at the end of each data series based on a difference in means. For data series based on survey data we are also able to indicate if the regional difference at the end of the series is statistically significant.

Table 9.2 Declining differences between the South and the North with a competitive party system in the South

Condition	Estimated change in difference per year	Difference at series end
Free speech (average)	−0.003**	0.07
Worry less about equality	−0.004	0.05
External efficacy	−0.227**	−1.49
Turnout	−0.005**	0.03*
Campaign activity	−0.002	0.00
Per capita income	−0.001**	1.19
School attendance	−0.01***	0.01
Family size	−0.01***	−0.04

* $p < .05$; ** $p < .01$.

Looking first at whether there has been a significant decline in regional differences over time, in all cases the parameter estimate is negative and in virtually all cases there has been a statistically significant, linear decline in the regional difference. In addition, according to the second column of results, the regional difference has become very small (turnout), nonexistent (most cases), or even negative (i.e., the South now scores "better" on efficacy and family size). And, thus, we conclude that the one thing that one really needs to know about political parties is that a system of competitive political parties is necessary for democracy.

Some may find that we paint too rosy a picture of the contemporary South. To be sure, the South faces its share of challenges with respect to inequality, but these are now, as we discuss below, many of the same challenges faced by the nation as a whole.

POSTSCRIPT

We hope that those who have made it to the end of our story will have gained a greater appreciation for the relationship between political parties, electoral competition, and effective democratic politics.

Electoral competition, we have argued for theoretically and shown to hold empirically, is a necessary condition for effective democratic politics. Competitive elections, which is to say elections where more than one candidate can be expected to receive more than a trivial amount of support, incentivize those who hold office to be attentive to the needs and concerns of the voters whose support is necessary to remain in office.

In turn, modern societies have identified no rival to a system of political parties as a means to achieve regularly competitive elections.

That is, not any competitive election will do. The competition fostered by political parties includes the feature that those in control of the levers of government can be held accountable by voters across different electoral units and different generations of politicians.

Before we conclude, we address two questions regarding the future of political parties, electoral competition, and thus effective democratic politics in the American South.

A New One-Party South?

For some, the resurgence of the southern GOP to become a regularly competitive party instead may be interpreted as a new-found one-party South, this time with the Democrats as the absent partner. For instance, a recent *New York Times* piece observed that "Mississippi is again dominated by one party with its rival blocs—except that it is Republicans who now enjoy near-total political control" (Martin 2014) In a scholarly treatment, Hayes and McKee (2008) examine the claim that the South has become a GOP-dominated one-party region. They point out that after GOP losses in the 2006 elections, the party held seven of thirteen southern governorships, twenty-one of twenty-six U.S. Senate seats, and eighty-five of 142 U.S. House seats. They attribute the strong position of the party in the region to the ideological congruence between the Republican Party and the region's electorate, the Republican trend among the region's younger voters, and the incumbency advantage accrued by current Republican officeholders.

In contrast, we agree with Black and Black (2003, 3) that "if the old solid Democratic South has vanished, a comparably solid Republican South has not developed. . . . Nor is one likely to emerge." In support of the view that a "comparably solid" GOP South has not emerged, we could first point to a reasonable degree of Democratic electoral success at the presidential level, where "Democrats are arguably doing their best in at least 20 years in three of the five most populous southern states"(Enten 2014).[8] In 2012, the South as a whole voted 2% more Republican for president than did the rest of the nation (one of the lowest differences since 1948—the lowest being a 1% difference [also more Republican, of course], in 2008; see Abramson, Aldrich, Gomez, and Rohde 2015, 128). At the congressional level, in 2013 southern House Republicans were much less numerous as a share of the total regional delegation (71%) than were southern Democrats in 1953 (94%), and not much greater in proportion than were the Democrats in 1981 (64%) (Abramson, Aldrich, Gomez, and Rohde, 2015, 230). In the Senate, GOP dominance of the southern delegation (73%) fell far short of the total control of southern Democrats in 1953 (100%), while still somewhat more dominant than were southern Democrats in 1981 (55%).[9] So, the South is not evenly balanced in preferences (the nation as a whole is what is more nearly evenly balanced), but as we will see no region is. The South is not exceptional in that. More to the point, it is much closer to symmetric, as we used that term above, and close enough so that Republicans need to be mindful of Democrats as potential competitors broadly across the region.

Second, if the South is not perfectly balanced in its partisanship, it is by no means a distinctive region in this regard. There are lots of places in the South where Republicans are going to win far more often than Democrats, just as Republicans struggle in New England and the Pacific coast states, Democrats in the mountain states, and so on. Each state and region is unique. The South is indeed still different in political preferences and beliefs, more conservative, more religious, and more rural. And as we have already observed, this has led to GOP advantages in its U.S. House and Senate delegations in recent years. However, the 2013 southern Senate delegation (again 73% GOP) was more balanced than was the delegation from the East (85% Democratic), and there was an imbalance in the West (62% Democratic) as well. Only in the Midwest was there partisan parity (Abramson, Aldrich, Gomez, and Rohde 2015, 230). In the U.S. House, it would have taken only four more Democratic wins, out of 138 southern House seats, to have the same balance in the House delegation from the South (71% Republican) as from the East (68% Democratic); the West (62% Dem) and Midwest (62% GOP) were also far from evenly partisan. All of this is not to say that in the aggregate partisan office holding in the South is anywhere near evenly balanced, but it does support the argument that the South is not much different from other regions in this regard.

Nor is the partisan balance in the South static. According to Atlantic.com, the demographics of the South are changing in ways that point toward a future of more even party competition: "The Southern states have America's fastest-growing Latino populations. Of 11 states whose Hispanic populations doubled between 2000 and 2011, nine—Virginia, the Carolinas, Georgia, Kentucky, Tennessee, Alabama, Mississippi, and Arkansas—were in the South. Black populations are also growing, thanks in part to a new migration of African-Americans back to the South. At current rates of growth, Georgia and Mississippi could be majority-minority states within a decade" (Ball 2013).

Even before these demographic changes have occurred, what differs in today's South from the old South is that preferences rooted in these demographics can inform southern votes in a way similar to the North—each has two distinct candidate choices and their political preferences shape their choices. That is new to the South; that is what makes the South "like" the North or, that is to say, ends that particular use of the "except in the South" phrase (more on this below). In the 1940s, 1950s, and 1960s, someone like, say, Adam Clayton Powell, could be elected from New York City thanks to a black voting majority in the district (Harlem), but were he from Atlanta, he would not have been able to run. Even if he could have run (and not have been lynched for trying), he would not have been able to win in 1945, even with a black majority in the congressional district, because Jim Crow made the South an exception. Civil rights hero John Lewis can win there repeatedly today.[10]

So, our contention is that while the GOP may have a working majority in much of the South, there is also a "competitive" Democratic Party that can win statewide offices under favorable, but not wildly unrealistic, conditions in nearly every southern state, even though the party may not really be "competitive" in lots of contests. The point is that even Republicans who are incumbent officeholders today need to pay attention to the Democratic Party and their candidates. It is through this systematic incentive for appealing seriously, in a competitive environment, to the general electorate that accountability works. This was not true for the Jim Crow South. It is true for the contemporary South. More generally, the current context is rather easily distinguishable as a competitive two-party system, compared to, say, 1936, when the Republican Party was competitive nationally, even though they were soundly defeated in a thoroughgoing landslide and had become in the national polls (i.e., in the Gallup Poll) clearly a minority in the nation. But this was far different from their position in the South. There, they were not competitive, because the legal and extralegal system was so rigged as to make it impossible for a second major party to emerge in the region.[11] It is when all politicians can ignore regularized competition from any party but their own that the system is not a competitive multiparty system. That is, the South did not lack a two-party system because southerners did not have an affinity for the second national party. The South did not have a two-party system because the institutional design of the system all but mandated an absence of even a second major political party. That is to say, the South did not have a two-party system because the South was not a democracy.

In sum, what makes the modern context so very different is that while the GOP may be dominant at the moment it must be mindful of the changing demographics of the region and of the parties' coalitions for there is nothing like the structural protections of the dominant party that were in place historically.

The End of Southern Politics?

Since the publication of V. O. Key's masterpiece *Southern Politics in State and Nation* in 1949, scholars of American politics have treated the region as a separate object of study. That is, studies of American politics regularly have excluded the South (e.g., Shannon 1968; Eismeier 1983; Alford and Hibbing 1981; Fiorina 1994; Berinsky and Lenz 2014; Cox and Katz 2002; Hansford and Gomez 2010; Clucas 2007), leaving the study of its politics for a separate group of scholars who studied the region in isolation (e.g., Ayers 1992; Key 1949; Aistrup 1996; Bullock 1981; Lublin 2004; Shadgett 2010; Stanley 1988). This bifurcation of the country by scholars was for many years justifiable based on the unique demographics, attitudes, and history of the South.

Across a wide variety of politically relevant metrics, however, we have documented that the South has become difficult to meaningfully separate from the remainder of the country as a unique region. As one study put it, "The growth of interparty competition is one reason why contemporary comparative analyses of state politics no longer automatically exclude southern states from the analysis" (Barghothi, Savchak, and Bowman 2010). This leads us to ask, as have others (Shafer and Johnston 2009), whether the study of southern politics has run its course.

The South is no longer exceptional and no longer unevenly balanced in preferences. More to the point, it is much closer to symmetric, as we used that term above, and close enough so that Republicans need to be mindful of Democrats broadly across the region. To be sure, courts and legislatures have been chipping away at the established symmetry of electoral law established in and after 1965 (Kousser 2008; Zengerle 2014),[12] but even if the Republicans were to win every instance, it would be a far cry from the asymmetry of Jim Crow.

In our view, southern politics as a field of inquiry is at its end. This should not be taken to mean that the residents of the southern states possess the same policy opinions as do the people of New England or the Pacific Coast. However, what it does mean, more importantly, is that the South is today, for the first time, fully integrated into the economic, social, and political fabric of this country. The South, that is, has a competitive two-party system, and it is the same two parties as in the rest of the country. And the parties compete in the North and South on the same issues and concerns. The southern party system has converged to equilibrium, and it is to the same equilibrium (albeit at different points along the liberal-conservative line of cleavage) as in the North. The United States thus has one, national, two-party system in equilibrium, and that is as true in the South as it is in the rest of the nation. The phrase "except in the South," so prevalent among prior studies of politics in this nation (e.g., Huntington 1974; Rusk 1974; Nagel and McNulty 1996; Fiorina 1997; Newman and Ostrom 2002; Carson and Roberts 2005), need never be used again.

ACKNOWLEDGMENTS

This project has been a labor of love for us. As such, we have been working on it for quite a long time, and that has, in turn, meant that we have built up a very large number of people and groups who have contributed immensely to this project. We are certain, we regret to say, to be unable to thank all of them by name. Even so, we are genuinely grateful for making this project much stronger than it would have been without your thoughts and assistance in so many ways. Because we have different relationships to the project, and we, of course, have different institutional affiliations, we offer our own acknowledgments. But one set of acknowledgments is fully shared. We want to thank the University of Chicago Press, starting with John Tryneski for his long and great support for us and this book. But he was only the first among equal supporters at the Press—we also thank Rodney Powell, Chuck Myers, Mark Reschke, and Holly Smith for getting us over the finish line.

John Aldrich: My role in this project began in 1999. I had the good fortune to be elected president of the Southern Political Science Association (SPSA), and the president gives an address. That year was the fiftieth anniversary of the publication of V. O. Key Jr.'s greatest book, *Southern Politics in State and Nation.* Professor Key was also one of the cofounders of the SPSA, I had recently published a book on political parties that rested on Key's various insights, and all together that meant that my address had to honor him and his work. Hence, I presented the address "Southern Parties in State and Nation" (*Journal of Politics* 62, no. 3 [2000]: 643–70). It turned out that Key and his work haunted me. It took a while and at least a 50% contribution by John Griffin, but this book is the culmination of that project. I might add that I gave another address to the SPSA at its annual conference (in my role as president of the American Political Science Association) in 2014 on this subject as the book neared completion.

The central question was whether Key's claim that a competitive party system was necessary to have a well-functioning democracy was correct. He, of course, was looking at the South when it was a one-party system (or, as he put it, a one-party system in the nation, a no-party system in the southern states), and there was no question (thanks to his work, among others) that it was not a well-functioning democracy. Now that the South had a genuine two-party system, was it the case that southern states had become a better functioning democracy?

One part of the way to answer that question was to see if the two parties in southern states had developed organizations of the sort usually associated with functioning party systems. The best way to do that was to replicate a survey of party organizations in the states (as reported in chapter 6). Brad Gomez and I conducted that survey, and indeed I could not (and would not) have done so without him. Rebecca Hatch has since conducted a newer survey for her doctoral dissertation and made the results available for John and I to use here.

Rebecca also served as a research assistant on the project, especially critical for the Granger analysis reported in chapter 7. Brendan Nyhan, Michael Brady, and Mark Dudley assisted us as well over the years. John and I are grateful for all of their contributions.

Bill Chafe, my great friend and colleague, offered the opportunity to jointly teach a graduate seminar on politics of the post-Reconstruction Jim Crow era South and the Progressive era nationwide. I learned a vast amount from him and from the entire class (including one John Griffin!), and I doubt this book would look at all like it does without his influence. He and my colleague Kerry Haynie served as coleaders of what was then known as the Faculty Fellows program through the Social Science Research Institute (SSRI) at Duke. This program gave a dozen faculty time and resources to work together on various aspects of the New South, which both allowed me time to reflect on the subject and John and I to present some of our work to the group. Wendy Wood was codirector of SSRI at the time, and this program was her idea and it was a terrific one. It is, of course, only one of many ways that Duke University supported the research going into this project.

I was honored (and rather surprised) to be a Guggenheim Fellow for the calendar year 2013. It was a wonderful thing, and it made possible the forward progress that actually led to the completion of this book. I greatly appreciate their support and apologize to the foundation for taking quite this long to finish the book.

John and I (either singly or jointly) gave a good number of presentations on this subject, such as at a conference at the University of Rochester to honor Richard Niemi and at a presentation at the University of South Carolina that had the very nice benefit of introducing me to graduate students there with whom I have had the pleasure of continuing to work (that is a shout-out to you, Paul White).

But, this manuscript was shaped most fully and directly by the extremely helpful reactions of the participants in the book seminar conducted under the auspices of the Political Institutions and Public Choice (PIPC) program headed by Dave Rohde. This multiday event culminated in a lengthy series of reactions from Dave, Jason Roberts, and Mark Dudley, with additional reactions across the set of graduate students associated with PIPC that year. While (or because) it took us nearly an extra year to complete the revisions their commentaries induced, the result is much better.

John Griffin: John has already trod much of the acknowledgment ground that needs covering. I wish just to add a few more expressions of thanks from my corner.

I began to work on this project as a graduate student at Duke University, and as it nears completion I am hoping to go up for promotion to full professor. While the duration of the manuscript's journey has its disadvantages, including several intervening elections requiring that the data (and corresponding tables and figures) be updated, there was one overriding benefit for me. Namely, for more than a decade and a half I have had the genuine pleasure to work first for, and then with, a generous, brilliant, and courageous colleague in John Aldrich. So my first thank-you goes to John for mentoring me while I figured out how to lend my voice to this manuscript, and for his patience and constant good cheer along the way. I feel so fortunate to have had this opportunity to work with you.

This project was supported in numerous ways while I was on the faculty at the University of Notre Dame, and more recently at the University of Colorado Boulder. My political science colleagues at both institutions provided valuable advice, especially Dianne Pinderhughes, David Campbell, Christina Wolbrecht, Scott Mainwaring, and Michael Coppedge.

In addition to receiving comments at professional meetings such as the Citadel Symposium on Southern Politics, portions of this project benefited from feedback at a number of departmental seminars (some noted in John's acknowledgments), but also the University of Chicago, University of Notre Dame American Politics Workshop, University of Pittsburgh, and Indiana University, among others.

I also want to thank my family. It is customary for authors to thank their spouse and children for putting up with their absences and distractedness while they focused on a manuscript. You'll see none of that here, because my family was not an obstacle to my work on this project but rather a tremendous source of support and inspiration. I began working on this project about the time that Amy and I had our daughter Elizabeth. She is now fifteen. Amy and Elizabeth, together with Jack and Natalie, have motivated me to contribute to something worthwhile, something they would be proud of. In this I hope that we have succeeded.

NOTES

CHAPTER ONE

1. For most of this book, we define the political South as the eleven states of the Confederacy. We do so following Key (1949) and because we are tracking the South from the nineteenth, and even the eighteenth century, on.

2. Found at http://web.utk.edu/~mfitzge1/docs/374/wallace_seg63.pdf, accessed February 6, 2015.

3. http://www.huffingtonpost.com/benjamin-r-barber/the-people-are-not-ready_b_821359.html.

4. http://seeingredinchina.com/2012/02/27/china-isnt-ready-for-democracy-vote-buying-low-quality-people-and-other-excuses/.

5. http://www.worldpolicy.org/journal/fall2012/big-question-what-biggest-threat-democracy.

6. http://wilsonquarterly.com/quarterly/winter-2013-is-democracy-worth-it/why-wait-for-democracy/.

CHAPTER TWO

A previous version of this chapter was published in Jan Leighley, ed., *Oxford Handbook of American Politics* (2010).

1. More accurately to quote someone to whom Churchill attributed the following: "Many forms of Government have been tried and will be tried in this world of sin and woe. No one pretends that democracy is perfect or all-wise. Indeed, it has been said that democracy is the worst form of government except all those other forms that have been tried from time to time." Speech in the House of Commons (November 11, 1947), published in 206–07 The Official Report, House of Commons (5th Ser.), 11 November 1947, vol. 444, or see Winston Churchill, speech, House of Commons, November 11, 1947, in *Winston S. Churchill: His Complete Speeches, 1897–1963*, ed. Robert Rhodes James, vol. 7 (1974), 7566.

2. Where "multi" means "at least two."

3. To us, this defines what we mean by a scientific theory—a logically sound argument with testable implications that provides evidence in support of (or in opposition to) a proposed answer to the fundamental question of science, "Why?"

4. Or, at least, central in democracies in extended republics, as Madison would put it, but that is only to say in virtually every democratic nation-state.

5. We stop just short of directly confronting this claim, as we contend that electoral competition is a necessary condition for effective governance and

a system of political parties is the only means that societies have invented to reliably produce competitive elections.

6. "The full development of the liberal democratic state in the West required that political criticism and opposition be incarnated in one or more opposition parties" (Hofstadter 1969, xii).

7. Of course, one or more parties will also generally seize the opportunity to compete on "valence" issues, but the logic of their competition shifts from "our policy is best" to "the opposition failed in governing well, we will do better, even on issues on which we all agree."

8. Absent a party system in equilibrium, we cannot reliably expect competitive elections to occur; it might happen from time to time and place to place, but there will not be sustained competition in which elected officials are held accountable.

9. Our theory does not indicate what "sustained" means in numbers of years, but we have in mind something like twenty years or more (Reed 1990).

10. On the other hand, Fiorina (1973) showed that more marginal districts did not tend to be represented by more moderate elected officials.

11. This view stands in some contrast to the notion of "issue ownership" in which the parties are viewed by voters as better able to advance particular policy areas, although Egan (2013) rather convincingly demonstrates that any such expectation on the part of voters is certainly not kept by the parties.

12. This follows from the fact of repeated elections, which parties as a collection of ambitious, office-seeking candidates (inter alia) consistently want to win. The idea is similar to the (restrictive) version Downs used (1957), conflating a party as equivalent to an infinite-lived individual candidate.

13. This is not to say, of course, that competitive elections uniquely bring good things to society. In a two-party system, competitive elections are equivalent to Richardson's arms' races, for example (Richardson 1960). Candidates are prone to run negative campaigns, for another, and the list can be extended.

14. Or as Gingrich has said, "Any time you have a dominant system, you begin to develop the competition inside the system" (Martin 2014).

15. For another argument from this perspective, see Bartels (2008).

16. In another noteworthy reminder that we should not be too quick to assume that political competition will yield outcomes more consonant with public opinion, Gerber and Lupia's (1995) theoretical examination of direct elections showed that competition over the proposed policy change was neither necessary nor sufficient to produce policy outcomes that are preferable to the public, without imposing additional conditions.

17. For instance, recent work shows that competitive elections produce more engaged and knowledgeable voters (Ensley, Carmines, and Evans 2014; Milazzo 2014).

18. The purpose for doing so, of course, is to seek to capture office and use its perquisites effectively. Note, of course, that there may be pockets—perhaps quite large pockets—of noncompetitive seats amidst a sea of competition, such as gerrymandered seats for many incumbents who stay within the same party for lengthy periods of time with little interparty competition, even when the overall composition of the assembly is closely contested.

19. Of course, the South was a one-party system in the nation and a zero-party system in the southern states according to Key (1949). Our argument, like his, is simply that effective democratic governance requires a party system of "two" or of "more than two," so that party "systems" of size zero and one are both associated with democratic failure.

20. This further suggests that what matters overall is not that every individual district need be competitive, but that the overall makeup be so.

21. That is, the set of "politicians" is divided into those whom Schlesinger (1975) referred to as "office seekers" and "benefit seekers."

22. In other electoral systems, parties may be evaluated in other terms. For example, in clientelistic systems, parties may be judged on how effective their local leaders are in distributing goods, services, and jobs to client/citizens. In ethnically fragmented lineage systems, judgments may be based on effectiveness of the integration of tribal or other social organization into the political system. Of course, distributive and identity politics are a part of the American political system, too.

23. Note that the category "activist" also includes formal and semiformal organizations of them, including in their contemporary manifestations such as "Super PACs."

24. At least if, as in these cases, the legislative defeat was due to the actions of members of the same party. Republicans defeating gun control measures in 2013 in Congress does not affect the value of the Democrats' label. There are too many veto points (in the sense of Tsebelis 2002) to be able to hold even a majority party fully accountable for inability to enact promised policies. Aldrich et al. (2014) find, however, that in the 2010 congressional elections, voters may not have blamed the Democratic Party for causing the "Great Recession," but they did hold them responsible for failing to do enough to end it, with their majority in both chambers and the presidency.

25. As Downs put it (1957), office seekers are political parties that formulate policy platforms to win election, rather than seek to win elections so that they can formulate policies.

26. Politicians who value only what the party stands for, that is, who evaluate the party label just as do the citizenry, are either called lucky politicians, lucky to value what is electorally propitious, or they are called former politicians.

27. Of course, some sought to avoid that fate by reemerging as Democrats.

28. That is, the behaviors of politicians motivated by policy are observationally equivalent to those motivated solely by office seeking. Or, in game-theoretic terms, politicians of either stripe are in a "babbling equilibrium," such that no voter could distinguish between the two types of politicians. On the other hand, no voter would care, since the politician's behavior is, indeed, observationally equivalent regardless of motivation.

29. In Caughey's analysis, Oklahoma and Kentucky are sometimes included; all Republican southern congressional districts are excluded, as are appointed officials.

30. While all stood for a unified south in the national government, to ensure northern forbearance necessary to maintain the Jim Crow system, that unanimity did not help the voter distinguish one politician from the other.

PART TWO

1. See Jillson and Wilson (1994) who show political differences for the period of the confederal Congress, and see Aldrich (2011) for demonstration, and reference to other studies conducted, about the early federal Congresses. See also Aldrich, Jillson, and Wilson (2002).

2. For entrée to this literature, see http://www.oxfordbibliographies.com /view/document/obo-9780199730414/obo-9780199730414–0048.xml.

3. As Franklin and Moss note (2000), indentured servitude was less economically viable than full slavery, and thus African American indentured servitude waned relatively quickly. This difference was, of course, exaggerated when the indentured servants were Europeans (among other reasons, they could run away and were far more difficult to recognize and recapture than African Americans). Enslaving Native Americans proved far less economically remunerative as well, in part due to their greater susceptibility to diseases brought by white colonialists and in part due to their lacking the social-cultural preparation to work as well in a plantation setting as Africans.

4. For a short account, see http://opinionator.blogs.nytimes.com/2013/03 /30/king-cottons-long-shadow/.

5. http://mapserver.lib.virginia.edu/, accessed April 2, 2013.

6. Here, for example, is what *Wikipedia* says about southern Baptists: "The word *Southern* in Southern Baptist Convention stems from its having been founded and rooted in the Southern United States. In 1845, members at a regional convention being held in Augusta, Georgia created the SBC, following a split from northern Baptists over the issue of forbidding churches in slaveholding states from sending missionaries to spread the gospel. After the American Civil War, another split occurred: most black Baptists in the South separated from white churches to set up independent congregations, regional associations, and state and national conventions, such as the National Baptist Convention, the second largest Baptist convention."

7. Dunn (1977, 2014) has compared slave life on plantations in Jamaica and Virginia, in which he argued that slavery in the Virginia plantation revolved primarily around the generation of "surplus" slaves to sell.

8. The Missouri Compromise was still in effect, anyway, not being repealed until 1854.

9. Charleston is where a number of major Federalist figures were from, such as the brothers Thomas Pinckney and Charles Coteswsorth Pinckney, candidates for vice president (and Charles for president as well) on the Federalist side.

10. McCormick (1960) is quoting the Beards (1933) by way of disputing their dating of the "flood" as 1824, while building his case for it to be in 1840 or so.

11. The degree of partisan polarization is, of course, a topic of current interest in and of itself. Our interest is the role it plays in the theory of conditional party government (CPG) proposed by Aldrich and Rohde (Rohde 1991; Aldrich 1995, 2011; Aldrich and Rohde 1996, 2000; Aldrich, Perry and Rohde, 2013). CPG highlights the circumstances in which parties will be more or less organized and effective, as parties, in the government and about how this condition is set in large part by electoral choice and thus, in large part, by the

strength of the party in elections, and the capabilities of the party organizations within and between these two spheres. See also Muirhead (2014).

CHAPTER THREE

1. John C. Calhoun was also so proposed but declined in order to concentrate on the vice presidency, as an office he believed (correctly) was one that he was more likely to win.

2. That is, electors were free by Constitution, law, and intention of the Founders to be able to vote for whomever they choose. The Jeffersonian caucuses and the Federalist counterparts were intended to offer focal points, coordinating the individual elector's "wisdom" in choosing to support John Adams's "most wise and good" candidates for president and vice president, following the guidance of the party in that quest.

3. The Twelfth Amendment ended the original design in which the vice president was the Electoral College runner up (with the vote of a majority of electors). It separated the electoral voting into two votes, one for each office, rather than each elector voting for two people for president. This amendment aligned with the new creation of political parties presenting a slate of candidates for president and for vice president and avoided the problems arising from the tied vote in 1800 between Jefferson and Burr, when all Jeffersonian electors, constituting a majority of the Electoral College, cast votes for both of them for president, and no non-Jeffersonians voted for either one. Once the 1800 election was finally resolved in the House, the Congress passed the amendment in 1803, and it was ratified in 1804.

4. The weight of scholarly opinion is that there was no bargain, although it is easy to see how Jacksonians could capitalize on the appearance of there being one.

5. Senator John Henry Eaton (TN) married a well-known DC resident and widow, Margaret O'Neale, but too soon after becoming a widower for the social mores of the time. Jackson had encouraged the marriage, and the controversy led many of his cabinet to resign (Jackson having appointed Eaton secretary of war) and was at least one of the considerations in play when Calhoun left the vice presidency.

6. Willie Mangum is generally listed as an independent candidate (or as an Independent candidate) but claimed to be the Whig Party of South Carolina candidate (even though he was from, and won, North Carolina).

7. Some argue for 1838 (e.g., Folsom 1973).

8. According to McCormick (1986, 178), "major political figures retained an unusual degree of freedom from party discipline."

CHAPTER FOUR

1. Or at least as best we can tell. Everyone could tell that the Democrats lost in 1854, but (due to fusion, secrecy of party affiliation, and general unsettledness [the Republicans did not yet have a name]) no one was quite sure who won.

2. The Free Soil platform claimed a "banner" of "Free Soil, Free Speech, Free Labor, and Free Men," in their presidential bids.

3. In 1860, the South, including slaves, had a population of 9 million, under a third of the nation's population (which was approximately 31.5 million), and only about a quarter of its wealth. This dramatic relative decline since the Revolution was part of the risk aversion motivating the white South. About 10% of the South lived in cities, compared to a quarter of northerners. See, for example, http://www.civilwar.org/education/history/civil-war-overview /northandsouth.html.

4. Electoral fusion is a tactic whereby two or more parties list the same candidate on the ballot and pool their support.

5. While Americans were creating fusion candidacies with Republicans (as well as with Democrats and with Whigs, and sometimes in several combinations), Republicans engaged in this practice less often than Americans, at least at higher levels of office. See Aldrich (2011).

6. Two conventions were required in part due to the use of the two-thirds rule for nominating the president, a rule (as noted in chapter 3) created to try to keep North and South together in the Democratic Party. The two southern candidates were John C. Breckinridge (KY) of the Southern Democratic Party and John Bell (TN) of the Constitutional Union Party. If everyone who voted for either of these candidates in the general election had voted for Douglas, he would have significantly outpolled Lincoln. This points out that while the Republicans could win a majority purely on the basis of northern votes, they would have to do very well there at least as long as they got no support out of the one-third of the nation that was the South.

7. Congressional elections still were spread over time in this period and continued into 1861.

8. See http://www.civilwar.org/education/history/primarysources/declaration ofcauses.html?referrer=https://www.google.com/.

9. Sherman was commander of the Military Division of the Mississippi and was particularly loathed by Confederates for his March to the Sea, from his departure from Atlanta on November 15 to his arrival at Savannah on December 21, 1864.

10. Along lands under Sherman's control; this was along the coast from Charleston, South Carolina, to St. John's River, Florida.

11. See Kennedy (1964 [1956]).

12. "Carpetbaggers" was the derogatory term southerners used to describe those who came south to run the former Confederacy.

13. http://www.aaregistry.org/historic_events/view/mississippi-plan-political -deviance.

14. While these were third parties in national politics, the effective demise of the Republican Party in most of the South indicates these were attempts at becoming the second major party in the state or broader region, even if being "only" a third-party movement nationally.

15. So severe was the panic that economists and political leaders adopted the euphemism "depression" to refer less scarily to what had heretofore been dubbed "panics."

16. "Where Republicans were elected from the periphery, their voting records—as was true in the Reconstruction era—would not have differed no-

ticeably from their northern comrades even though the economic interests of their constituencies would have been radically different" (Bensel 1984, 76).

17. "The Georgia Republicans had by this time degenerated into a quarrelsome lot of office-holders, office-seekers, and contentious factionalists. . . . In the tenth district the Republican convention, preferring to concentrate on the presidential ticket, unanimously resolved not to run a candidate for Congress nor make any local opposition to the Democrats" (Ward 1943, 209).

"The Republican attempt to aid the Independent movement brought violent internal convulsions within the Republican party in Georgia. . . . This factional bickering led one correspondent to write: 'The Republican party was never so dead in Georgia as it is today'" (Ward 1943, 203).

18. We include in the count of uncontested races a relatively small number of races in which the party fielded a candidate who received less than 10% of the vote.

CHAPTER FIVE

1. There were other, earlier third parties that logically could have done what the Populists were trying to do, that is, to become a major player in elections, often on at least roughly similar policy and coalitional bases as the Populists, such as the Greenback Party. Only the Populists, however, succeeded in becoming anything like a serious threat in the South and in the nation.

2. The 1957 bill was the next national civil rights law enacted after the "force bill" of 1870.

3. That is, it permitted a law to stand that mandated separate facilities in public transportation.

4. This last point was, of course, the centerpiece underlying the reversal of "separate but equal" in the 1954 *Brown v. Board* case. The defense of this separate provision was that it was "equal" in the sense that it provided both whites and blacks seats on public transportation or schools. It was true, of course, that provision of any such matters was progress at this time.

5. A comprehensive coverage of laws that constitute what is commonly referred to as "Jim Crow" can be found in several places, perhaps most famously, Murray (1997 [1951]).

6. Epperly et al. (2016) report, in part, that "we find that lynchings increased as elections approached and that they were most common when and where black political participation was most threatening to white, Democratic elites. We observe, however, that these relationships between political variables and lynchings disappear once the Southern states developed institutionalized means of voter suppression."

7. That set of issues was chosen by 34% of the public, followed by the threat of communism/Russia/Cuba at 20% and "international problems" at 10%, as reported in *The Public Perspective*, May/June 1993, 15; http://www.ropercenter.uconn.edu/public-perspective/ppscan/44/44010.pdf.

8. Perhaps the first civil rights sit-in was on August 21, 1939, in the Alexandria (VA) Library. See http://www.alexandria.lib.va.us/client/en_US/home/?rm=1939+LIBRARY+S0%7C%7C%7C1%7C%7C%7C0%7C%7C%7Ctrue&dt=list.

9. Note, however, that the South was too small to be able to hold a majority of the Democratic delegation in years when the Democrats controlled a full majority of the House. Thus, there were limits to their national strength. Of course, they need only ally with conservative Republicans to defeat liberal Democratic policies, a strategy they used after 1936 when they were able to form a conservative coalition.

CHAPTER SIX

1. At least three Presidential Addresses of the Southern Political Science Association have dealt primarily with this topic (Bullock 1988b; Black 1998; Aldrich 2000).

2. According to Key, this included an organized Democratic Party. Key was thus careful to refer to the Democratic Party in the South itself as a no-party, rather than one-party, system.

3. It could be argued that, while the Whigs were a mass-based party by 1840 and their sweep of national offices, they could win national election only with war hero presidents and that the separation between northern and southern wings kept them from being as fully developed as the Jacksonian Democrats or as today's Democratic and Republican Parties are. This is also consistent with our finding that both of the parties were divided by region essentially to the same extent that the parties divided the nation; see chapter 3.

4. As Patterson (1981) points out, the huge Democratic majority may be dated from before the Seventy-Fifth Congress (1937–40), and southerners did seek Republican support, as well as votes from conservative Democrats from outside the South, before the 1936 landslide. The stakes were raised substantially after 1936, however, so we mark this as our point of origin.

5. These data are taken from Manley (1973).

6. Goldwater's belief in states' rights provided his justification for his vote against the Civil Rights Bill in 1964, but "states' rights" was also a code word of leading southern Democrats for retaining white dominance.

7. The data actually begin in 1993, but from 1993 to 1995 the data are missing forty-five, forty-six, and thirty-seven states, respectively.

8. We use forty-nine states (Nebraska has a nonpartisan legislature) and use the lower house for them and the U.S. Congress. By "standardization," we mean that each legislature is set so that their scaled voting scores have the same variance as each other. We cannot say from examining the data this way whether Vermont Republicans are more liberal or conservative than, say, those in New Mexico. We can observe, however, whether Republicans voted more consistently conservative than their Democratic opponents in one state than was true in another state.

9. As usual the ability to relate one set of scaling to another, such as a state legislature to the national one, depends upon specific data requirements. In this case, it is the "bridging observations" of members of the state legislature who become members of the U.S. Congress. Their solution is perfectly fine, with a good number of bridging observations (roughly half of all MCs were once state legislators), but it is a set of assumptions that could be wrong, and, of course, there are no real bridging observations to compare across states.

10. Where Gibson et al. reported mean party organizational strength by region for the Northeast, Midwest, South, and West, we collapse the data for the three northern regions.

11. We (together with Brad Gomez) conducted a mail survey of the one hundred state party chairs in the summer of 1999. Sixty-five surveys were returned, after several prompts, twenty-six from Republican Party state chairs and thirty-nine from Democratic Party state chairs.

12. In Gibson et al.'s original analysis, they retained three factors; however, they included more variables in their analysis, which likely explains the slightly different results. In the factor analysis for the 2011 data, the "Candidate support" and "Infrastructure" dimensions did not emerge as clearly, likely due to the need for new measures of organizational strength (Hatch 2016).

13. Chairpersons were classified by period based on their final reported year of service.

14. One of these is preprimary endorsement, perhaps because endorsement is less likely to be allowed in the South.

15. The ANES item used to generate these data is the standard party identification question: "Generally speaking, do you usually think of yourself as a Republican, a Democrat, an Independent, or what?" Would you call yourself a strong (REP/DEM) or a not very strong (REP/DEM)? (IF INDEPENDENT, OTHER [1966 AND LATER: OR NO PREFERENCE]:) Do you think of yourself as closer to the Republican or Democratic Party?

16. Specifically, the ANES asks, "Do you think there are any important differences in what the Republicans and Democrats stand for?"

17. The proportion of voters who recognize a difference between the parties is quite a bit larger in presidential election years than in midterm elections (Weisberg 2002). However, because both southern and northern whites exhibit this tendency, we include regional comparisons in midterm years in figure 6.17.

PART THREE

1. For example, see Sartori (1977); Miller (1983); Strom (1990); Griffin (2006); Jones (2013).

2. As V. O. Key put it (1949, 310), "ruling groups have so inveterate a habit of being wrong that the health of a democratic order demands that they be challenged and constantly compelled to prove their case." See also Riker (1982).

3. Certainly, sometimes it may be one set of voters who are aided more than another set (e.g., Cingranelli 1981; Gerber and Lewis 2004), but over time, those losers can become winners. Miller (1983) offers a formal discussion of this and related issues. The major point is that it is the need to seek ways to form majorities of the public that favors competitive democracies over other, nonmajoritarian, that is, nondemocratic, systems.

4. Bueno de Mesquita and others argue that officeholders respond to the "selectorate," those whose support is needed to attain and retain office. In this view, democracy is distinct in being the particular form of government with the broadest selectorate—the whole electorate, that is, as compared to

nondemocratic systems that are distinct in having a vastly smaller selectorate and thus being responsive to the few rather than the many. See Bueno de Mesquita et al. (1999).

5. In Mexico, before full democratization, the authoritarian dominant party, the Institutional Revolutionary Party (PRI), supported the National Action Party (PAN) as a "manufactured opposition," rather similar to the way the Washington Nationals were a "manufactured opposition" to the Harlem Globetrotters. The PRI's decision to allow full competition led their manufactured opposition party to become a major opponent, one that replaced them in the presidential election of 2000.

CHAPTER SEVEN

1. In most of these periods, "he" is the correct word. Only recently would it be "she or he."

2. 5 Stat. 491 (1842).

3. We are grateful to Craig Goodman for providing these data (Goodman 2003).

4. In contrast, Seagull (1970) observed that the Goldwater breakthrough in 1964 did *not* produce GOP success in U.S. Senate races in 1966 or 1968 in the same locales.

5. Note, though, that Aistrup's data do not begin until 1968, after much of the "action" in figure 7.5 has commenced. Moreover, the data end in 1989, before the full emergence of the southern GOP. Aistrup's estimations also curiously exclude U.S. House elections, as well as Louisiana voters and black voters. Finally, this analysis does not estimate whether any simultaneous, "upward" effects exist.

6. This theory was also that of Key (1956), who noted that "the broad fluctuations in national politics sweep the states along in their presidential voting but the solidly entrenched local party, with its advantage *in organization, in traditional loyalties,* and often in leadership, can at least for a time maintain its local position" (37, emphasis added). Although Key was describing why Roosevelt's popularity only slowly improved northern Democratic candidates' prospects in state office races, the arguments apply analogously to the South. Black and Black (1989) also focus their explanation of the GOP's success in the South on the changes among voters.

7. A first analysis of the state-to-national development of party competition was presented by Aldrich (2000).

8. The 1968 result reflects the percentage difference in the popular vote for the top two candidates, due to George Wallace's candidacy.

9. Data for 1850–1980 provided by Brady and Grofman (1991). Engstrom and Kernell (2005) have updated the measure through 2004, by which time there is complete regional convergence.

10. In additional analyses, we found that when we estimated the model using data obtained since 1994 (the year of the southern Republican takeover of the House), the estimated effect of party contacting was positive (.150) and statistically significant ($p < .01$).

11. There are also two ways we can count things, either by looking at the

percentage vote or the proportion of seats won. The details of this are re-counted in the appendixes to chapter 8.

12. We limit the analysis to voting and seats that were Democrat or were Republican, Populist, or both (fusion).

13. Jacobson (1989) now argues that a sufficient measure is the revealed ability to raise a large campaign war chest. Such a measure is simply unavailable systematically before the most recent period.

14. See, for example, a discussion of the Nunn dynasty in Georgia: http://www.nytimes.com/2014/01/25/us/politics/familiar-name-tries-to-reverse-democrats-slide-in-georgia.html?nl=us&emc=edit_cn_20140124.

CHAPTER EIGHT

1. There are a number of additional technical issues about the calculations with respect to the House. We report these in the appendixes to this chapter.

2. The comparable figure for the House is similar, and we report only one chamber per time period in this way for that reason. Of course, for the House, there is a slightly upward-sloping line for the South, and an even more upward-sloping line for the North than in this figure. Note that for this figure and all parallel figures to follow, the line of fit only ranges over the range of observable data.

3. We estimated probit models of senator party affiliation as a function of state support for the Democratic presidential candidate in the most recent election and found that the estimated relationship in the North (5.6) was about four times as large as the relationship in the South (1.4).

4. Because there were too few Republicans and Populists in office (unlike the stronger showing of the Whigs), we report regressions using party dummy variables and separating the data by party for the House.

5. "Southern planters, industrialists, farmers, artisans, merchants, professionals—all found themselves on one party, their divergent interests papered over by white unity" (Ayers 1992, 50).

6. The line for northern legislators does not range over the entire ideological space because there were no sufficiently liberal northern legislators in this period. Stated another way, the lines for the two regions do not cross.

7. Citing J. G. de Roulhac Hamilton, *North Carolina since 1860* (Chicago and New York, 1919), 192–93; *North Carolina House Journal*, 1876–77, 875–76; *Raleigh Daily Caucasian*, February 10, 1895; William A. Mabry, *The Negro in North Carolina Politics since Reconstruction*, in Trinity College Historical Society, Historical Papers, Ser. 23 (Durham, 1940), 18–19.

8. Citing Eldridge R. Collins, "The Florida Constitution of 1885" (M.A. thesis, University of Florida, 1939), 7, 89–92, 676.

9. Citing *Jackson Clarion-Ledger*, September 11, 1890.

10. Our conclusion that southern legislators were less responsive than northern legislators to constituents' preferences prior to 1980 but not afterward may be challenged on several grounds. A first alternative interpretation of these results is that there was much less variation in southern than northern preferences among citizens prior to 1980 and/or less variation in southern than northern officials' roll call behavior prior to 1980. From this perspective,

when the variation in opinion and/or roll call voting became more similar in each region, the effect of opinion on roll call voting became more equal. Comparing the standard deviations of regional ideology showed that there was not less variance in southern (.14) than northern (.13) congressional district preferences or southern (.13) than northern (.10) state preferences in the pre-1980 period. Indeed, there was somewhat less variation in southern (.12) than northern (.14) congressional district liberalism in the *post*-1980 period, when representatives were somewhat more responsive in the South than the North. Southern states, too, were more homogenous as a group than northern states only after 1980 (the standard deviation of southern states' liberalism after 1980 was .06, compared to a standard deviation of .09 for northern states).

On the other hand, there was less variation in the roll call voting of southern (s.d. = .23) than northern (.36) representatives and southern (.26) than northern (.37) senators prior to 1980, but not much afterward. The standard deviation of northern representatives post-1980 was .41, compared to a standard deviation of .38 for southern MCs. The data for senators after 1980 are similar. So, limited variance in the dependent variable prior to 1980 might be driving our results. To estimate the importance of the lesser roll call variation among southern representatives for our results, we standardized the distributions of pre-1980 roll call liberalism so that southern and northern representatives would exhibit the same amount of variation and reestimated the models. Specifically, we divided the values for northern MCs by the standard deviation of the pre-1980 northern distribution and the values for southern MCs by the standard deviation of its pre-1980 distribution, so that both distributions shared a standard deviation of 1. After doing so, we continued to find that northern representatives were much more responsive than southern representatives.

11. https://library.cqpress.com/cqalmanac/toc.php?mode=cqalmanac-appendix&level=2&values=CQ+Key+Votes+Tables.

12. $156 in 2010 dollars.

13. U.S. Census Bureau, Consolidated Federal Funds Report, 2005.

14. https://earmarks.omb.gov/earmarks-public/.

15. As a recent *New York Times* article asked, "Do voters hate spending even when it is spending that comes home to them?" (Fausset 2014).

16. The Volden and Wiseman Legislative Effectiveness Scores reflect bill sponsorship, bill attention in committee, bill passage out of committee, bill floor passage, and bill enactment into law.

17. In unreported results we found that at the beginning of this period constituents in the two regions were equally satisfied with their House member's response to their request for help. Beginning in 1986, however, and continuing every year except 1992, southern constituents reported being more satisfied with the response than did northern constituents.

CHAPTER NINE

1. Border states are defined here, as per usual, as Kentucky, Delaware, Maryland, West Virginia, and Missouri.

2. West Virginia, under Union control, had unique rules about slavery.

3. A belief in the desirability of democracy does not exist in isolation from other beliefs. For most people it is a part of a cluster of beliefs. Included in this cluster is the belief that freedom of expression "is desirable in itself" (Dahl 1998, 50–51).

4. As a side note, in midterm years and within the South among whites, reported turnout increased from about 45% in 1958 to 67% as recently as 2002 (ANES data 1958–98, CCES data in 2002). Outside the South, reported turnout in midterm elections increased much more modestly, from 70% in 1958 to 75% in 2002.

5. The ANES has only asked this item in presidential election years, resulting in a smaller case count.

6. For example, scholars have long observed that economic and democratic performance go hand in hand (Lipset 1959). Some emphasize the influence of economic development on democracy (Burkhart and Lewis-Beck 1994), others the effect of democracy on economic growth (Leblang 1997).

7. "Reasonably good health in the face of poverty is not a puzzle it is something observed in other societies that have low population density but abundant arable land remote from commercial centers" (Ferleger and Steckel 2000, 174).

8. This Fivethirtyeight.com post goes on to add "President Obama won Florida two consecutive times. In 2008, Obama was the first Democratic presidential candidate to win in North Carolina since Jimmy Carter in 1976. . . . Obama [is] the first Democrat to win Virginia since 1964."

9. Again, Democratic success has been greater outside the Deep South, with two Democratic senators in Virginia in 2015 for the first time since 1973 (Enten 2014). And "Even as Obama lost the Tar Heel State in 2012, Democratic House candidates there won a majority of the vote [as did state assembly candidates, even though they won few seats]" (Enten 2014).

10. Four of the "battleground" states for the 2016 presidential race in Realclearplitics.com were former Confederate states (Florida, Georgia, North Carolina, and Virginia), with Clinton carrying Virginia. In North Carolina, with its veto-override dominance of Republicans in the state legislature, the incumbent Republican governor was defeated for reelection in a very close race against the then-incumbent attorney general.

11. Hayes and McKee (2008) acknowledge that the full enfranchisement of African American voters places an upper bound on GOP control, as compared to the years Key (1949) recounted prior to 1950.

12. Also notable are the turn toward voter ID in Texas and North Carolina, and the 2013 suspension by the Supreme Court of Section 4 (and thus by implication 5) of the Voting Rights Act.

REFERENCES

Abramowitz, Alan I. 1988. "Explaining Senate Election Outcomes." *American Political Science Review* 82(2):385–403.

Abramson, Paul R., and John H. Aldrich. 1980. "The Decline of Electoral Participation in America." *American Political Science Review* 76(3):502–21.

Abramson, Paul R., John H. Aldrich, and David W. Rohde. 1987. "Progressive Ambition among United States Senators: 1972–1988." *Journal of Politics* 49(1):3–35.

Acharya, Avidit, Matthew Blackwell, and Maya Sen. 2016. "The Political Legacy of American Slavery." *Journal of Politics* 78(3):621–41.

Achen, Christopher H. 1978. "Measuring Representation." *American Journal of Political Science* 22(3):475–510.

Adams, James, Thomas L. Brunell, Bernard Grofman, and Samuel Merrill III. 2013. "Do Competitive Districts Necessarily Produce Centrist Politicians?" In *Advances in Political Economy: Institutions, Modelling and Empirical Analysis*, ed. Norman Schofield, Gonzalo Caballero, and Daniel Kselman, 331–50. New York: Springer Press.

Adler, Scott E., and John D. Wilkerson. 2012. *Congress and the Politics of Problem Solving.* New York: Cambridge University Press.

Aistrup, Joseph A. 1996. *The Southern Strategy Revisited: Republican Top-Down Advancement in the South.* Lexington: University Press of Kentucky.

Aldrich, John H. 1995. *Why Parties? The Origin and Transformation of Party Politics in America.* Chicago: University of Chicago Press.

Aldrich, John H. 1999. "Political Parties in a Critical Era." *American Politics Research* 27(1):9–32.

Aldrich, John H. 2000. "Southern Parties in State and Nation" *Journal of Politics* 62(3):643–70.

Aldrich, John H. 2005. "The Election of 1800: The Consequences of the First Change in Party Control." In *Establishing Congress: The Removal to Washington, D.C., and the Election of 1800*, ed. Kenneth R. Bowling and Donald R. Kennon, 23–38. Athens: Ohio University Press (for the United States Capitol Historical Society), 2005.

Aldrich, John H. 2011. *Why Parties? A Second Look.* Chicago: University of Chicago Press.

Aldrich, John H. 2015. "Did Hamilton, Jefferson, and Madison 'Cause' the US Government Shutdown? The Institutional Path from an Eighteenth Century Republic to a Twenty-First Century Democracy." *Perspectives on Politics* 13(1):7–23.

Aldrich, John H., Mark Berger, and David W. Rohde. 2003. "Historical Variability in Conditional Party Government, 1877–1994." In *Party, Process, and Political Change in Congress: New Perspectives on the History of Congress*, ed. David Brady and Mathew D. McCubbins, 17–35. Stanford, CA: Stanford University Press.

Aldrich, John H., and William T. Bianco. 1992. "A Game-Theoretic Model of Party Affiliation of Candidates and Office Holders." *Mathematical and Computer Modeling* 16(8–9):103–16.

Aldrich, John H., Bradford H. Bishop, Rebecca S. Hatch, D. Sunshine Hillygus, and David W. Rohde. 2014. "Blame, Responsibility, and the Tea Party in the 2010 Midterm Elections." *Political Behavior* 36(3): 471–91.

Aldrich, John H., Brad Gomez, and John D. Griffin. 1999. *State Party Organizations Study*. State Party Chair Questionnaire. Duke University.

Aldrich, John H., Calvin C. Jillson, and Rick W. Wilson. 2003. "Why Congress? What the Failure of the Confederation Congress and the Survival of the Federal Congress Tell Us about the New Institutionalism." In *Party, Process, and Political Change in Congress: New Perspectives on the History of Congress*, ed. David W. Brady and Mathew D. McCubbins, 315–42. Stanford, CA: Stanford University Press.

Aldrich, John H., and Daniel J. Lee. 2016. "Why Two Parties? Ambition, Policy, and the Presidency" *Political Science Research and Methods* 4(2): 275–92.

Aldrich, John H., Brittany N. Perry, and David W. Rohde. 2013. "Richard Fenno's Theory of Congressional Committees and the Partisan Polarization of the House." In *Congress Reconsidered*, vol. 10, pp. 193–220. Washington, DC: CQ Press.

Aldrich, John H., and David W. Rohde. 1996. *A Tale of Two Speakers: A Comparison of Policy Making in the 100th and 104th Congresses*. Michigan State University, Institute for Public Policy and Social Research.

Aldrich, John H., and David W. Rohde. 2000. "The Republican Revolution and the House Appropriations Committee." *Journal of Politics* 62(1):1–33.

Aldrich, John H., and Danielle M. Thomsen. 2017. "Party, Policy, and the Ambition to Run for Higher Office." *Lesislative Studies Quarterly* 42(2): 321–43.

Alford, John R., and John R. Hibbing. 1981. "Increased Incumbency Advantage in the House." *Journal of Politics* 43(4):1042–61.

Al-Nafjan, Eman, "Saudi Arabia: The Unknown." In "The Big Question: What Is the Biggest Threat to Democracy?" http://www.worldpolicy.org /journal/fall2012/big-question-what-biggest-threat-democracy. Accessed May 29, 2016.

Altman, David, and Aníbal Pérez-Liñán. 2002. "Assessing the Quality of Democracy: Freedom, Competitiveness and Participation in Eighteen Latin American Countries." *Democratization* 9(2):85–100.

Ansolabehere, Stephen, and Shanto Iyengar 1994. "Of Horseshoes and Horse Races: Experimental Studies of the Impact of Poll Results on Electoral Behavior." *Political Communication* 11(4):413–30.

Ansolabehere, Stephen, James M. Snyder Jr., and Charles Stewart III. 2001.

"Candidate Positioning in US House Elections." *American Journal of Political Science* 45(1):136–59.

Arnold, R. Douglas. 1993. "Can Inattentive Citizens Control Their Elected Representatives?" In *Congress Reconsidered*, ed. Lawrence Dodd and Bruce Oppenheimer, 401–16. Washington, DC: CQ Press.

Arnold, R. Douglas. 2004. *Congress, the Press, and Political Accountability*. Princeton, NJ: Princeton University Press.

Ayers, Edward L. 1992. *The Promise of the New South: Life after Reconstruction*. Oxford: Oxford University Press.

Ball, Molly. 2013. "Can Democrats Win Back the Deep South?" http://www .theatlantic.com/politics/archive/2013/06/can-democrats-win-back-the -deep-south/277123/.

Barber, Benjamin R. 2011. "'The People Are Not Ready for Democracy!' Announces the Tyrant." http://www.huffingtonpost.com/benjamin-r -barber/the-people-are-not-ready_b_821359.html. Accessed January 31, 2015.

Barghothi, A. J., Elisha Carol Savchak, and Ann O'M. Bowman. 2010. "Candidate Quality and the Election of Republican Governors in the South, 1950–2004." *American Politics Research* 38(3):563–85.

Bartels, Larry M. 2000. "Partisanship and Voting Behavior, 1952–1996." *American Journal of Political Science* 44(1):35–50.

Bartels, Larry M. 2008. *Unequal Democracy: The Political Economy of the New Gilded Age*. Princeton, NJ: Princeton University Press.

Beard, Charles A., and Beard, Mary R. 1933. *The Rise of American Civilization*, new ed., 2 vols. in 1. New York: Macmillan Company.

Beckel, Deborah. 2010. *Radical Reform: Interracial Politics in Post-Emancipation North Carolina*. Charlottesville: University of Virginia Press.

Benedict, Michael Les. 1985. "Factionalism and Representation: Some Insight from the Nineteenth-Century United States." *Social Science History* 9(4):361–98.

Bensel, Richard Franklin. 1984. *Sectionalism and American Political Development, 1880–1980*. Madison: University of Wisconsin Press.

Berinsky, Adam J., and Gabriel S. Lenz. 2014. "Red Scare? Revisiting Joe McCarthy's Influence on 1950s Elections." *Public Opinion Quarterly* 78(2):369–91.

Berkowitz, Daniel, and Karen B. Clay. 2011. *The Evolution of a Nation: How Geography and Law Shaped the American States*. Princeton, NJ: Princeton University Press.

Besley, Timothy, Torsten Persson, and Daniel M. Sturm. 2010. "Political Competition, Policy and Growth: Theory and Evidence from the US." *Review of Economic Studies* 77(4):1329–52.

Bickers, Kenneth N., and Robert M. Stein. 1996. "The Electoral Dynamics of the Federal Pork Barrel." *American Journal of Political Science* 40(4):1300–26.

Black, Earl. 1998. "Presidential Address: The Newest Southern Politics." *Journal of Politics* 6(3):591–612.

Black, Earl, and Merle Black. 1989. *Politics and Society in the South*. Cambridge, MA: Harvard University Press.

Black, Earl, and Merle Black 2003. *The Rise of Southern Republicans*. Cambridge, MA: Harvard University Press.

Black, Gordon S. 1972. "A Theory of Political Ambition: Career Choices and the Role of Structural Incentives." *American Political Science Review* 66(1):144–59.

Blais, André, and Marc André Bodet. 2006. "Does Proportional Representation Foster Closer Congruence between Citizens and Policy Makers?" *Comparative Political Studies* 39(10):1243–62.

Brady, David W., and Charles S. Bullock. 1980 "Is There a Conservative Coalition in the House?" *Journal of Politics* 42(2):549–59.

Brady, David W., and Bernard Grofman. 1991. "Sectional Differences in Partisan Bias and Electoral Responsiveness in US House Elections, 1850–1980." *British Journal of Political Science* 21(2):247–56.

Brunell, Thomas L. 2006. "Rethinking Redistricting: How Drawing Uncompetitive Districts Eliminates Gerrymanders, Enhances Representation, and Improves Attitudes toward Congress." *PS: Political Science & Politics* 39(1):77–85.

Brunell, Thomas L. 2008. *Redistricting and Representation: Why Competitive Elections Are Bad for America*. New York: Routledge.

Brunell, Thomas L., and Justin Buchler. 2009. "Ideological Representation and Competitive Congressional Elections." *Electoral Studies* 28(3):448–57.

Brunell, Thomas L., and Harold D. Clarke. 2012. "Who Wants Electoral Competition and Who Wants to Win?" *Political Research Quarterly* 65(1):124–37.

Buchler, Justin. 2005. "Competition, Representation and Redistricting: The Case Against Competitive Congressional Districts." *Journal of Theoretical Politics* 17(4):431–63.

Buchler, Justin. 2007. "The Social Sub-Optimality of Competitive Elections." *Public Choice* 133(3):439–56.

Bueno De Mesquita, Bruce, James D. Morrow, Randolph M. Siverson, and Alastair Smith. 1999. "An Institutional Explanation of the Democratic Peace." *American Political Science Review* 93(4):791–807.

Bullock, Charles S., III. 1981. "Congressional Voting and the Mobilization of a Black Electorate in the South." *Journal of Politics* 43(3):662–82.

Bullock, Charles S. 1988a. "Creeping Realignment in the South." In *The South's New Politics: Realignment and Dealignment*, edited by Robert H. Swansbrough and David M. Brodsky, 220–37. Columbia: University of South Carolina Press.

Bullock, Charles S. 1988b. "Regional Realignment from an Officeholding Perspective." *Journal of Politics* 50(3):553–74.

Burden, Barry C. 2004. "Candidate Positioning in US Congressional Elections." *British Journal of Political Science* 34(2):211–27.

Burkhart, Ross E., and Michael S. Lewis-Beck. 1994. "Comparative Democracy: The Economic Development Thesis." *American Political Science Review* 88(4):903–10.

Cain, Bruce E., John A. Ferejohn, and Morris P. Fiorina. 1984. "The Constituency Service Basis of the Personal Vote for US Representatives and British Members of Parliament." *American Political Science Review* 78(1):110–25.

Cain, Bruce, John Ferejohn, and Morris Fiorina. 1987. *The Personal Vote: Constituency Service and Electoral Independence*. Cambridge, MA: Harvard University Press.

Calvert, Randall L. 1985. "Robustness of the Multidimensional Voting Model: Candidate Motivations, Uncertainty, and Convergence." *American Journal of Political Science* 29(1):69–95.

Campbell, Angus, Philip E. Converse, Warren E. Miller, and Donald E. Stokes. 1960. *The American Voter*. Ann Arbor: University of Michigan Press.

Canes-Wrone, Brandice, Michael C. Herron, and Kenneth W. Shotts. 2001. "Leadership and Pandering: A Theory of Executive Policymaking" *American Journal of Political Science* 45(3):532–50.

Canon, David T. 1990. *Actors, Athletes, and Astronauts: Political Amateurs in the United States Congress*. Chicago: University of Chicago Press.

Canon, David T. 1999. *Race, Redistricting, and Representation: The Unintended Consequences of Black Majority Districts*. Chicago: University of Chicago Press.

Carmines, Edward G., and James A. Stimson. 1989. *Issue Evolution: Race and the Transformation of American Politics*. Princeton, NJ: Princeton University Press.

Caro, Robert A. 2009. *Master of the Senate: The Years of Lyndon Johnson*. New York: Random House.

Carson, Jamie L., and Jason M. Roberts. 2005. "Strategic Politicians and U.S. House Elections, 1874–1914." *Journal of Politics* 67(2):474–96.

Carson, Jamie L., and Jason M. Roberts. 2013. *Ambition, Competition, and Electoral Reform: The Politics of Congressional Elections across Time*. Ann Arbor: University of Michigan Press.

Caughey, Devin. 2014. "Representation without Parties: Reconsidering the One-Party South." MIT unpublished paper, November 3.

Cecelski, David S., and Timothy B. Tyson, eds. 1998. *Democracy Betrayed: The Wilmington Race Riot of 1898 and Its Legacy*. Chapel Hill: University of North Carolina Press.

Cingranelli, David L. 1981. "Race, Politics and Elites: Testing Alternative Models of Municipal Service Distribution." *American Journal of Political Science* 25(4):664–92.

Clemens, Elisabeth. 1997. *The People's Lobby—Organizational Innovation and the Rise of Interest Group Politics in the United States, 1890–1925*. Chicago: University of Chicago Press.

Clinton, Joshua, Simon Jackman, and Douglas Rivers. 2004. "The Statistical Analysis of Roll Call Data." *American Political Science Review* 98(2): 355–70.

Clotfelter, Charles T. 2011. *After Brown: The Rise and Retreat of School Desegregation*. Princeton, NJ: Princeton University Press, 2011.

Clubb, Jerome M., William H. Flanigan, and Nancy H. Zingale. 1986. *Electoral Data for Counties in the United States: Presidential and Congressional Races, 1840–1972*. Inter-university Consortium for Political and Social Research. Ann Arbor: University of Michigan.

Clucas, Richard A. 2007. "Legislative Professionalism and the Power of State House Leaders." *State Politics & Policy Quarterly* 7(1):1–19.

Cohen, Marty, David Karol, Hans Noel, and John Zaller. 2009. *The Party Decides: Presidential Nominations Before and After Reform.* Chicago: University of Chicago Press.

Coleman, John J., and Paul Manna. 2007. "Above the Fray? The Use of Party System References in Presidential Rhetoric." *Presidential Studies Quarterly* 37(3):399–426.

Collier, David, and Steven Levitsky. 1997. "Democracy with Adjectives: Conceptual Innovation in Comparative Research." *World Politics* 49(3):430–51.

Converse, Philip E. 1964. "The Nature of Belief Systems in Mass Publics." In *Ideology and Discontent,* ed. David Ernest Apter, 206–61. New York: Free Press.

Cooper, James Fenimore. 2010. *The American Democrat: The Social and Civic Relations of the United States of America.* New Brunswick, NJ: Transaction Publishers.

Coulter, Ellis Merton. 1950. *The Confederate States of America, 1861–1865.* Baton Rouge: Louisiana State University Press.

Cox, Gary W. 1997. *Making Votes Count.* New York: Cambridge University Press.

Cox, Gary W., and Jonathan N. Katz. 2002. *Elbridge Gerry's Salamander: The Electoral Consequences of the Reapportionment Revolution.* Cambridge: Cambridge University Press.

Cox, Gary W., and Mathew D. McCubbins 1993. *Legislative Leviathan: Party Government in the House.* Berkeley: University of California Press.

Cox, Gary W., and Michael C. Munger. 1989. "Closeness, Expenditures, and Turnout in the 1982 U.S. House Elections." *American Political Science Review* 83(1):217–31.

Dahl, Robert A. 1971. *Polyarchy: Participation and Opposition.* New Haven, CT: Yale University Press.

Dahl, Robert A. 1998. *On Democracy.* New Haven, CT: Yale University Press.

Dahl, Robert A. 2003. *How Democratic Is the American Constitution?* New Haven, CT: Yale University Press.

Dailey, Jane Elizabeth. 2000. *Before Jim Crow: The Politics of Race in Postemancipation Virginia.* Chapel Hill: University of North Carolina Press.

Delli Carpini, Michael X., and Scott Keeter. 1996. *What Americans Know about Politics and Why It Matters.* New Haven, CT: Yale University Press.

DeSantis, Victor S., and T. Renner. 1991. "Contemporary Patterns and Trends in Municipal Government Structure." *The Municipal Year Book.* Washington, DC: International City/County Management Association.

Diamond, Larry. 2013. "Why Wait for Democracy?" http://wilsonquarterly.com/quarterly/winter-2013-is-democracy-worth-it/why-wait-for-democracy/. Accessed January 31, 2015.

Diamond, Larry, and Richard Gunther. 2001. *Political Parties and Democracy.* Baltimore: Johns Hopkins University Press.

Downey, Douglas B. 1995. "When Bigger Is Not Better: Family Size, Parental Resources, and Children's Educational Performance." *American Sociological Review* 60(5):746–61.

Downs, Anthony. 1957. *An Economic Theory of Democracy*. New York: Harper and Row.

Dropp, Kyle, and Zachary Peskowitz. 2012. "Electoral Security and the Provision of Constituency Service." *Journal of Politics* 74(1):220–34.

Dunn, Richard S. 1977. "A Tale of Two Plantations: Slave Life at Mesopotamia in Jamaica and Mount Airy in Virginia, 1799 to 1828." *William and Mary Quarterly: A Magazine of Early American History* 34(1):32–65.

Dunn, Richard S. 2014. *A Tale of Two Plantations: Slave Life in Jamaica and Virginia* Cambridge, MA: Harvard University Press.

Egan, Patrick J. 2013. *Partisan Priorities: How Issue Ownership Drives and Distorts American Politics*. New York: Cambridge University Press.

Eismeier, Theodore J. 1983. "Votes & Taxes: The Political Economy of the American Governorship." *Polity* 15(3):368–79.

Engstrom, Erik J., and Samuel Kernell. 2005. "Manufactured Responsiveness: The Impact of State Electoral Laws on Unified Party Control of the Presidency and House of Representatives, 1840–1940." *American Journal of Political Science* 49(3):531–49.

Epperly, Brad, Ryan Strickler, Paul White, and Christopher Witko. 2016. "Rule by Violence, Rule by Law: Voter Suppression and the Rise and Fall of Lynching in the U.S. South." Unpublished paper, May 11, University of South Carolina.

Erikson, Robert S. 1971. "The Advantage of Incumbency in Congressional Elections." *Polity* 3(3):395–405.

Erikson, Robert S. 1978. "Constituency Opinion and Congressional Behavior: A Reexamination of the Miller-Stokes Representation Data." *American Journal of Political Science* 22(3):511–35.

Erikson, Robert S., and Gerald C. Wright. 2000. "Representation of Constituency Ideology in Congress." In *Continuity and Change in Congressional Elections*, edited by David Brady and John Cogan, 149–77. Stanford, CA: Stanford University Press.

Evans, Heather K., Michael J. Ensley, and Edward G. Carmines. 2014. "The Enduring Effects of Competitive Elections." *Journal of Elections, Public Opinion & Parties* 24(4):455–72.

Fausset, Richard. 2014. "In Mississippi, Largess Helped a Senator, until It Hurt Him," *New York Times*, June 18, A14.

Ferejohn, John A., and Morris P. Fiorina. 1975. "Closeness Counts Only in Horseshoes and Dancing." *American Political Science Review* 69(3): 920–25.

Ferleger, Luis A., and Richard H. Steckel. 2000. "Measuring the South: Health, Height, and Literary Myths." In *Slavery, Secession, and Southern History*, edited by Robert L. Paquette and Lou Ferleger, 163–77. Charlottesville: University of Virginia Press.

Finkelman, Paul. 2014. *Slavery and the Founders: Race and Liberty in the Age of Jefferson*. London and New York: Routledge.

Fiorina, Morris. 1973. "Electoral Margins, Constituency Influence and

Policy Moderation: A Critical Assessment." *American Politics Quarterly* 1:479–98.

Fiorina, Morris P. 1981. *Retrospective Voting in American National Elections.* New Haven, CT: Yale University Press.

Fiorina, Morris P. 1994. "Divided Government in the American States: A Byproduct of Legislative Professionalism?" *American Political Science Review* 88(2):304–16.

Fiorina, Morris P. 1997. "Professionalism, Realignment, and Representation." *American Political Science Review* 91(1):156–62.

Folsom, Burton W. 1973. "Party Formation and Development in Jacksonian America: The Old South." *Journal of American Studies* 7:217–29.

Foner, Eric. 1971. *Free Soil, Free Labor, Free Men: The Ideology of the Republican Party before the Civil War.* Oxford: Oxford University Press.

Foner, Eric. 2011. *Reconstruction: America's Unfinished Revolution, 1863–1877.* New York: Harper Collins.

Fowler, James H. 2006. "Altruism and Turnout." *Journal of Politics* 68(3): 674–83.

Franklin, John Hope, and Alfred A. Moss Jr. 2000. *From Slavery to Freedom: A History of African Americans.* New York: Alfred A. Knopf.

Frantzich, Stephen. 1979. "Who Makes Our Laws? The Legislative Effectiveness of Members of the US Congress." *Legislative Studies Quarterly* 4(3):409–28.

Froman, Lewis A. 1963. *Congressmen and Their Constituencies.* Berkeley, CA: Rand McNally.

Gamm, Gerald, and Kenneth Shepsle. 1989. "Emergence of Legislative Institutions: Standing Committees in the House and Senate, 1810–1825." *Legislative Studies Quarterly* 14(1):39–66.

Garreton, Merino Manuel Antonio. 1995. "Redemocratization in Chile." *Journal of Democracy* 6(1):146–58.

Gerber, Elisabeth R., and Jeffrey B. Lewis. 2004. "Beyond the Median: Voter Preferences, District Heterogeneity, and Political Representation." *Journal of Political Economy* 112(6):1364–83.

Gerber, Elisabeth R., and Arthur Lupia. 1995. "Campaign Competition and Policy Responsiveness in Direct Legislation Elections." *Political Behavior* 17(3):287–306.

Gibson, James L., Cornelius P. Cotter, John F. Bibby, and Robert J. Huckshorn. 1983. "Assessing Party Organizational Strength." *American Journal of Political Science* 27(2):193–222.

Gienapp, William E. 1987. *The Origins of the Republican Party, 1852–1856.* New York: Oxford University Press.

Goodman, Craig. 2003. "Congressional Elections and Legislative Responsiveness during the Populist Era." Annual Meeting of the Midwest Political Science Association, Chicago.

Goodwyn, Lawrence. 1978. *The Populist Moment: A Short History of the Agrarian Revolt in America.* Oxford: Oxford University Press.

Griffin, John D. 2006. "Electoral Competition and Democratic Responsiveness: A Defense of the Marginality Hypothesis." *Journal of Politics* 68(4):909–19.

Griffin, John D., and Patrick Flavin. 2011. "How Citizens and Their Legislators Prioritize Spheres of Representation." *Political Research Quarterly* 64(3):520–33.

Grynaviski, Jeffrey D. 2004. "The Impact of Electoral Rules on Factional Competition in the Democratic South, 1919–48." *Party Politics* 10(5):499–519.

Grynaviski, Jeffrey D. 2010. *Partisan Bonds*. New York: Cambridge University Press.

Grzymala-Busse, Anna. 2007. *Rebuilding Leviathan: Party Competition and State Exploitation in Post-Communist Democracies*. Cambridge: Cambridge University Press.

Hall, Melinda G. 2007. "Voting in State Supreme Court Elections: Competition and Context as Democratic Incentives." *Journal of Politics* 69(4):1147–59.

Hansen, John Mark. 1991. *Gaining Access: Congress and the Farm Lobby, 1919–1981*. Chicago: University of Chicago Press.

Hansford, Thomas G., and Brad T. Gomez. 2010. "Estimating the Electoral Effects of Voter Turnout." *American Political Science Review* 104(2):268–88.

Hatch, Rebecca S. 2016. "Party Organizational Strength and Technological Capacity: The Adaptation of the State-Level Party Organizations in the United States to Voter Outreach and Data Analytics in the Internet Age." *Party Politics* 22(2):191–202.

Hayes, Danny, and Seth C. McKee. 2008. "Toward a One-Party South?" *American Politics Research* 36(1):3–32.

Herbst, Susan. 2010. *Rude Democracy: Civility and Incivility in American Politics*. Philadelphia: Temple University Press.

Hicks, John Donald. 1931. *The Populist Revolt: A History of the Farmers' Alliance and the People's Party*. Minneapolis: University of Minnesota Press.

Hofstadter, Richard. 1969. *The Idea of a Party System: The Rise of Legitimate Opposition in the United States, 1780–1840*. Berkeley: University of California Press.

Holbrook, Thomas M., and Emily Van Dunk. 1993. "Electoral Competition in the American States." *American Political Science Review* 87(4):955–62.

Holt, Michael F. 1999. *The Rise and Fall of the American Whig Party: Jacksonian Politics and the Onset of the Civil War*. Oxford: Oxford University Press.

Huber, John D., and G. Bingham Powell. 1994. "Congruence between Citizens and Policymakers in Two Visions of Liberal Democracy." *World Politics* 46(3):291–326.

Huddleston, John. 2002. *Killing Ground: Photographs of the Civil War and the Changing American Landscape*. Baltimore: Johns Hopkins University Press.

Humes, Brian D., Elaine K. Swift, Richard M. Valelly, Kenneth Finegold, and Evelyn C. Fink. 2002. "Representation of the Antebellum South in the House of Representatives: Measuring the Impact of the Three-Fifths Clause." In *Party, Process, and Political Change in Congress: New Perspectives on the History of Congress*, ed. David W. Brady and Mathew D. McCubbins, 452–66. Stanford, CA: Stanford University Press.

Huntington, Samuel P. 1974. "Paradigms of American Politics: Beyond the One, the Two, and the Many." *Political Science Quarterly* 89(1):1–26.

Hutchings, Vincent L. 1998. "Issue Salience and Support for Civil Rights Legislation among Southern Democrats." *Legislative Studies Quarterly* 23(4):521–44.

Jackman, Robert W. 1987. "Political Institutions and Voter Turnout in the Industrial Democracies." *American Political Science Review* 81(2):405–24.

Jacobson, Gary C. 1989. "Strategic Politicians and the Dynamics of US House Elections, 1946–86." *American Political Science Review* 83(3):773–93.

Janda, Kenneth, Jeffrey Berry, Jerry Goldman, and Deborah Schildkraut. 2012. *The Challenge of Democracy.* Boston, MA: Cengage Learning.

Jenkins, Jeffrey A. 1999. "Examining the Bonding Effects of Party: A Comparative Analysis of Roll-Call Voting in the U.S. and Confederate Houses." *American Journal of Political Science* 43:1144–65.

Jenkins, Jeffrey A., and Timothy P. Nokken. 2000. "The Institutional Origins of the Republican Party: Spatial Voting and the House Speakership Election of 1855–56." *Legislative Studies Quarterly* 25(1):101–30.

Jenkins, Jeffery A., and Charles Stewart III. 2012. *Fighting for the Speakership: The House and the Rise of Party Government.* Princeton, NJ: Princeton University Press.

Jenkins, Jeffery A., and Marc Weidenmier. 1999. "Ideology, Economic Interests, and Congressional Roll-Call Voting: Partisan Instability and Bank of the United States Legislation, 1811–1816." *Public Choice* 100(3): 225–43.

Jillson, Calvin C., and Rick K. Wilson. 1994. *Congressional Dynamics: Structure, Coordination, and Choice in the First American Congress, 1774–1789.* Stanford, CA: Stanford University Press.

Johannes, John R., and John C. McAdams. 1981. "The Congressional Incumbency Effect: Is It Casework, Policy Compatibility, or Something Else? An Examination of the 1978 Election." *American Journal of Political Science* 25(3):512–42.

Jones, Philip Edward. 2013. "The Effect of Political Competition on Democratic Accountability." *Political Behavior* 35(3):481–515.

Kaiser, Henry F. 1958. "The Varimax Criterion for Analytic Rotation in Factor Analysis." *Psychometrika* 23(3):187–200.

Karol, David. 2009. *Party Position Change in American Politics: Coalition Management.* Cambridge: Cambridge University Press.

Kennedy, John Fitzgerald, and Allan Nevins. 1964. *Profiles in Courage.* New York: Harper & Row.

Kernell, Samuel. 1977. "Toward Understanding 19th Century Congressional Careers: Ambition, Competition, and Rotation." *American Journal of Political Science* 21(4):669–93.

Key, V. O., Jr. 1956. *American State Politics: An Introduction.* New York: Knopf.

Key, V. O., Jr. 1961. *Public Opinion and American Democracy.* 1st ed. New York: Knopf.

Key, V. O., Jr. 1964 [1942]. *Politics, Parties, and Pressure Groups.* New York: Thomas Crowell.

Key, V. O., Jr. 1984 [1949]. *Southern Politics in State and Nation*. Knoxville: University of Tennessee Press.

Keyssar, Alexander. 2009. *The Right to Vote: The Contested History of Democracy in the United States* New York: Basic Books.

Kingdon, John W. 1989. *Congressmen's Voting Decisions*. Ann Arbor: University of Michigan Press.

Klepper, Robert. 1974. "The Economic Bases for Agrarian Protest Movements in the United States, 1870–1900." *Journal of Economic History* 34(1):283–85.

Kleppner, Paul. 1979. *The Third Electoral System, 1853–1892: Parties, Voters, and Political Cultures*. Vol. 2. Chapel Hill: University of North Carolina Press.

Klingman, David, and William W. Lammers. 1984. "The 'General Policy Liberalism' Factor in American State Politics." *American Journal of Political Science* 28(3):598–610.

Kousser, J. Morgan. 1974. *The Shaping of Southern Politics: Suffrage Restriction and the Establishment of the One-Party South, 1880–1910*. New Haven, CT: Yale University Press

Kousser, J. Morgan. 2008. "The Strange, Ironic Career of Section 5 of the Voting Rights Act." *Texas Law Review* 86:667–775.

Kuklinski, James H. 1977. "District Competitiveness and Legislative Roll-Call Behavior: A Reassessment of the Marginality Hypothesis." *American Journal of Political Science* 21(3):627–38.

Kuklinski, James H., Michael D. Cobb, and Martin Gilens. 1997. "Racial Attitudes and the 'New South.'" *Journal of Politics* 59(2):323–49.

Lamis, Alexander P. 1999. *Southern Politics in the 1990s*. Baton Rouge: Louisiana State University Press.

Larson, Edward J. 2007. *A Magnificent Catastrophe: The Tumultuous Election of 1800, America's First Presidential Campaign*. New York: Simon and Schuster.

Lawson, Chappell. 2000. "Mexico's Unfinished Transition: Democratization and Authoritarian Enclaves in Mexico." *Mexican Studies/Estudios Mexicanos* 16(2):267–87.

Lazarsfeld, Paul F., Bernard Berelson, and Hazel Gaudet. 1948. *The People's Choice*. New York: Columbia University Press.

Leblang, David A. 1997. "Political Democracy and Economic Growth: Pooled Cross-Sectional and Time-Series Evidence." *British Journal of Political Science* 27(3):453–72.

Lee, Frances E., and Bruce I. Oppenheimer. 1999. *Sizing Up the Senate: The Unequal Consequences of Equal Representation*. Chicago: University of Chicago Press.

Lee, David S., Enrico Moretti, and Matthew J. Butler. 2004. "Do Voters Affect or Elect Policies? Evidence from the US House." *Quarterly Journal of Economics* 119(3):807–59.

Levine, Renan. 2000. "Readjuster Party of Virginia," In *Encyclopedia of Third Parties in America*, ed. Immanuel Ness and James Ciment. Armonk, NY: M. E. Sharpe.

Levitsky, Steven, and A. Cameron Maxwell. 2003. "Democracy without

Parties? Political Parties and Regime Change in Fujimori's Peru." *Latin American Politics and Society* 45(3):1–33.

Lijphart, Arend. 1999. *Patterns of Democracy: Government Forms and Performance in Thirty-Six Democracies*. New Haven, CT: Yale University Press.

Lindert, Peter H., and Jeffrey G. Williamson. 2012. *American Incomes, 1774–1860*. No. w18396. Cambridge, MA: National Bureau of Economic Research.

Lipset, Seymour Martin. 1959. "Some Social Requisites of Democracy: Economic Development and Political Legitimacy." *American Political Science Review* 53(1):69–105.

Lodge, Milton, Marco R. Steenbergen, and Shawn Brau. 1995. "The Responsive Voter: Campaign Information and the Dynamics of Candidate Evaluation." *American Political Science Review* 89(2):309–26.

Logan, Rayford Whittingham. 1965. *The Betrayal of the Negro, from Rutherford B. Hayes to Woodrow Wilson*. Cambridge, MA: Da Capo Press.

Lublin, David. 2004. *The Republican South: Democratization and Partisan Change*. Princeton, NJ: Princeton University Press.

Lupia, Arthur, and Matthew D. McCubbins. 1998. *The Democratic Dilemma: Can Citizens Learn What They Need to Know?* Cambridge: Cambridge University Press.

MacRae, Duncan. 1952. "The Relation between Roll Call Votes and Constituencies in the Massachusetts House of Representatives." *American Political Science Review* 46(4):1046–55.

Magaloni, B., and R. Kricheli. 2010. "Political Order and One-Party Rule." *Annual Review of Political Science* 13:123–43.

Majewski, John. 1996. "Commerce and Community: Internal Improvements in Virginia and Pennsylvania, 1790–1860." *Journal of Economic History* 56(2):467–69.

Manley, John F. 1973. "The Conservative Coalition in Congress." *American Behavioral Scientist* 17(2):223–47.

Mann, Thomas E., and Raymond E. Wolfinger. 1980. "Candidates and Parties in Congressional Elections." *American Political Science Review* 74(3):617–32.

Martin, Jonathan. 2014. "One Party, Two Factions: South's Republicans Look a Lot Like Its 1970s Democrats." *New York Times*, http://www.nytimes.com/2014/06/03/us/politics/one-party-two-factions-souths-republicans-look-a-lot-like-its-1970s-democrats.html?_r=0.

Martin, Paul S. 2003. "Voting's Rewards: Voter Turnout, Attentive Publics, and Congressional Allocation of Federal Money." *American Journal of Political Science* 47(1):110–27.

Mayhew, David R. 1974. "Congressional Elections: The Case of the Vanishing Marginals." *Polity* 6(3):295–317.

McCormick, Richard L. 1986. *Party Period and Public Policy: American Politics from the Age of Jackson to the Progressive Era*. Oxford: Oxford University Press.

McCormick, Richard P. 1960. "New Perspectives on Jacksonian Politics." *American Historical Review* 65(2):288–301.

McGerr, Michael. 1986. *The Decline of Popular Politics: The American North, 1865–1928*. Oxford: Oxford University Press.

McPherson, James M. 1992. *Abraham Lincoln and the Second American Revolution*. Oxford: Oxford University Press.

McVeigh, Rory, David Cunningham, and Justin Farrell. 2014. "Political Polarization as a Social Movement Outcome: 1960s Klan Activism and Its Enduring Impact on Political Realignment in Southern Counties, 1960 to 2000." *American Sociological Review* 79(6):1144–71.

Mickey, Robert. 2015. *Paths Out of Dixie: The Democratization of Authoritarian Enclaves in America's Deep South*. Princeton, NJ: Princeton University Press.

Milazzo, Caitlin. 2014. "Voters in Marginal Constituencies Know More about Parties' Policy Positions than Those in Safe Seats." *Democratic Audit Blog*.

Milbrath, Lester W. 1965. *Political Participation: How and Why Do People Get Involved in Politics?* Chicago: Rand McNally.

Miller, Nick. 1983. "Pluralism and Social Choice." *American Political Science Review* 77(3):734–47.

Miller, Warren E. 1991. "Party Identification, Realignment, and Party Voting: Back to the Basics." *American Political Science Review* 85(2):557–68.

Miller, Warren E., and Donald E. Stokes. 1963. "Constituency Influence in Congress." *American Political Science Review* 57(1):45–56.

Moger, Allen W. 1942. "The Origin of the Democratic Machine in Virginia." *Journal of Southern History* 8(2):183–209.

Moon, Bruce E., Jennifer Harvey Birdsall, Sylvia Ciesluk, Lauren M. Garlett, Joshua J. Hermias, Elizabeth Mendenhall, Patrick D. Schmid, and Wai Hong Wong. 2006. "Voting Counts: Participation in the Measurement of Democracy." *Studies in Comparative International Development* 41(2):3–32.

Moyers, Bill. 2006 "There Is No Tomorrow." *Minneapolis Star Tribune*, January 1, 30.

Muirhead, Russell. 2014. *The Promise of Party in a Polarized Age*. Cambridge, MA: Harvard University Press.

Murray, Pauli. 1997 [1951]. *States' Laws on Race and Color*. Athens: University of Georgia Press.

Mushkin, Selma. 1957. "Federal Grants and Federal Expenditures." *National Tax Journal* 10(3):193–213.

Nagel, Jack H., and John E. McNulty. 1996. "Partisan Effects of Voter Turnout in Senatorial and Gubernatorial Elections." *American Political Science Review* 90(4):780–93.

Nelson, Garrison. 2005. Committees in the U.S. Congress, 1947–1992. http://hdl.handle.net/1721.1/18166. June 24.

Newman, Brian, and Charles Ostrom Jr. 2002. "Explaining Seat Changes in the U.S. House of Representatives, 1950–98." *Legislative Studies Quarterly* 27(3):383–405.

Niemi, Richard G., and Patrick Fett. 1986. "The Swing Ratio: An Explanation and an Assessment." *Legislative Studies Quarterly* 11(1):75–90.

Packard, Jerrold M. 2003. *American Nightmare: The History of Jim Crow*. New York: Macmillan.

Palfrey, Thomas R. 1984. "Spatial Equilibrium with Entry." *Review of Economic Studies* 51(1):139–56.

Parsons, Stanley B., William W. Beach, and Michael J. Dubin. 1986. *United States Congressional Districts and Data, 1843–1883*. Vol. 2. Westport, CT: Greenwood Publishing Group.

Parsons, Stanley B., William W. Beach, and Dan Hermann. 1978. *United States Congressional Districts, 1788–1841*. Westport, CT: Greenwood Publishing Group.

Patterson, James T. 1981. *Congressional Conservatism and the New Deal: The Growth of the Conservative Coalition in Congress, 1933–1939*. Westport, CT: Greenwood Press.

Pildes, Richard H. 2000. "Democracy, Anti-Democracy, and the Cannon." *Constitutional Commentary* 17:295–320.

Polsby, Nelson W. 2003. *How Congress Evolves: Social Bases of Institutional Change*. Oxford: Oxford University Press.

Poole, Keith T., and Howard Rosenthal. 1997. *Congress: A Political-Economic History of Roll Call Voting*. Oxford: Oxford University Press.

Powell, G. Bingham, Jr. 1982. *Contemporary Democracies: Participation, Stability, and Violence*. Cambridge, MA: Harvard University Press.

Powell, G. Bingham, Jr. 1986. "American Voter Turnout in Comparative Perspective." *American Political Science Review* 80(1):17–43.

Powell, G. Bingham, Jr. 2004. "Political Representation in Comparative Politics." *Annual Review of Political Science* 7:273–96.

Przeworski, Adam. 1991. *Democracy and the Market: Political and Economic Reforms in Eastern Europe and Latin America*. Cambridge: Cambridge University Press.

Przeworski, Adam, Susan C. Stokes, and Bernard Manin, eds. 1999. *Democracy, Accountability, and Representation*. Vol. 2. Cambridge: Cambridge University Press.

Ranney, Austin. 1965. *Pathways to Parliament: Candidate Selection in Britain*. Madison: University of Wisconsin Press.

Ranney, Austin. 1976. "'The Divine Science': Political Engineering in American Culture." *American Political Science Review* 70(1):140–48.

Redding, Kent, and David R. James. 2001. "Estimating Levels and Modeling Determinants of Black and White Voter Turnout in the South: 1880 to 1912." *Historical Methods* 34(4):141–58.

Reed, Steven R. 1990. "Structure and Behaviour: Extending Duverger's Law to the Japanese Case." *British Journal of Political Science* 20(3):335–56.

Richardson, Lewis Fry. 1960. *Arms and Insecurity: A Mathematical Study of the Causes and Origins of War*. Chicago: Boxwood Press.

Riker, William. 1982. *Liberalism against Populism: A Confrontation between the Theory of Social Democracy and the Theory of Social Choice*. San Francisco: W. H. Freeman.

Rodrik, Dani. 1999. "Where Did All the Growth Go? External Shocks, Social Conflict, and Growth Collapses." *Journal of Economic Growth* 4(4):385–412.

Rohde, David W. 1991. *Parties and Leaders in the Postreform House*. Chicago: University of Chicago Press.

Rosenblum, Nancy L. 2010. *On the Side of the Angels: An Appreciation of Parties and Partisanship*. Princeton, NJ: Princeton University Press.

Rosenstone, Steven, and John Mark Hansen. 1993. *Mobilization, Participation and Democracy in America*. New York: Pearson.

Rusk, Jerrold G. 1974. "Comment: The American Electoral Universe; Speculation and Evidence." *American Political Science Review* 68(3):1028–49.

Sacher, John M. 1999. "The Sudden Collapse of the Louisiana Whig Party." *Journal of Southern History* 65(2):221–48.

Sartori, Giovanni. 1968. "Representational Systems." *International Encyclopedia of the Social Sciences* 13:470–75.

Sartori, Giovanni. 1977. *Parties and Party Systems: A Framework for Analysis*. Cambridge: Cambridge University Press.

Schaffner, Brian F., Matthew Streb, and Gerald Wright. 2001. "Teams without Uniforms: The Nonpartisan Ballot in State and Local Elections." *Political Research Quarterly* 54(1):7–30.

Schattschneider, E. E. 1942. *Party Government*. New York: Farrar and Rinehart.

Schattschneider, E. E. 1960. *The Semisovereign People*. New York: Holt, Rinehart and Winston.

Scheiner, Ethan. 2006. *Democracy without Competition in Japan: Opposition Failure in a One-Party Dominant State*. Cambridge: Cambridge University Press.

Schiller, Wendy J. 1995. "Senators as Political Entrepreneurs: Using Bill Sponsorship to Shape Legislative Agendas." *American Journal of Political Science* 39(1):186–203.

Schlesinger, Joseph A. 1966. *Ambition and Politics: Political Careers in the United States*. Chicago: Rand McNally.

Schlesinger, Joseph A. 1975. "The Primary Goals of Political Parties: A Clarification of Positive Theory." *American Political Science Review* 69(3):840–49.

Schmitter, Philippe C., and Terry Lynn Karl. 1991. "What Democracy Is . . . and Is Not." *Journal of Democracy* 2(3):75–88.

Schumpeter, Joseph. 1962. *Capitalism, Socialism and Democracy*. New York: Harper and Row.

Schweiger, Beth Barton. 1991. "Putting Politics Aside: Virginia Democrats and Voter Apathy in the Era of Disenfranchisement." In *The Edge of the South: Life in Eighteenth-Century Virginia*, ed. Edward L. Ayers and John C. Willis. Charlottesville: University of Virginia Press.

Seagull, Louis M. 1970. "Southern Republicanism: Party Competition in the American South, 1940–1968." Diss., University of Chicago.

Sen, Amartya. 1999. "Democracy as a Universal Value." *Journal of Democracy* 10(3):3–17.

Shadgett, Olive Hall. 2010. *The Republican Party in Georgia: From Reconstruction through 1900*. Athens: University of Georgia Press.

Shafer, Byron E. 1991. *The End of Realignment? Interpreting American Electoral Eras*. Madison: University of Wisconsin Press.

Shafer, Byron E., and Richard Johnston. 2009. *The End of Southern Exceptionalism: Class, Race, and Partisan Change in the Postwar South.* Cambridge, MA: Harvard University Press.

Shannon, Wayne. 1968. "Electoral Margins and Voting Behavior in the House of Representatives: The Case of the Eighty-Sixth and Eighty-Seventh Congresses." *Journal of Politics* 30(4):1028–45.

Sharp, James Roger. 2010. *The Deadlocked Election of 1800: Jefferson, Burr, and the Union in the Balance.* Lawrence: University Press of Kansas.

Shepsle, Kenneth A., and Barry R. Weingast. 1987. "The Institutional Foundations of Committee Power." *American Political Science Review* 81(1): 85–104.

Shor, Boris, and Nolan McCarty. 2011. "The Ideological Mapping of American Legislatures." *American Political Science Review* 105(3):530–51.

Silbey, Joel H. 1991. "Beyond Realignment and Realignment Theory: American Political Eras, 1789–1989."

Silbey, Joel H. 1994. *The American Political Nation: 1838–1893.* Stanford, CA: Stanford University Press.

Snyder, James M., Jr., and Michael M. Ting. 2003. "Roll Calls, Party Labels, and Elections." *Political Analysis* 11(4):419–44.

Stanley, Harold W. 1988. "Southern Partisan Changes: Dealignment, Realignment or Both?" *Journal of Politics* 50:64–88.

Stewart, Charles, III, and Jonathan Woon. "Congressional Committee Assignments, 103rd to 112th Congresses 1993–2011." http://hdl.handle.net/1721.1/18172. June 24, 2005. *Senate.* https://dspace.mit.edu/handle/1721.1/18172.

Stimson, James A. 1975. "Belief Systems: Constraint, Complexity, and the 1972 Election." *American Journal of Political Science* 19(3):393–417.

Stokes, Susan. 1999. "Political Parties and Democracy." *Annual Review of Political Science* 2:243–67.

Stover, John F. 1969. "American Railroad Politics, 1914–1920: Rates, Wages, and Efficiency." *American Historical Review* 74(5):1742–43.

Strom, Kaare. 1990. "A Behavioral Theory of Competitive Political Parties." *American Journal of Political Science* 34(2):565–98.

Struble, Robert, Jr. 1979. "House Turnover and the Principle of Rotation" *Political Science Quarterly* 94(4):649–67.

Sullivan, John L., and Eric M. Uslaner. 1978. "Congressional Behavior and Electoral Marginality." *American Journal of Political Science* 22(3):536–53.

Thorpe, Francis Newton, ed. 1909. *The Federal and State Constitutions, Colonial Charters, and Other Organic Laws of the State, Territories, and Colonies Now or Heretofore Forming the United States of America: Kentucky; Massachusetts.* Vol. 3. Washington, DC: U.S. Government Printing Office.

Thurstone, Louis Leon. 1947. *Multiple Factor Analysis.* Chicago: University of Chicago Press.

Tsebelis, George. 2002. *Veto Players: How Political Institutions Work.* Princeton, NJ: Princeton University Press.

Umfleet, LeRae Sikes. 2009. *A Day of Blood: The 1898 Wilmington Race Riot.* Raleigh: North Carolina Office of Archives and History.

Valelly, Richard M. 2004. *The Two Reconstructions: The Struggle for Black Enfranchisement*. Chicago: University of Chicago Press.

Verba, Sidney, and Norman H. Nie. 1972. *Participation in America*. New York: Harper & Row.

Verba, Sidney, and Gary R. Orren. 1985. *Equality in America*. Cambridge, MA: Harvard University Press.

Verba, Sidney, Kay L. Schlozman, and Henry E. Brady. 1995. *Voice and Equality: Civic Voluntarism in American Politics* Cambridge, MA: Harvard University Press.

Volden, Craig, and Alan E. Wiseman. 2014. *Legislative Effectiveness in the United States Congress: The Lawmakers*. Cambridge: Cambridge University Press.

Ward, James A. 1973. "A New Look at Antebellum Southern Railroad Development." *Journal of Southern History* 39(3):409–20.

Ward, Judson C. 1943. "The Republican Party in Bourbon Georgia, 1872–1890." *Journal of Southern History* 9(2):196–209.

Wawro, Gregory. 2001. *Legislative Entrepreneurship in the US House of Representatives*. Ann Arbor: University of Michigan Press.

Weisberg, Herbert F. 2002. "Partisanship and Incumbency in Presidential Elections." *Political Behavior* 24(4):339–60.

Whitby, Kenny J. 2002. "Bill Sponsorship and Intraracial Voting among African American Representatives." *American Politics Research* 30(1):93–109.

Wiebe, Robert H. 1967. *The Search for Order, 1877–1920*. New York: Hill and Wang.

Wikipedia Contributors. 2014. "Southern Baptist Convention." *Wikipedia*, http://en.wikipedia.org/wiki/Southern_Baptist_Convention.

Wilson, Clyde N. 2000. "'Free Trade: No Debt: Separation from Banks': The Economic Platform of John C. Calhoun." In *Slavery, Secession, and Southern History*, ed. R. L. Paquette and L. A. Ferleger, 84. Charlottesville: University of Virginia Press.

Wittman, D. 1983. "Candidate Motivation: A Synthesis of Alternative Theories." *American Political Science Review* 77(1):142–57.

Woodward, C. Vann. 1971 [1951]. *Origins of the New South, 1877–1913*. Baton Rouge: Louisiana State University Press.

Woodward, C. Vann. 2001 *The Strange Career of Jim Crow*. Oxford: Oxford University Press.

Wray, Joe D. 1971. "Population Pressure on Families: Family Size and Child Spacing." In *Rapid Population Growth: Consequences and Policy Implications*, edited by National Academy of Sciences, Office of the Foreign Secretary, Study Committee, 403–61. Baltimore: Johns Hopkins Press.

Wright, Gavin. 2013. *Sharing the Prize*. Cambridge, MA: Harvard University Press.

Yiannakis, Diana Evans. 1981. "The Grateful Electorate: Casework and Congressional Elections." *American Journal of Political Science* 25(3): 568–80.

Zengerle, Jason. 2014. "The New Racism." *New Republic*, August 10, http://www.newrepublic.com/article/119019/civil-rights-movement-going-reverse-alabama.

INDEX

Page numbers ending in an *f* or a *t* indicate a figure or table, respectively.

CHICAGO STUDIES IN AMERICAN POLITICS

A series edited by Benjamin I. Page, Susan Herbst, Lawrence R. Jacobs, and Adam J. Berinsky

Series titles, continued from frontmatter:

Trading Democracy for Justice: Criminal Convictions and the Decline of Neighborhood Political Participation by Traci Burch

White-Collar Government: The Hidden Role of Class in Economic Policy Making by Nicholas Carnes

How Partisan Media Polarize America by Matthew Levendusky

The Politics of Belonging: Race, Public Opinion, and Immigration by Natalie Masuoka and Jane Junn

Political Tone: How Leaders Talk and Why by Roderick P. Hart, Jay P. Childers, and Colene J. Lind

The Timeline of Presidential Elections: How Campaigns Do (and Do Not) Matter by Robert S. Erikson and Christopher Wlezien

Learning While Governing: Expertise and Accountability in the Executive Branch by Sean Gailmard and John W. Patty

Electing Judges: The Surprising Effects of Campaigning on Judicial Legitimacy by James L. Gibson

Follow the Leader? How Voters Respond to Politicians' Policies and Performance by Gabriel S. Lenz

The Social Citizen: Peer Networks and Political Behavior by Betsy Sinclair

The Submerged State: How Invisible Government Policies Undermine American Democracy by Suzanne Mettler

Disciplining the Poor: Neoliberal Paternalism and the Persistent Power of Race by Joe Soss, Richard C. Fording, and Sanford F. Schram

Why Parties? A Second Look
by John H. Aldrich

News That Matters: Television and American Opinion, Updated Edition
by Shanto Iyengar and Donald R. Kinder

Selling Fear: Counterterrorism, the Media, and Public Opinion
by Brigitte L. Nacos, Yaeli Bloch-Elkon, and Robert Y. Shapiro

Obama's Race: The 2008 Election and the Dream of a Post-Racial America
by Michael Tesler and David O. Sears

Filibustering: A Political History of Obstruction in the House and Senate
by Gregory Koger

In Time of War: Understanding American Public Opinion from World War II to Iraq
by Adam J. Berinsky

Us against Them: Ethnocentric Foundations of American Opinion
by Donald R. Kinder and Cindy D. Kam

The Partisan Sort: How Liberals Became Democrats and Conservatives Became Republicans by Matthew Levendusky

Democracy at Risk: How Terrorist Threats Affect the Public
by Jennifer L. Merolla and Elizabeth J. Zechmeister

Agendas and Instability in American Politics, Second Edition
by Frank R. Baumgartner and Bryan D. Jones

The Private Abuse of the Public Interest
by Lawrence D. Brown and Lawrence R. Jacobs

The Party Decides: Presidential Nominations Before and After Reform
by Marty Cohen, David Karol, Hans Noel, and John Zaller

Same Sex, Different Politics: Success and Failure in the Struggles over Gay Rights
by Gary Mucciaroni